SUEZ
1956

SELWYN LLOYD

SUEZ

1956

A personal account

MAYFLOWER BOOKS, INC.,
575 LEXINGTON AVENUE,
NEW YORK CITY 10022.

11-79   B+J   1095

Contents

Illustrations

FIGURES

MAP

Acknowledgments

The author and publishers wish to thank the following for permission to reproduce copyright material: Mr Alexander Murray for two letters written by Professor Gilbert Murray; HMSO for extracts from speeches made in Parliament and reproduced here from Hansard; Osbert Lancaster and John Murray (Publishers) for two cartoons from *The Year of the Comet* by Osbert Lancaster, published by Gryphon Books; Airborne Forces Museum, Aldershot, for Plate 15; Associated Press Ltd for Plates 3, 14, 21; Camera Press Ltd for Plate 25; Central Press Photos Ltd for Plate 11; the Imperial War Museum for Plate 16; the Israeli Embassy for Plate 4; Keystone Press Agency Ltd for Plates 7, 10, 17, 19, 22, 24, and the jacket photograph; Popperfoto/UPI for Plates 1, 5, 6, 12; Press Association Ltd for Plates 18, 27; Leo Rosenthal for Plate 23; Syndication International for Plate 20; *The Times* for Plate 2; Topix for Plates 9, 13; United Press Association for Plate 26.

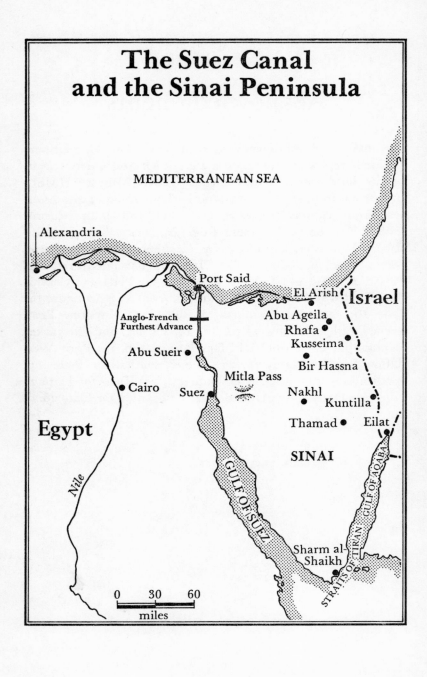

The Suez Canal and the Sinai Peninsula

MEDITERRANEAN SEA

Alexandria

Port Said

El Arish

Israel

Anglo-French
Furthest Advance

Abu Ageila

Rhafa

Kusseima

Abu Sueir

Bir Hassna

Mitla Pass

Cairo

Suez

Nakhl

Kuntilla

Thamad

Eilat

Egypt

SINAI

Nile

GULF OF SUEZ

GULF OF AQABA

Sharm al-
Shaikh

STRAITS OF TIRAN

0   30   60

miles

Preface

This book should have been written a long time ago. But I felt that, in view of the violent controversies about the events of 1956, it was necessary first to give myself time to go through my own papers and the official records.

Under our rules only a Minister himself may have access during the closed period to his own and Cabinet or Foreign Office papers affecting his time in office. He cannot send in a research student to do the work for him. This made it impracticable for me to begin while a Minister or while I was playing an active part in politics and business, or until I had resigned from the Speakership. Also, during the last twenty years there has been no lack of published reading material which had to be studied.

By the same token, it has not been possible for me to indicate sources in every case.

One of the advantages of the rule about official papers to which I have just referred is that no one but myself can be blamed for the result. Any faults or errors of commission or omission are mine and mine alone. Several friends have read my drafts and made helpful comments upon them. By preserving their anonymity I spare them possible embarrassment, but that does not diminish my gratitude.

I must put on record my appreciation of the staff of the Cabinet Office and in the Library and Records Department of the Foreign and Commonwealth Office, to whom I must have become an almost intolerable nuisance. I cannot express too strongly my gratitude for their courtesy and helpfulness.

I must also name two friends, Miss Susan Carter in London and Mrs Jessica Harkness in Wirral, who have given me invaluable help in the typing and retyping of the text.

I have referred throughout to Lord Avon as Eden, the name by which he was then known, and for the sake of simplicity I have dropped all descriptive titles such as 'President', 'Lord', 'Sir' or 'Mr'. Appendix I lists the members of the Cabinet in 1956, and, in addition, gives the offices held at the time by others frequently referred to in the text.

In transliterating Russian and Arabic names I have been conscious of the difficulty of reconciling customary usage with recent scholarship.

SL

Introduction

The year 1956 was one of particular difficulty for Britain at home and abroad but it was not a year of disaster.

For the Conservatives after their narrow victory at the General Election in 1951, things had gone well for a time. The dismantling of controls, the ending of rationing, the reductions in taxation, and the almost too successful house-building programme had given great satisfaction. Overseas, the Indo-China agreement at Geneva had been an outstanding example of Eden's sure touch in foreign affairs. The Trieste problem had been solved after many months of patient work. The Western European Union had been formed out of the wreckage of the European Defence Community, again largely due to Eden. The Coronation of the Queen, head of the Commonwealth and still sovereign over a vast colonial Empire, had given the nation the cause and the occasion for rejoicing. In May 1953 the Government had actually gained a seat at a by-election in Sunderland.

Then in 1955 the Conservatives began to experience rougher waters. By July it was apparent that all was not well on the economic and financial fronts. Overseas there was trouble in Cyprus. The Soviet Union was supplying arms to Egypt and Syria and only a spark was needed for a major conflagration in the Middle East. The balance at the United Nations was turning against the West.

In the Labour Party there were some able and eager young men determined to make their reputations in Opposition by the fierceness of their attacks upon Ministers. No possible complaint can be made about that. It is the essence of our form of Parliamentary democracy. But it does not make things easier for the Government of the day.

Then into this situation was injected Nasser's challenge, with his nationalisation of the Suez Canal Company. At the time of the first House of Commons debate, there was general resentment at the nationalisation of the Canal and the way in which it had been done, shared also by the press and the public. With that measure of agreement at the beginning of August, it seems extraordinary that the year should have ended as it did. Plenty of explanations of this have been put forward.

In the following pages I try to give for the first time in detail my personal account of these traumatic months. The temptation which obviously besets anyone doing this after twenty years is to use hindsight. I have done my best to avoid it and, wherever possible, I have relied on records made at the time.

I want to make it clear that my hostility to Nasser did not and does not extend to the Egyptian people. I have dealt with many Egyptians whom I respected. I much admire the courage of President Sadat, not only in exposing the facts of the Nasser regime to his people, but also in his bid for peace in the Middle East. As for my criticism of the American leadership, I have many close American friends, and I remain convinced that Anglo-American friendship and co-operation, in spite of the difference in our material strength, remain essential for the well-being of our two countries.

Chapter I

The Heritage

My appointment as Minister of State — United Nations General Assembly in Paris 1951 — the Sudan — abrogation of 1936 treaty — Anglo-Egyptian agreement February 1953 — my visit to Sudan 1953 — Sudanese leaders — meetings with Neguib and Nasser in Cairo — my visit to Sudan 1954 — riots.

After the narrow Conservative victory at the General Election in October 1951 and the return of Churchill as Prime Minister, I was appointed Minister of State.

I had been concerned in Opposition with financial affairs and, as one of the secretaries of the Conservative Finance Committee in the Commons, had had a great deal to do with organising the opposition to the budgets of Stafford Cripps and Gaitskell. I had been tipped for office in the Treasury or perhaps the Board of Trade. I did not want to become a Law Officer. At the Bar I had been interested in advocacy but never in the intricacies of case law and legal theory.

After the election I drove down from my Cheshire constituency to London for the opening of Parliament, and I stopped on the way to stay at Bruern with Michael Astor. Various Ministerial appointments were being announced. I heard on the radio that Maxwell-Fyfe was to be Home Secretary and that Walter Monckton was to be Minister of Labour. They were our two leading lawyers in the Commons. I began to be apprehensive about what was in store for me. Would I be asked to be a Law Officer?

On arrival at 10 Eccleston Square, where I then had a flat, I rang Albert Stanner, my Clerk in Chambers in the Temple,

to ask whether there was any message. He said that the Prime
Minister wished me to go at once to Chartwell. I knew that all
the Cabinet posts had not yet been filled. I also knew that there
was not the slightest chance of one of them for me. Law Officers,
however, are not Members of the Cabinet, and I could not
think why I had been sent for so soon unless it was to offer me
a Law Office because some tricky legal problem had already
arisen. I went off in some apprehension because, if the offer was
that I should be Solicitor-General, I intended to refuse. If it
was to be Attorney-General, the head of the profession, I felt
that I would have to accept although with serious doubts about
my capacity to do it well.

When I reached Chartwell my fears were very soon laid to
rest. I was ushered into Churchill's room. He was wearing one
of his blue siren suits, a kind of overall with a zip all the way up
the front of it. I congratulated him on the victory and upon
becoming Prime Minister again. He was obviously tired but
happy. He murmured something about it being a crown of
thorns and went on to say that, although we had had little
contact with one another during the past six years of Labour
Government, he had heard well of me and wanted me to go to
the Foreign Office as Minister of State.

I was flabbergasted. I wondered whether it was a case of
mistaken identity. There followed this exchange: I said, 'But,
Sir, I think there must be some mistake. I do not speak any
foreign language. Except in war, I have never visited any
foreign country. I do not like foreigners [a view which I very
soon changed]. I have never spoken in a Foreign Affairs debate
in the House. I have never listened to one.' He replied, 'Young
man, these all seem to me to be positive advantages.' He then
said that I would be made a Privy Councillor and that Eden
wanted me urgently at the Foreign Office.

I went out in a daze. James Stuart, Harry Crookshank and
Patrick Buchan-Hepburn were in an outer room. James charac-
teristically sought to augment his congratulations with a whisky
and soda. I needed it.

When I arrived at the Office, Michael Hadow, the Minister of State's Private Secretary, met me. For some reason, the Minister of State at the Foreign Office was then called throughout Whitehall just 'Minister of State'. The other Ministers of State were named with their Departments. This ended when Gerald Reading, the Foreign Office Minister in the House of Lords, was upgraded from Under-Secretary to Minister of State. We both became Ministers of State at the Foreign Office. Hadow took me to my room overlooking St James's Park and the lake. I think there was a portrait of Sir Edward Grey in it. Not long ago I read that when, much to his surprise because of his lack of relevant experience, Grey was made Under-Secretary at the Foreign Office, he said, 'Well, it will be very jolly watching the wild fowl on the lake.'

I found that the reason for my speedy appointment was the fact that the General Assembly of the United Nations was to begin its session in a few days' time in Paris. It was meeting there at the Palais de Chaillot because the new building in New York was not finished. Although the Foreign Secretary was named as leader of the United Kingdom delegation and usually attended to make a speech in the general debate at the General Assembly, the actual leader over the weeks or months of the sittings was always the Minister of State. It was necessary for me to receive urgent briefing on the various items likely to be on the agenda.

I was asked to go along to the Foreign Secretary's room, easily the most pleasant Ministerial room which I ever occupied. Little did I think then that I would be there myself for nearly five years. It looks out not only over St James's Park but also the Horse Guards Parade. Anthony Eden was there holding an office meeting on Iran. The Iranian Government had seized the Anglo-Iranian Company's installations at Abadan earlier that year. After a division of opinion in the Attlee Cabinet, so I have always been led to believe, the Labour Government had decided not to use force to restore the situation. It was a problem at the top of the agenda for the new Government.

The office meeting, as it used to be conducted in the Foreign Office then and for all I know may still be the case, was one of the most effective and agreeable methods of discussing a problem. The Secretary of State would be there with any junior Ministers concerned, probably the Permanent Under-Secretary of State (the most senior official in the Foreign Office), one or two other senior officials, and then those immediately concerned with the details, the head of the Department and one or two of his juniors. It might well be that most of the talking would be done by the most junior present, the one who knew all the details of the relevant telegrams and dispatches, and the records of any former meetings.

The Abadan crisis was my first experience of the attitude of many in the American State Department to British interests in the Middle East. McGhee, an Oklahoma millionaire, had steadily undermined our position in Iran. It was said that McGhee told the Iranians that they would get a much better deal out of the United States than from us, and incited them to start the trouble which led to Abadan. I am afraid that this was quite true. Although the matter did not, so far as I remember, come on to the agenda of the Assembly, there were private talks between Eden and Dean Acheson, the United States Secretary of State.

I was present at all these discussions between Eden and Acheson. It was the first time that I had met Acheson. He was impressive, with a fine intellect, courage — as his contribution to the Alger Hiss defence fund showed — and in many ways very sound judgment. He seemed a little jealous of Eden at that time. He had not relished the extraordinary welcome given to Eden by the representatives of many countries at his reappearance on the international scene. Unfortunately, in the following years I fell out with Acheson in New York over Korea. I disagreed with the rigidity of the United States's position over an Armistice and put Acheson in the position of having to give way. He made a remark to me just afterwards, when Eden had come for a brief visit to New York, which I have never forgotten. Eden had supported me 100 per cent. Acheson, after a diatribe against me and several dry Martinis, said, 'Selwyn, one day you will find that it never pays to win victories over your friends.' Perhaps it was not surprising that those words came to my mind again in November and December 1956.

Acheson was pressing us all the time to settle with Musaddiq, on the ground that if he fell, the next Iranian leader would be much worse. Acheson was quite wrong. We resisted his pressure. Musaddiq did fall in 1953, and the next Iranian Government was a much better one. A reasonably satisfactory settlement was reached over the Anglo-Iranian Oil Company's interests.

To return to the United Nations in 1951, not much was said about Middle Eastern affairs. The main topic was the cold war between East and West. Vyshinsky, the Soviet Permanent Representative, launched a bitter attack upon the West in reply to disarmament proposals presented by Dean Acheson on behalf of the United States, France and Britain. Eden answered next day in a speech which made a deep impression. One could feel the thrill that went through the Assembly as it witnessed a masterly debating speech. Vyshinsky was sunk without trace. Unfortunately, Soviet policy did not sink with him. It remained unchanged.

We did, however, have some success in getting talks on disarmament started. My proposal for a sub-committee of five was approved. It consisted of Phil Jessup for the United States, Jules Moch for France, Vyshinsky for the Soviet Union, and myself for Britain, with Padillo Nervo of Mexico, the President of the General Assembly for that session, as chairman. Even though little came of it, the Soviet Union was kept on the defensive for the next year or two by our initiatives in that sub-committee. Jessup and Moch were splendid colleagues.

A few years earlier when I had been to an Inter-Parliamentary Union Meeting in Stockholm in, I think, 1949, the Egyptian delegation there had talked a lot about 'unequal treaties'. By that they meant treaties concluded when one party was not really a free agent. They maintained that our treaty of

1936 with Egypt was not valid because Egypt was not a free agent at the time. That certainly was not the whole truth. Egypt wanted the treaty because of her fears of Mussolini. But one heard the phrase 'unequal treaties' repeated from time to time. However, in 1951 matters had got beyond arguments between international lawyers.

On 5th October 1951, King George VI had granted Attlee's request and dissolved Parliament. Nahas Pasha, the Prime Minister of Egypt, thought that the moment had come to act unilaterally. On 8th October he put three measures or decrees before the Egyptian Parliament, the first abrogating the Anglo-Egyptian Treaty of 1936, and the Sudan Condominium Agreements of 1899. The second decree declared Egypt and the Sudan to be one country and the King of Egypt to be the King of Egypt and the Sudan. The third gave the King of Egypt the right to dismiss Sudanese Ministers and to dissolve their Parliament; it vested in the King powers to refuse approval of Sudanese legislation and gave him control of foreign affairs, defence and currency matters. These decrees came out of the blue, so far as Britain and the Sudan were concerned.

It was from these events in the year 1951 onwards that the crisis of 1956 was to emerge. Therefore, I must deal with what happened in the Sudan over self-government and self-determination. The Agreement regarding the Suez Canal Base, initialled in July 1954, was the next important factor; and the Baghdad Pact, the Egyptian purchases of arms from behind the Iron Curtain, the Aswan Dam project, the happenings in Jordan, all were stepping stones to Nasser's disastrous act of nationalising the Suez Canal Company in July 1956.

First, as to the Sudan, it had been misruled from Cairo from about 1820 to 1885. Muhammad Ahmad, the Prophet, the Mahdi, had led the revolt which ended in success when General Gordon was killed in the palace at Khartoum. The Mahdi himself died soon after, to be succeeded by his lieutenant Abdullah, the Khalifa, a ruthless and militant character. He threatened Egypt with invasion from time to time; he fought with all his neighbours; he was eventually overthrown by an Anglo-Egyptian army under Kitchener in 1898 after the battle of Omdurman.

The question then arose of what to do with the country. After Cairo's record of appalling misgovernment and inefficiency, it seemed impossible to return it to Egyptian rule. Britain did not want to annex it, partly not to upset other European powers but probably, in the main, for financial reasons. Accordingly, the idea of an Anglo-Egyptian Condominium was thought up, defined as conjoint sovereignty, with full authority vested in the Governor-General appointed by Britain. The Condominium agreements were signed in 1899 between the British Government and the Government of His Highness the Khedive of Egypt. The Sultan of Turkey was still the nominal suzerain and entered a mild and ineffectual protest.

In 1914, when Turkey came into the First World War on the German side, Britain declared a Protectorate over Egypt. The Khedive became Sultan. In 1922, Egypt was declared independent and the Sultan became King Fuad I. Nationalist opinion in Egypt maintained that he should be called King of Egypt and the Sudan. The argument continued with disturbances of varying magnitude. Ramsay MacDonald's Government refused to give way, MacDonald himself making a firm statement to that effect in October 1924. Then in November of that year, Sir Lee Stack, the Governor-General of the Sudan, was murdered in Cairo.

Lord Allenby, the High Commissioner in Egypt, acted decisively. All elements of the Egyptian Army were ordered out of the Sudan except for one battalion quartered in Khartoum as a token of the Condominium. A British battalion was also quartered there for the same reason. The Sudan Defence Force was formed out of Sudanese elements in the Egyptian Army. Egypt was allowed to have little or no say in Sudanese affairs. This was bitterly resented by Egyptian nationalists. It was a blow to their pride. It also deprived Egypt of three very valuable assets—vast areas where surplus Egyptian population might be settled, Sudanese manpower for her armed forces, and control over the waters of the Nile.

Consistently thereafter, over the next thirty years Egyptian leaders of every persuasion had claimed that the Sudan was part of Egypt.

We took a very different view of the position. We believed that we had preserved the Sudan from Egyptian imperialism and exploitation. We wanted the Sudan ultimately to choose independence, not absorption into Egypt. We had hoped that an independent Sudan would join the Commonwealth, but it became clear that that was not a feasible policy for any Sudanese leader to propose in the atmosphere of heady nationalism then prevailing and because of the belief among many that Commonwealth still meant Empire.

When, therefore, the British Parliament met again after the General Election, the King's Speech on 6th November 1951 contained this sentence:

> My Government regard abrogation by the Egyptian Government of the Anglo-Egyptian Treaty of Alliance of 1936 and the Sudan Condominium Agreements of 1899, as illegal and without validity.

A few days later, Eden stated that the Sudan was rapidly moving in the direction of self-government as a prelude to self-determination.

In May 1952, the Sudanese administration submitted a draft self-government statute for examination by the British and Egyptian Governments. It provided for elections to a Sudanese Parliament, and for a Sudanese Council of Ministers to take office after the elections and be responsible to that Parliament. The draft statute had been approved by the Sudanese Legislative Assembly.

The following October, the British Government, as one of the Condomini, announced their acceptance of the statute, and said that they looked forward to the Sudanese exercising the right of self-determination in the near future. The Egyptian Government, the other Condomini, had expressed no views. There was an obvious and understandable reason for delay on their part. On 26th July, King Farouk had been forced to abdicate. In his place, his infant son had been proclaimed King of Egypt and the Sudan. A Council of Regency had been formed. Ali Maher, an experienced politician with a gift for survival, had been appointed Prime Minister.

All this was, in reality, only a façade. Farouk's overthrow was the result of a conspiracy between younger officers in the armed forces, led by men like Nasser. They never had any intention of allowing the monarchy to survive. They discarded Ali Maher as quickly as they decently could because he was a symbol of the old regime. General Neguib took his place.

Because of this upheaval, we could not complain too much about the Egyptian delay in commenting on the draft statute. But it was inconvenient. We wanted to get on, and we knew that Egyptian efforts to subvert the Sudanese were increasing. There was, however, one important development. The new Egyptian rulers did announce a change of policy, conceding what had never been conceded before: that the Sudanese should have the right of self-determination. Eden, hoping for a turn for the better in Anglo-Egyptian relations, made a friendly gesture in the House of Commons. He paid a tribute to Neguib and his colleagues for their courageous efforts to cut through the tangle of maladministration at home and international disputes which were the legacy of previous Egyptian Governments. More specifically, he welcomed their new approach to Egyptian-Sudanese relations, and their apparent acceptance of self-government and self-determination for the Sudan.

It was not until the following February, 1953, that at long last the agreement was signed between Egypt and ourselves. The situation had been somewhat complicated by the fact that the Sudanese political parties thought it prudent to go to Cairo and see what bargains they could make in their own interests. It was a form of reinsurance which did nothing to clarify the situation, to speed the agreement or, in fact, to benefit any of the Sudanese parties.

However, on 12th February, Eden announced the signing of the agreement.

It provided for a transitional period of three years, after a Sudanese Parliament had been elected, during which the Sudanese would govern themselves. The issue of sovereignty would be reserved. At the end of the three-year period, they could determine their future. There were special provisions for the southern provinces. The Governor-General's powers were fixed. For some matters, he required the approval of a Commission with a Pakistani chairman. There was to be an Electoral Commission with an Indian chairman, and a Sudanisation Committee to deal with the administration and defence forces. It was rather complicated, but welcomed both in Britain and the Sudan. It did not, however, usher in a new era of co-operation between the two Condomini.

Egyptian propaganda against us increased in intensity. Neguib talked of cleansing the Nile of British imperialist filth. There was deadlock on the composition of the Governor-General's commission. Egypt would not accept the Sudanese nominations, even though approved by all the Sudanese parties. She was obviously playing for time, to undermine our influence and to set the scene for victory for those Sudanese who wanted union with Egypt.

Eden decided that I should go out to the Sudan to assess the situation. I was to try to break the deadlock over the Governor-General's commission and smooth the way for early elections. I spent a week there, from 21st to 27th March, and a day in Cairo on my way home.

While in Khartoum I saw representatives of all the parties and groups, beginning with the two great men, Sayyad Abdul Rahman al Mahdi and Sayyad Ali al Mirghani. They were called S.A.R. and S.A.M. respectively. S.A.R. was a posthumous son of the Mahdi of Gordon's time, head of the Ansar Sect. S.A.M. was head of Khatmia Sect. Both, however, in addition to being religious leaders, were much involved in politics and secular affairs. S.A.R. was a tall, impressive extrovert, living in great state, incurably extravagant and pro-British. S.A.M. was quieter and more reserved. He was careful not to be precise as to where his loyalties lay. I do not think that he was as much against us as his opponents would have had us believe.

I also had talks with almost all the other political leaders in the north, and with some from the south. I met Salah Salem, one of the Egyptian junta, called the Dancing Major because he had been photographed doing a dance with some Sudanese. He was down on a visit to Khartoum when I was there, I suspect in order to shadow me. I talked to some non-party people, to the French representative who bore a historic name, Count de Lesseps, a member of the family of the de Lesseps who built the Suez Canal, and to Sweeney, the American liaison officer. I could have no confidence in the advice the latter might give to the Sudanese administration. He was out-spokenly anti-British. His favourite theme, I was told, was that Britain had done nothing for the Sudan, and we were finished anyhow.

The quality of the British public servants was outstanding. I had known of the high repute of the Sudan Civil Service. I had met privately that splendid proconsular figure Sir John Maffey, later Lord Rugby, Governor-General from 1926 to 1934, who had developed the use of the native authorities, the tribal chiefs and shaikhs, in public administration. My expectations were fully confirmed by the British administration when I met in Khartoum the Governors of some of the provinces: Carmichael in charge of finance, General Scoones commanding the Sudan Defence Force and, in particular, William Luce, the political secretary to the Governor-General.

I also had a long talk with Dardiri, the man whom the Egyptians were insisting on as the Khatmia representative on the Governor-General's commission. My judgment of him was that he is very pleasant, rather pompous in a not unpleasing way and, if handled rightly, may not always do what the Egyptians tell him. I am told that he is incorruptible.

After all these talks, and long discussions with Sir Robert Howe, the Governor-General, my conclusion was that we had been right to make the agreement of 12th February. It was too late to take any other course. Some have called this appeasement. I think that it was recognition of the facts. Sudanese nationalism was developing rapidly and would soon be too powerful for us to hold back without very large forces, even if we had wanted to hold it back. One estimate was that we would have needed five divisions. The new regime in Egypt had led to a resurgence of Egyptian nationalism. If we tried to maintain ourselves as rulers of the Sudan, we would drive Sudanese nationalism into the arms of the Egyptians. If we extricated ourselves, Sudanese nationalism would be too strong for Egypt and we would have an independent Sudan.

On the way back to London I stopped for some hours in Cairo. I went with Michael Creswell, the Minister at our Embassy, to see General Neguib. He was a short, squat man, half-Sudanese I was told, with a good military record. He was pleasant to talk to and friendly, in spite of what he had said about imperialist filth. We had a general discussion about Anglo-Egyptian relations and the Sudan. It was then said that the British Government would like to start talks about defence. I was not certain how good his English was, and how much he understood, but he seemed rather naïve politically.

After my meeting with Neguib, I was told that my aircraft was considerably delayed. I said that I would much like to meet Colonel Nasser, if that was possible. Trefor Evans, who had earlier been Lord Killearn's Private Secretary in the 1930s, was Oriental Counsellor at our Embassy. That meant, among other things, that he was responsible for contact with the Egyptian leaders. He was very intelligent and on good terms with them; a good Arabist. Later he had a rather disappointing career. After being Ambassador in Algeria, Syria and Iraq, his Foreign Office career petered out. He went to Aberystwyth as Professor of International Politics and died prematurely. On this occasion, he promptly fixed at his home a meeting with Nasser. I think that Nasser had gone to bed and was woken up and asked to come. He arrived with Hakim Amer, then a major, who later commanded the Egyptian armed forces.

I was favourably impressed by Nasser, as so many were on first meeting him. He seemed to want to be friendly. He was much pleasanter than Hakim Amer, who sat there for most of the time with his utterly expressionless face, and when he spoke, it was to say something rather stupid and bitter.

We discussed Egyptian propaganda against Britain in the Sudan. Nasser then talked about defence, the need for us to evacuate the British Military Base in the Suez Canal Zone, air defence, military equipment and regional defence arrangements. When I mentioned the need for regional defence pacts in peacetime, one of them said, 'We cannot understand why you are worrying about these matters now. We will be friends with you when the attack comes; we will make a pact then.' I explained what infrastructure was, and how useless a last-moment pact would be if there had been no preliminary arrangements over stockpiling, uniformity of equipment and the like. Nasser seemed genuinely interested. He ended by saying that if we would trust them and withdraw, they would negotiate with us afterwards about regional defence. Britain and the United States might be associated with the Arab League in some form. I said that I thought it would all have to be rather more definite than that, but thanked him sincerely for having come to see me at such short notice.

I gave a fuller account of my talks with Neguib and Nasser to the House of Commons in the Foreign Affairs debate in May.

During the rest of 1953, matters proceeded slowly. We accepted Dardiri as a member of the Governor-General's commission. The commission was appointed. The Egyptians successfully stalled the elections, making difficulties in the electoral commission. The elections eventually took place in November. Without doubt, they were affected by Egyptian influence, propaganda and money. The result was a victory for the parties which looked to Egypt rather than to Britain. The Umma Party, headed by S.A.R., which was friendly towards us, did quite well, but I was later told did not win a single seat in the areas of the country suppressed and devastated by the ruthless Khalifa sixty or seventy years before. So long are memories.

Al Azhari, leader of the National Unity Party (N.U.P.), became Prime Minister. We encouraged the Umma Party to form an effective opposition in Parliament and, meanwhile, started to build our bridges to Azhari and the N.U.P. As frequently happens, once the N.U.P. leaders had the smell of independence and power, they drew away from Egypt. Azhari was saying to Luce in February, 'You must not suppose that anyone in his senses, having thrown off one master, would put himself under a new master.' He intended that the Sudan should be friendly with Egypt but independent. They would be friendly with Britain after we had left the Sudan.

It was decided that the new Parliament should be opened on 1st March. Eden asked me to go to represent Britain. I bought a grey morning coat for the occasion and went off to Khartoum with Tony Duff, my Private Secretary, the morning coat and a grey top hat.

During the flight, varying stories were coming in from Cairo. Neguib had been ousted by his colleagues with the backing of the army. Next, Neguib was back again, the cavalry regiments having rallied to his support, but the situation was uncertain. When we reached Cairo, I did not leave the airfield. By then Neguib was thought to be firmly back in control, but it was uncertain whether he would go to Khartoum to represent Egypt at the opening of the Sudanese Parliament. It depended on how secure he felt himself to be. I reached Khartoum and went to the Governor-General's palace, built on the site of General Gordon's, destroyed in 1885.

After some hours' sleep, at about 10.30 a.m. I heard shouts and clapping from the road below my windows, where a crowd had gathered at the west gate of the palace to make a pro-Neguib demonstration. One or two cheer-leaders were very much in evidence. I went downstairs and found Neguib sitting there having a cup of coffee. He had been driven by an unexpected route from the airfield and there had been no trouble. I asked him about the situation in Cairo. He replied that young men like Nasser thought they knew everything, but he had them exactly where he wanted them. He had brought Salah Salem with him to make sure of his good behaviour. Neguib, poor chap, little knew that about six months later, Nasser, having cunningly got the pro-Neguib cavalry out of the way, would stage another coup, as a result of which Neguib himself would have to spend many years under house arrest.

I joined the Governor-General on the verandah, and soon it was clear that something untoward was happening. The police had moved the pro-Neguib demonstration away, but there were sounds of trouble. I returned to my room, and just as I got there I heard what sounded like shots. I went up onto the flat roof, from which I had a good view of Kitchener Square. There was a huge mob there. Sporadic fighting was taking place. The police were shooting and using tear gas. Dead and wounded were being carried through the west gate, and some bodies were being fished out of the Nile. The crowd were supporters of S.A.R. and the Umma Party. They had been allowed to come into Khartoum on the promise that they would bring no arms and be peaceful and orderly. They had meant to demonstrate against Neguib and for independence as he drove from the airfield to the palace. They were infuriated when they found that he had been taken there by another route and they marched on the palace.

It was a nasty situation. The British Chief of Police and his Ansar deputy were soon stabbed to death. So much for no arms. The official casualty list given out later stated that 8 police had been killed and 64 wounded, 20 civilians had been killed and

33 wounded. I am sure that the figure for civilians was a considerable underestimate.

I went down to see the Governor-General. On the landing I met Neguib. The main staircase splits into two half-way up. I said to Neguib how thoughtful I felt the architect had been when the palace was rebuilt after its destruction by the Mahdi. Gordon had been stabbed to death at the top of a single staircase. We were there representing the two Condomini—there was a place for both of us, one at the head of each staircase. He did not seem very amused. It has been said that I added, 'Gordon had the Gordon College for boys named after him. Do you think they will found a Lloyd-Neguib College for girls in our memory?' I am afraid that that is apocryphal. I didn't think of it until afterwards.

About this time, Luce, a fluent Arabist and man of strong character, left the palace and walked through the Ansar crowd, cursing them in Arabic as he went, to see S.A.R. and get him to restrain his followers. It was a brave thing to do.

There were amusing factors in our situation. Tony Duff had been a submarine commander in the war and been awarded a D.S.O. and D.S.C. I had spent six years in the army. On this occasion all that we could muster between us by way of defensive armament were our nail scissors. I wondered whether I ought to be doing something. It was not at all clear that the police and guards would be able to keep the mob out of the palace. Some of them were getting over the wall into the garden, where they were being dealt with by the guards. I then remembered the two token battalions, one Egyptian and one British. The British one, the 1st Bn the York and Lancaster Regiment, was in barracks not very far away.

I went down to see the Governor-General. He was placidly sitting in his study doing nothing in particular, a masterly display of British phlegm. Very tentatively I asked whether it was true that this British battalion was still there. He said, 'Yes.' I then asked, still tentatively, 'Have they by any chance been told of what is going on here?' He replied, 'I don't think so but they always have a company standing by in case of trouble.' I said, 'Do you think they ought to know about the trouble here?' He replied, 'Oh, perhaps they should,' and said he would have a message sent. To this day I do not know whether he was pulling my leg. The company was never, in fact, required. Luce's mission to S.A.R. was successful. The row subsided. Neguib was very subdued at dinner, and next day went back to Egypt on the Governor-General's insistence.

The Egyptian press said that the riots had been imperialist-inspired; that they had been carried out by Umma supporters on behalf of British imperialism.

I stayed on for a few days and then came back to England. At a press conference as I was leaving I wished the self-governing Sudan well. Their difficulty in the future was not going to be to get rid of the British but to keep them to help run the country. Churchill saw me on my return and said that he had not liked that bit at all, but I think that he had read a rather garbled report. Nevertheless, he gave me a copy of his book, *The River War*, suitably inscribed, which has been a treasured possession ever since.

The three years of self-government continued with Egyptian propaganda and intrigue, but the Sudanese were not going to tolerate Egyptian rule in exchange for British, and Nasser's efforts came to nought. On 13th November 1955, the last British and Egyptian troops were withdrawn, with our encouragement. On 19th December, the Sudanese Parliament passed a unanimous resolution in favour of immediate and full independence. On 1st January 1956, Britain and Egypt recognised the independent Sudan. We had frustrated Nasser's ambitions, something for which he never forgave us. It remained a constant irritant. He continued to accuse us of turning the Sudan against him, over the Nile waters, over the division of sterling balances and of disrupting Arab unity.

3

Chapter II

Middle East Alliances

Suez Base agreement July 1954—Baghdad Pact February 1955—meeting between Eden and Nasser in Cairo March 1954—Nasser's purchases of Czech arms September 1955—Aswan Dam—Jordan and Baghdad Pact—Templer's mission December 1955—Sudanese independence.

On the whole, our policy in the Sudan was accepted in Britain. One or two Members of Parliament like Captain Charles Waterhouse, Member for Leicester South-east, and a respected former Minister, criticised it, but I think that most people agreed that we were right to aim at an independent Sudan, and that our tactics to achieve that aim were correct. Attlee, in a debate on 29th July 1954, accused us of having sold the Sudanese down the river and prophesied that there was very great danger of the Sudanese falling again into the hands of the Egyptians. That view was an unusual error of judgment on his part and I do not think that it was widely shared.

There were much stronger feelings about the Suez Canal Base and the agreement that our troops should leave it, initialled on 27th July 1954. There were the usual polemics between the two main parties. The Tories had accused the Labour Government of 'scuttling' from imperial responsibilities. Now, said Labour Members, the Tories were scuttling, although it was right to leave the Base. The Tories replied that if it was right to go, why had the Labour Government stayed and actually increased the number of troops in the Base until there were 80,000 there in 1951. That was normal party stuff and not significant.

A much more serious breach existed within the Conservative Party itself. There were fierce arguments at party meetings. Field-Marshal Lord Alexander, the Minister of Defence, and Antony Head, the Secretary of State for War, supported the decision to take troops out of the Base.

Their case was that the advent of the hydrogen bomb had altered the position. The likelihood of large-scale land operations requiring a large base was considerably reduced. Turkey's entry into NATO had made a more forward defence possible, on Turkey's right flank. The facilities within the Base were useless if Egypt was hostile. The Army was overstrained, yet the equivalent of two and one-third divisions were locked in the Base — 80,000 troops in all — which made the building up of a needed strategic reserve impossible. Moreover, service in the Base was unpopular and bad for recruiting.

On the other hand, respected figures in the Conservative Party such as Waterhouse, Assheton, Christopher Holland Martin and Guy Lloyd, were against, as were several active younger Members, like Julian Amery, Harry Legge-Bourke, Hinchingbrooke and Angus Maude. In addition, there were many doubters. I was one of them. I felt that we probably had to go in the long-run, but I would have preferred a much slower process. I was not so concerned with prestige and scuttling as with giving up a key strategic position before an Arab-Israeli settlement had been made, and while Israeli ships were being denied passage through the Canal.

When going through my papers while writing this book, I came across a note of a discussion which I had in the Foreign Office on 6th January 1954 with Ministers and officials:

Great discussions about our future policy in Egypt. There is considerable support in the Office for the announcing of our intention to leave the Canal Zone, winding up the Base in our own time but eventually clearing out altogether ... After 3 meetings I have persuaded them all, I think, that this course is politically unacceptable, and that if no agreement is reached, we should announce our intention to wind up the Base, but say that so far as facilities in war and the stationing of troops in the Canal Zone in peace are concerned, we shall rely upon our rights under the 1936 Treaty, and that we are prepared to discuss arbitration upon these matters.

Gerald Reading has been a strong help, also Kirkpatrick, both favouring a rather earlier offer of arbitration than I myself would have done. Under this plan, if the Cabinet should accept it, we get rid of the white elephant of the Base, declare our adherence to the rule of law, keep our troops for some time in Egypt and, I believe, save our faces to a considerable extent. The Egyptians will hate this plan.

Under the Anglo-Egyptian Treaty of Friendship and Alliance of 1936 negotiated by Eden and representatives of all the Egyptian political parties when Mussolini was a threat, Egypt's independence had been recognised and the international character of the Suez Canal reaffirmed, and the British right to retain up to 10,000 troops in the Canal Zone accepted. At the end of the period of the treaty in 1957 there had to be agreement as to what should replace it.

The matter was repeatedly discussed in Cabinet. These discussions were rather complicated from my point of view because there was a conference of Foreign Ministers in Berlin from 25th January to 18th February 1954, and the Geneva Conference on Indo-China from 26th April to 21st July. These conferences meant that Eden was unable to be present at many of the Cabinet discussions. He strongly favoured an agreement with Egypt if it could be obtained on reasonable terms. The courses open to us if we failed to get an agreement were:

(a) to stay on in the Base indefinitely. This was open to the disadvantage of no economy in men and money; the progressive deterioration of the Base; awkward international repercussions and growing Egyptian hostility;

(b) to announce liquidation of the Base, evacuation of the Canal Zone and redeployment of our troops in our own time. This would be represented as a scuttle. It would damage the Government's position at home and British prestige abroad. It would be tantamount to admitting that the Egyptians had been too strong for us;

(c) to take the course which I outlined in my note above. We should decide to liquidate the Base and redeploy in our own time. But we should maintain our rights under the 1936 treaty, offering to submit any matters of disagreement about revision of this treaty to international arbitration of some sort. We should offer to enter into discussions with the Egyptians with a view to these matters going to arbitration. This course would be disliked by the Egyptians. They would not get the advantage of the Base nor would they be rid of British troops in the Canal Zone unless they agreed to a long and complicated international lawsuit (and perhaps not even then). On the other hand, we would get no co-operation in winding up the Base and that task would be more difficult.

This third course would be defensible with British opinion. Our international position would be sounder than if we adopted the first course and stayed on indefinitely. It would enable us to keep troops in Egypt for several critical years. If eventually we had to go, it would only be because we were conforming to the ruling of an international tribunal.

During Eden's absences, I had several talks with Churchill himself. He disliked very much the idea of taking all our troops out of Egypt after so many years. He was attracted to the third course. It was said against it that our reduced number of troops, the 10,000 allowed under the treaty, would have been beleaguered. It would have been impossible to supply them, and they could not have protected or secured the working of even a small part of the Base. I had not thought of their role being to protect the Base or any part of it. They would have been garrisons occupying key points. The Egyptians would have seen most of our troops depart, and it could have been said to them that, if they attacked those remaining during the period of the arbitration about a new treaty, it would be regarded by us as an act of war. In Eden's opinion, however, and he was strongly backed by the Chiefs of Staff, this plan was not feasible. They may well have been right, but I thought it the least of the evils although fraught with difficulties.

The United States Government were strongly in favour of an agreement and this time did put pressure on Nasser. They said that unless he accepted reasonable terms, they would stop all economic aid. The negotiations dragged on.

The agreement was to provide for the withdrawal of British forces within twenty months, the upholding of the 1888 Canal Convention, and for part of the Base to be kept in efficient working order and capable of immediate use in the event of armed attack upon Egypt or any other members of the Arab League. This would be done by British and Egyptian technicians. It was to last for seven years. Eventually only two points were outstanding; first, whether we could reactivate the Base in the event of an attack upon Turkey; second, whether the British technicians could wear uniform. Nasser gave way on the first. It seemed impossible to me to refuse an agreement by insisting on the second. Accordingly, it was initialled on 27th July 1954.

Churchill remained unhappy about it, but was convinced in the end that the Base had lost much of its strategic value. Eden announced the agreement in the House of Commons on 28th July 1954. Attlee asked Churchill whether he had consented to it. Churchill replied, 'I am convinced that it is absolutely necessary.' The next day, the agreement was debated. Antony Head opened for the Government. He was followed by Attlee, who showed how much he had resented the charge of scuttling. Eden wound up for the Government.

During the debate there was a remarkable incident. Paget accused Churchill of conspiring with a 'back-bench cabal' against the policy favoured by Eden and Head. Churchill rose to his feet and made an intervention, which was in fact a miniature speech. It raised the tone of the debate and contained within about half a column of *Hansard* an exposition of the strategic considerations, ending on a note of deep emotion. It was extempore and Churchill was only a few months from his eightieth birthday. I quote:

I behaved with perfect correctness in my relations with my colleagues and Members of the House. I have not in the slightest degree concealed in public speech how much I regretted the course of events in Egypt. But I had not held my mind closed to the tremendous changes that have taken place in the whole strategic position in the world which makes the thoughts which were well formed and well knit together a year ago utterly obsolete and which have changed the opinions of every competent soldier that I have been able to meet.

I am not going to attempt, in interrupting the honourable and learned Gentleman, to lay this argument before the House, but I should be prepared to do so and to show how utterly out of proportion to the Suez Canal and the position which we held in Egypt are the appalling developments and the appalling spectacle which imagination raises before us. Merely to try to imagine in outline the first few weeks of a war under conditions about which we did not know when this Session commenced, and about which we had not been told—merely to portray that picture and submit it to the House would, I am sure, convince honourable Gentlemen of the obsolescence of the Base and of the sense of proportion which is vitally needed at the present time, not only in military dispositions, but in all our attempts to establish human relationships between nation and nation.

The effect was dramatic. It uplifted the debate. In the end
the Government won the vote by 259 to 28, including the two
tellers on each side. A handful of Liberals and Labour Members
voted with the Government; those against were all Conservatives.

It was hoped that the conclusion of this agreement, following
upon that about the Sudan in February 1953, would remove the
two main obstacles to friendly relations between Britain and
Egypt, and mark the beginning of a new chapter in a long story.
It was not to be.

Towards the end of 1954, Nuri-es-Said, the Prime Minister of
Iraq, was anxious to strengthen the Arab League Pact by
bringing in Turkey. We were extremely interested in this. It had
taken some months to persuade Nasser that an attack upon
Turkey would entitle us to reactivate the Suez Canal Base, and
that had been included in the agreement regarding the Base.
Nuri pursued his idea with Menderes, the Turkish Prime
Minister, and with Nasser. Menderes was in favour but Nasser
was very much against. He was extremely jealous of Nuri and
afraid that Iraq would challenge Egypt for leadership of the
Arab states. In view of Nuri's age — he was nearly seventy — this
jealousy was rather unnecessary, but nevertheless it was an
obsession with Nasser.

His hostility did not prevent an agreement being signed
between Turkey and Iraq on 24th February 1955, with strong
American encouragement. We were also in favour for two
reasons. It was strengthening the defences of the Middle East
against Soviet attack. Also, the Anglo-Iraqi Treaty of 1930
would expire in 1957. After the disastrous failure in 1948 to
negotiate a new treaty, we had to proceed carefully. If we
joined the Baghdad Pact, it offered the opportunity of a new
agreement under the umbrella of the Pact, an arrangement
between equals which would be palatable in Iraq. Its success,
however, depended very much on continuing American
support.

In March 1954, Eden discussed the Pact when passing through

Cairo on his way to a meeting of the South-East Asia Treaty Organisation (SEATO), about the formation of which I say more on p. 38, Chapter III.

There have been varied accounts of this meeting. Eden told me that it had been quite friendly but Nasser had annoyed him by suddenly holding hands as the photographer was about to photograph them. Heikal's account is much more critical of Eden and said that he treated Nasser as an inferior. This became an obsession with Nasser in later years and he kept returning to the theme that Eden had behaved in an intolerable fashion. One of the British officials who was present has categorically denied this to me, and it certainly would be very unlike Eden to be rude to a foreigner. At all events, it seems fairly common ground that Nasser said that as a soldier he understood the importance of the Northern tier. His interest and sympathy were with the West but the Pact between Turkey and Iraq was bad. It had set back effective collaboration between the Arab states and the West. As political leader of Egypt, whatever he thought as a soldier, he could not possibly join it.

Nevertheless, for the reasons which I have stated, it was decided by the British Cabinet that we should adhere to it, and we did so on 4th April. Pakistan joined in July, and Iran in October. This was satisfactory, but the weakness lay in the ambiguity of the United States's approach. Dulles kept shying off full membership. He said that it was not possible to get the two-thirds majority in the Senate required for formal accession. He did not think that Jewish opinion in America would be favourable. Once what he described as a Palestine settlement had been achieved, it would be different and he would recommend full American membership. He agreed, however, to send military and political observers to the meetings. I believe that the real reason was that he wanted to have it both ways — to have a defensive alliance created on the Soviet southern frontier, but not by joining to incur the hostility of Nasser and those in other Arab states who thought as Nasser did.

We joined the Baghdad Pact on the day before Churchill resigned as Prime Minister. Eden succeeded him. Macmillan became Foreign Secretary. I moved from the Ministry of Supply to which Churchill had appointed me the previous October and became Minister of Defence. Parliament was dissolved and, after a comparatively peaceful General Election in May, Eden came back to power with an increased majority.

That Dulles gained nothing by his refusal to join the Baghdad Pact was shown by Nasser's next move. He proceeded to buy large quantities of arms from the Czech Government. He announced in September that Egypt was to receive MIG fighters, Ilyushin jet bombers, Stalin Mark III tanks, Czech T34 tanks and other heavy equipment. This dramatically changed the balance of power in the Middle East. It was enthusiastically received in other Arab countries. The Arabs attributed Egypt's defeat by Israel in 1948 to the failure of Farouk's corrupt regime to arm the Egyptian Army with modern weapons. The Western powers had been stingy in doling out arms to them since. Therefore, the prospect of vast quantities of modern weapons from behind the Iron Curtain delighted them. The Israelis felt that their backs were now to the wall. This arms deal of Nasser's was certainly one of the causes of what happened in October 1956. Fortunately for the Israelis, the Arabs thought that possessing the weapons was all-important, learning how to use them was a different matter, a miscalculation which revealed itself in no uncertain fashion later in 1956, and in the Six-Day War in 1967. What also depressed the Israelis was the fact that the Russian weapons were comparatively cheap. Their price for a MIG was $400,000, while a French Mirage cost over $1 million. What was more, the Russian long-term credits were granted at 1½ per cent.

The Czech arms deal convinced Eden that it was vitally necessary for the West to take over responsibility for the Aswan Dam scheme. This was a large-scale project to improve the irrigation of the Nile Valley and to produce electric power. There was already a dam at Aswan. The scheme was to build a new high dam, three miles long, south of the existing one, at a total cost of some $1,300 million. There was talk of Soviet help for this, following up the arms deal. Eden felt that this would mean an undesirable extension of Soviet influence in Africa. Macmillan, now Foreign Secretary, agreed with Eden's view and talked about it to Dulles at the abortive Foreign Ministers' meeting in Geneva at the end of October and beginning of November. In Macmillan's words 'they decided to try to get the Aswan Dam for a Western group by some means or other'. Accordingly, on 15th December there was a joint offer by the United States and British Governments and the International Bank to lend the Egyptian Government $400 million towards the total cost of the project. That sum was calculated to be the foreign exchange liabilities which Egypt would have to meet in connection with the project.

Not everyone was convinced of the wisdom of this. Eagerness on our part to undertake this onerous liability before Nasser had made the deal over arms was understandable, but after he had done that some people were in favour of letting him have to go to the Russians for help. They did not think that the presence of large numbers of Russians in Egypt would endear them to the Egyptians. The Saudi royal family was strongly anti-Communist, and Russians in Egypt might cool Saudi-Egyptian relations. Whether that was right or wrong it is impossible to say. When the Russians did come to build the dam, circumstances were quite different.

While discussions were taking place about the Aswan Dam project, it was suggested that Jordan should join the Baghdad Pact. Early in November the Turkish President had paid a state visit to Jordan accompanied by Zorlu, the acting Turkish Foreign Minister. They had strongly pressed Jordan to join. King Hussein was in favour. He told our Ambassador, Charles Duke, that he was willing to join provided he was given the necessary backing by us. In practice that meant the expansion of the Jordanian Army and more money and arms. The time was ripe for a revision of the Anglo-Jordan Treaty. A memorandum of Jordan's needs was drawn up and given to us.

About the same time, Macmillan, then Foreign Secretary, went to a meeting of the Pact countries in Baghdad. He found the Turks gloomy. They considered that by the arms deal with Egypt the Russians had obtained a firm foothold in the Middle East. All the members were strongly in favour of Jordan being invited to join. Macmillan came back to urge this course upon his colleagues. 'Could we not now', he says in *Tides of Fortune*,* 'make a fresh attempt to draw the Arab World away from the growing ambitions of Nasser and the increasing temptations dangled before them by the Soviet Government?' He had no difficulty. We were already working on the list given to Duke by the Jordanian Government. I remember Macmillan asking me outside the Cabinet Room at No. 10 whether I, as Minister of Defence, would agree to Templer, the C.I.G.S., going to Jordan. He spoke with some vehemence of the importance of this. I willingly agreed.

Templer arrived in Amman early in December and offered substantial help in equipment and money to expand the Arab Legion. Then the trouble began. Nasser knew what had happened in Amman and Baghdad and turned the full fury of his propaganda machine on to Jordan. Every kind of allegation was made by the Voice of the Arabs. The intention they said was that the Arab security pact should be broken; Israel was going to become a member of the Baghdad Pact; Jordan would be partitioned.

The four West Bank Ministers in the Jordan Cabinet resigned. They said that anyone who took their places would be a traitor. It was thought that they had been heavily bribed by the Saudis. The Egyptian military attaché was openly urging sedition and revolt. It was a case of the 'strong winds of Arab nationalism scented with Saudi gold', as someone put it. The

* Macmillan, 1969.

Jordan Government resigned. Hazza al Majali, a keen supporter of Jordan joining the Pact, formed a Government. The
pressure grew. Riots began. Three Ministers resigned and
Hazza felt that he could not continue. There is a graphic
description in General Glubb's book of these few days. King
Hussein's own position began to be threatened. It was clear
that Jordan's membership was out of the question. The
Templer mission had failed, through no fault of his.

Muhammad Heikal in his Papers* says that the British
action was a breach of a pledge which I had given: 'In August,
1955, Selwyn Lloyd had been appointed Foreign Secretary and
told the Egyptian Ambassador that Britain would stop all
further efforts to pull Arab countries into the Pact if Egypt
stopped her propaganda against the Pact.' Of course, I was not
Foreign Secretary in August 1955. Heikal must have been confused over his dates. Whether or not it was an error of judgment to try to bring Jordan in at that stage is uncertain.
Humphrey Trevelyan, our Ambassador in Cairo, thought that
it was a mistake.

However that may be, Nasser had triumphed and his
victory was well publicised. It was true that he had suffered at
the same time a setback over the Sudan. Although it was we
who had advised Azhari to declare for independence, not
surprisingly we got no credit for this from Radio Cairo.
Publicly Nasser tried to pretend that it had happened as a
result of an Egyptian initiative. Privately he described it as a
British plot.

The Sudanese Parliament's unanimous declaration in favour
of independence was made on 19th December 1955. Three days
later I was sworn in as Foreign Secretary.

* *Nasser: The Cairo Documents* (known as the 'Heikal Papers'), (New English
Library, 1972).

Chapter III

Minister at Large

*My appointment as Foreign Secretary — Middle Eastern problems —
visits with Eden to Washington and Ottawa — my tour of the
Middle East and India March 1956 — meeting with Nasser.*

I think that Eden asked me to go back to the Foreign Office for
two reasons. The financial situation had deteriorated. After
taking sixpence off income tax in April, Butler had been compelled to have a further Budget in October. That had involved
various cuts in expenditure and increases in taxation which
were unpopular. The imposition again of purchase tax on some
kitchen utensils led to it being called the 'Pots and Pans Budget'.
It was not certain that the situation had been restored. Eden
felt that Butler was tired. Butler had had four successful years
as Chancellor of the Exchequer but he had been much distressed by the painful illness and death of his first wife, Sydney.
Eden wanted a fresh mind for the Treasury. Macmillan obviously was the man for that. Second, Eden was not at all averse
to a change at the Foreign Office. He and Macmillan had not
found it easy to work with each other. During my three years
as Minister of State, and for my shorter time as Minister of
Defence, Eden and I had worked very closely and harmoniously
together. Owing to my long periods at the United Nations, I
had got to know almost all the leading figures handling Foreign
Affairs in other countries and was familiar with the details of a
wide range of overseas problems.

I myself was not at all anxious to move from the Ministry of
Defence. I had been very happy there. I thought I was making
some progress. For the first time since the war, the three

Services were being compelled to examine their programmes for five or more years ahead and to cost them. By the creation of a new post of Chairman of the Chiefs of Staff Committee responsible to the Minister of Defence, I had taken the first step towards the inevitable fusing of the three Service Ministries. The reduction of the length of National Service by three months was the beginning of the end of something which, while providing valuable training and character-building for the young, was beyond our economic means. I had negotiated a satisfactory agreement with South Africa over the Simonstown Base. I was deeply involved in a major battle with the Treasury over pay, allowances and conditions of service for the men in the armed forces.

I also had misgivings about a Minister with only eight months' experience in the Cabinet taking over the very senior post of Foreign Secretary. On the other hand, I knew the Foreign Office well through my time as Minister of State, and it is a wonderful place in which to work because of the continuing contacts with so many members, of all ranks, in the Foreign Service. I felt that I had Eden's confidence and he mine.

Also, I hoped for a measure of goodwill from the Opposition. In October 1964, when I had just changed from Minister of State at the Foreign Office to Minister of Supply, Attlee in that abrupt and clipped manner of his, had been kind enough to say as he passed me in a corridor in the House, 'Great loss to the Foreign Office', hurrying on before I could answer.

Obviously, I could not refuse the offer. I was sworn in and received the seals of office from the Queen at Buckingham Palace on 22nd December 1955.

The most urgent set of problems facing me concerned the Middle East. The outlook was unsatisfactory.

Nasser's aims were set out in his book *The Philosophy of the Revolution*.* Egypt, he thought, held a most important strategic

---

* Cairo: Mondiale Press, undated; U.S. edition published as *Egyptian Liberation: The Philosophy of the Revolution* (Washington: Public Affairs Press, 1955).

position; it was the meeting place, the crossroads, the military corridor of the world. Therefore, Egypt must be the head of the Arab states, the Arab Circle, with oil as its motive power. Second, the white man must be eliminated from the Middle East and Africa. Third, a universal Islamic Empire must be created, with limitless power.

Those aims Nasser was determined to achieve by hook or by crook. In his first objective, the leadership of the Arab world, he regarded Nuri as his principal opponent. I have already referred to his strong feelings about the Baghdad Pact. I discuss later whether Nasser should be likened to Hitler or Mussolini. He certainly possessed a propaganda machine which even Doctor Goebbels would have envied. I have referred to its success over Jordan. It poured out a cascade of abuse of Britain and anything British in the Middle East and further afield; any friends of Britain, like Nuri and the Rulers in the Gulf, were continuously assailed. Day after day the cry was— death to the British and their friends wherever they may be found. Glubb, the British Commander of the Arab Legion in Jordan, was an obvious target and in the early weeks of 1956 special attention was given to him. Nasser regarded him as an obstacle to his control of Jordan and was preparing the way for his departure.

The Governments in all the surrounding countries, except perhaps Syria, were afraid of Nasser and distrusted him. If any of their leaders stood up to him, they were promptly denounced as being secret allies of Israel. One of them, after saying to me what he thought of Nasser, added, 'If I spoke out like that against him publicly, I should be assassinated.' He was assassinated later.

Israel itself knew the form. Elath, the Israeli Ambassador in London, told me on his first visit after my appointment that Nasser intended to attack Israel in the summer, as soon as the British had left the Canal Base. Among the documents captured the following autumn was an operation order to Egyptian commanders in the Third Division dated 15th February 1956:

Para. III: Every Commander should be prepared and prepare his troops for unavoidable wars with Israel in order to achieve our supreme objective, namely, annihilation of Israel and its complete destruction in as little time as possible, and by fighting against her as brutally and cruelly as possible.

There is more of the same stuff in other captured documents. It was no consolation to the Israelis to know that Nasser's hostility came more from the desire to secure thereby leadership of the Arab nations than from a belief in the necessity from the Arab point of view for the extermination of Israel.

Before determining our future policy, I thought it wise to meet face-to-face all our Ambassadors in Middle Eastern countries. I wanted to hear their views and also to assess them personally. Accordingly I summoned them to a two-day meeting in London on 4th January. While they were on their way I tried to think things out myself: how to play our hand in the Middle East. Independence for the Indian Empire had deprived us of the firm base from which in the past our military efforts in the Middle East had been supported at no great cost to ourselves. The Suez Canal Base was no substitute. It depended on local labour which faded away when relations between us and Egypt were strained. It was obsolescent and beyond our financial means, so it had to go—although, as I have indicated earlier, I should have preferred a slower departure.

In the Sudan, the plan of letting Sudanese nationalism and Egyptian imperialism meet head-on had been successful. I had thought the result would be an independent and friendly Sudan. This, in fact, happened.

Our bases could not have remained in Iraq on the old footing. Our military help or presence had to be under the umbrella of the Baghdad Pact. With Turkey, Iran and Pakistan as members, together with U.S. support, it could not plausibly be described as an instrument of British imperialism, and it ensured a presence for us.

In Jordan we had to be prepared for the end of the dominance of the Arab Legion. But again, under a revised treaty our influence might be maintained for a long time. In the other areas in the Middle East where we had control—Kuwait, Bahrain and other shaikhdoms in the Gulf—we should seek to create politically viable entities buttressed by a comparatively scanty military presence on our part, a warship or two at Bahrain, some aircraft at Sharja, and less than 100 British officers and other ranks providing key men for the Trucial Oman Levies, renamed Scouts later that year.

Along those lines I believed that we could reduce our commitments in an orderly fashion but retain our influence and capacity to intervene in an emergency. With Iran also a member of the Baghdad Pact, trouble there was unlikely.

There were difficulties about this strategy. The Arab-Israeli dispute poisoned the atmosphere. We had to be ready to take chances to get that settled. Nasser would probably go to any lengths to disrupt our plans. The Sudan agreement, that over the Suez Canal Zone Base, concessions over sterling balances and the possibility of help over the Aswan Dam had done little to improve our relations. The United States blew hot and cold; Dulles promoted and welcomed the Baghdad Pact but refused to join it. The old jealousy of Britain seemed to persist, certainly among some of his advisers. The Americans were, on the face of it, loyal and dependable allies but underneath there was in many American hearts a dislike of colonialism, a resentment of any authority left to us from the great days of our Empire, and a pleasure, only half-concealed, at seeing us done down.

The final difficulty was the paucity of our resources. At a later stage it was alleged that one result of Suez was to make us realise that we could not act independently. The fact was that we knew that all the time. We were very well aware of our economic weakness and of the strain on our resources of expenditure overseas affecting our balance of payments. We had, however, to conceal that knowledge. If an army in war is going to conduct a strategic withdrawal it does not trumpet that abroad or say precisely what it is going to do with exact timings. That way would indeed lie disaster.

With these ideas in mind, I began the discussions with the Ambassadors in the Middle East. Those attending the meeting were: Trevelyan (Egypt), Wright (Iraq), Parkes (Saudi Arabia), Burrows (Political Resident in the Persian Gulf), Gardiner (Syria), Duke (Jordan), Nicholls (Israel) and Chapman Andrews (Lebanon). After three hours of discussion and plain speaking it was agreed that our policy should be:

(a) to support the Baghdad Pact as strongly as we could but to make no direct effort to bring other Arab states into it;

(b) to press the United States to take some urgent initiative about a settlement of the Arab-Israeli dispute;

(c) to press the United States to persuade King Saud of Saudi Arabia not to throw his money about as he was doing;

(d) to maintain our influence in all the ways open to us — technical assistance, cultural relations, teaching English, educational facilities, etc.;

(e) to make one more attempt to come to terms with Nasser and that I should try to do that myself.

I therefore set about arranging a Middle Eastern tour. But Eden wanted me to go first to Washington and Ottawa with him at the end of January. I was anxious to do that for several reasons. I wanted to renew my acquaintance with Eisenhower. As a staff officer in the British Second Army I had served under him in the war. Before and during the campaign in Normandy and the subsequent advance I had met him frequently. He was still in Paris commanding the North Atlantic Treaty Organisation (NATO) forces when I went there in 1951 as Minister of State. I liked him; he was, in my opinion, a better general than many thought and a master of diplomacy in dealing with his various military subordinates and his political chiefs.

Dulles I had first met at the New Zealand Embassy in Washington in the winter of 1952. That year the United Nations General Assembly had sat until nearly Christmas. Leslie Monroe, the New Zealand Ambassador in Washington, and his wife Olga invited me to spend Christmas with them. While I was there I heard that Dulles was also in Washington. Eisenhower, as Republican candidate, had won the 1952 Presidential election and had appointed Dulles as Secretary of State. Dulles had not, however, yet taken up his appointment. I sent him a message of good wishes and said that I was available in Washington if he wanted to see me. He came almost at once and spent three hours asking me many questions and taking voluminous notes. He showed a gratifying interest in my views. After that I had met him briefly before the formation of SEATO in 1954, and I felt that the proposed visit would be an opportunity to get to know him better and also to ascertain United States intentions in the Middle East.

After Washington, we were to go on to Ottawa. I had not met St Laurent, the Prime Minister, personally but Mike Pearson, the Canadian Minister of External Affairs, was an old friend whom I had known before I became a Minister and of whom I had become very fond at the four meetings of the United Nations General Assembly which I had attended as Minister of State. It would be well on into February before we returned from Ottawa. There was to be a meeting of SEATO at Karachi on 5th March. This had been set up under United States leadership in 1954 after the Geneva agreement on Indo-China. Thereby had hung a story. It was my first personal experience of Dulles saying one thing and doing another. He had definitely agreed at a meeting with Eden and myself in London not to announce this new move until we had had time to consult with other possible members, in particular Australia and New Zealand. Forty-eight hours later he publicly announced the formation of the organisation, without any further notice to us. The members were the United States, France, Australia, New Zealand, Pakistan, Thailand, the Philippines and ourselves. It was never a great success but it certainly did something to maintain morale among its Asiatic members. It withered away when the United States withdrew from Vietnam.

I decided to arrange my Middle East tour around this SEATO meeting. On the way out I would see Nasser and then visit Nehru, the Indian Prime Minister, so as to avoid resentment if I went to Pakistan without also going to India. After Karachi I planned to go to Iraq, Iran, Turkey, Israel and Libya, and to come home on 14th March.

Eden and I were to sail in the *Queen Elizabeth*. Before that there was a lot to be done to prepare for the journey. One tiresome matter took up a great deal of time. It was discovered that some used or surplus war material was being shipped to the Middle East, some of it through third parties in other countries. The Opposition made a great fuss and demanded a debate on it. There also had been a furore in the press. It had been extremely difficult to ascertain the facts. However, we had produced a White Paper and interest in the topic had diminished by the time of the debate. It therefore broadened out into a more general discussion of the Middle East. The usual recriminations began. This was something which very much distressed me. In the period 1945–51, and then when I was Minister of State confronted by Attlee and Morrison, the tone of Foreign Affairs debates had seemed quite different.

Gaitskell, however, in his speech did make one concession. He admitted rather grudgingly that I had rightly claimed that in the past five years the efforts of the United States, France and ourselves to control the supply of arms to the Middle Eastern countries had not been unsuccessful. He said that he was worried about the future. I replied that I hoped that his tribute would carry authority in the Labour Party. It did not—the complaints continued just the same.

In this debate I put forward an idea which when Minister of State I had discussed with the Secretary-General of the United Nations. It was that United Nations forces—or to use a horrible but neutral word, personnel—should be deployed in the de-militarised zones to keep the peace. The forty or so 'observers' then stationed there were not enough and their function was limited to observing.

The talks in Washington with Eisenhower and Dulles were rather disappointing. I have always been doubtful about highly publicised meetings between heads of government. These doubts do not arise from any fear that these undermine the position of a Foreign Secretary in relation to the Prime Minister. In the modern world, those two must work as a team, agreed about policy and with complete confidence in each other. When this is not the case, all is not well; for example, Lloyd George and Curzon, Neville Chamberlain and Eden, Attlee and Morrison. On the other hand, the confidence between Attlee and Bevin, Churchill and Eden (although they had their occasional differences between 1951 and 1955) and, in my opinion for what it is worth, between Eden and myself, Macmillan and myself, and Macmillan and Home, made the relationship work. Which of them gets most of the limelight does not much matter. It depends on personalities. With heads of government like the United States President, the French President under de Gaulle's constitution, and the U.S.S.R. head of government, the British Prime Minister must play a large public part. This must be the case. The Foreign Secretary appears a lesser figure. I did not object to Summits on that account.

However, they have their dangers. On the one hand, they give the impression of action. They enable useful personal contacts to be made. If there has been full preparation before and there is some specific and realisable objective they may be successful. After a good dinner at the Embassy in Moscow in 1959 I told Khrushchev and Macmillan what I thought of them. I said:

If one side says 3 and the other side says 5, you Heads of Government are competent to agree on 4. If it is more complicated than that, you have not the time to prepare adequately or to be properly briefed on detail; you will probably do more harm than good.

I do not think that either was very pleased, but it is so, and when it is seen that nothing important has been achieved at a Summit Meeting there will be a feeling of anti-climax.

This applied to our meeting in Washington. We discussed the Chinese seat at the United Nations. We were told that the United States would leave the organisation if the Peking Government was allowed to take that seat. There was a long discussion about the Buraimi oasis. It was in the territory of the Sultan of Muscat, with whom we had a treaty. It was thought that there might be oil there. The Saudis had moved in to occupy the oasis. In 1953, with the intervention of a detachment of the Trucial Oman Levies and the help of the Emir Zaid, brother of the ruler of Abu Dhabi, the Saudis had been turned out. There had then been an arbitration but irregularities had been proved. We had withdrawn from it and were maintaining our position in the oasis. It had become a running sore in our relations with Saudi Arabia but there was nothing which we could do about it without throwing over our friends. The United States Government, because of their strategic base at Dhahran and the importance of their Aramco oil interests in Saudi Arabia, continuously brought pressure to bear on us to give in. We did our best to convince the President and Dulles that this was out of the question. At last they did seem to understand our position and also to realise that King Saud was using his wealth foolishly and in such a way as to damage the West and to help the Communists.

They agreed with us about Nasser's propaganda. We learned, I think for the first time, of doubts about the Aswan Dam project. Dulles told us that Black, of the International Bank, had said that his talks with Nasser were almost at breaking point. Black felt that the dam was too grandiose for Egypt's fragile economy and shaky political base.

Dulles was cautious and unenthusiastic about the Tripartite Declaration by Britain, France and the United States in 1950 to prevent breaches of the Arab-Israeli armistice. The United States Government would have to get Congressional approval for definite action. Rather reluctantly he allowed a reference to further military discussions about it being put in the communiqué. I think that this was the first time that I realised that the Tripartite Declaration had nothing like the efficacy which it was thought to have. Similarly, the Americans could not join the Baghdad Pact, although they promised substantial military and other help. Perhaps the best feature of the visit was Eden's brilliant speech in Congress, which was widely reported.

Those who contend that Suez was a watershed in our national history often maintain that Eden's Government still regarded Britain as capable of independent action on a global scale. It needed Suez, they say, to convince us that we were no longer a Great Power. This is very wide of the mark. We knew the facts only too well. During our talks in Washington, Eden put in a paper on our economic situation. The Second World War had turned us from the world's greatest creditor to the world's greatest debtor. We could not undertake any more external commitments. Our gold and dollar reserves only covered three months' imports. All this made the safeguarding of our supplies of oil from the Middle East the more important. What we did not foresee were the actions that would be taken against us by the United States Government. Perhaps we were all personally on too good terms, influenced too much by our previous close and friendly relations with Eisenhower. We felt that we might argue away like members of a family but at the end of the day would never seriously fall out. Not having the Americans on the same side, or at least benevolently neutral, was unthinkable.

There followed a very pleasant visit to Ottawa, the high spot of which was another successful speech by Eden, this time to the Canadian Parliament. I am sure that if Ministers visit the United States they should make a point of going on to Ottawa to tell Canadian Ministers what, if anything, has transpired.

On the way to Ottawa I made a detour to Chicago to speak to a luncheon club there. It was rather a strain but amply compensated for by a brief visit to a Toulouse-Lautrec exhibition. They said that never again would so many of his works be gathered in the same place.

In Canada we stayed with Vincent Massey, the Governor-General. He was a charming host. In the course of the visit I dropped a frightful brick. Our High Commissioner was General Sir Archibald Nye. I spoke to the Canadian Women's Club, with Mrs Mike Pearson in the chair. I sat on her right with Nye on my other side. There was a microphone in front of me. Towards the end of lunch I found that it had been live all the time. The guests could have listened in to my conversation with Mrs Pearson and Nye. Perhaps they did. I started my speech by referring to the microphone having been live and said to Nye, tapping him on the shoulder, 'It just shows, General, doesn't it, how careful you have to be about what you say!' There was a kind of quiver from the audience. They did not laugh very much. I sensed that something was not quite right. Afterwards I was told that Nye had been severely criticised that morning in the Canadian press for having made some very controversial statement, quite unintentionally of course, on some subject of considerable topical interest. It was thought that I had deliberately given him a public rebuke. The lesson indeed was that one can never be too careful about what one says in public.

There was another Foreign Affairs debate on 27th February, just before I left for my Middle Eastern tour. I restated the objectives of our policy in that area. The first task, apart from the keeping of the peace, was to assist in an Arab-Israeli settlement; second, we should maintain our position in the Persian Gulf; third, we should support our friends in the area; fourth, we should be loyal to our alliances; fifth, we should persuade those who might succumb to Soviet blandishments of the dangers involved for their political freedom and their religious life; and finally — and very important — we should try to improve the standards of living of those who dwell in the area.

There was little criticism of these objectives and little help as to how they might be achieved. But at least I received good wishes for my mission from most on both sides of the House.

As to the rest of the debate, I have no wish to provoke unnecessary controversy. I would merely suggest that those interested in the political attitudes of the time should read the speeches of one or two Members who later were to hold high office.

On arrival in Cairo, I had a meeting during the afternoon of 1st March with Fawzi, the Egyptian Minister for Foreign Affairs. He was a smooth and rather slippery customer but had good manners and personally was pleasant to deal with. He was also an extremely skilful negotiator, but at that time was working his passage with the Egyptian ruling clique. It was difficult to place a proper value on what he might say.

We talked first about the Baghdad Pact. Fawzi said that the Arab world should have been allowed 'to get together on their own account from their centre in Cairo' — a revealing comment! The Pact had divided the Arab world, but Egypt did not wish to eliminate genuine British interests or influence in the Middle East. I explained the dangers of Soviet infiltration. Middle East oil was vital to us and to other countries of Western Europe. We had not started the Baghdad Pact: it was the nations on the northern perimeter which had done so. I said that we would help, if asked, over the Nile waters. I hoped that the Aswan Dam project would go through. The supply of arms was a difficult problem. Fawzi said that Egypt was firmly anti-Communist but must be free to get arms where she could. Every Government had a duty to provide for the security of its own people — but no Egyptian Government would ever be so mad as to use arms in an aggressive attack upon Israel.

It was a good-tempered conversation. In it, Fawzi only made two statements of doubtful veracity. The first was that Egypt did not wish to eliminate British influence in the Middle

East. Everything Egypt did belied that. Second, the statement that no Egyptian Government would attack Israel reads strangely alongside the operational orders for the extermination of Israel which had already been issued to the Egyptian Army (see p. 34).

In the evening there took place the notorious dinner with Nasser. He, Hakim Amer (the Egyptian Commander-in-Chief) and Fawzi on one side, and I, Humphrey Trevelyan and Harold Caccia on the other side.

Nasser greeted me courteously. It was suggested that we should discuss Anglo-Egyptian problems later. As we were going in to dinner I said that I would be most interested to hear how he had attained his present position as ruler of Egypt. He proceeded to give us a fascinating account. It had begun with his deep resentment at the insult inflicted upon King Farouk and Egypt by the British action when Lampson (later Lord Killearn) during the war went with military detachments, including tanks, to the Abdin Palace to force the King to abdicate, unless he agreed at once to appoint Nahas Pasha as Prime Minister with freedom to choose his own Ministers. Nasser had immediately begun to conspire against the British, but he soon realised that his resentment against them could only be satisfied if Farouk were eliminated. Therefore, he next began to conspire against Farouk. That conspiracy was successful, but Neguib was not sufficiently anti-British, so Nasser had to conspire in turn against Neguib. His life had been conspiracy after conspiracy and we must understand that fact.

After dinner we discussed the situation on the borders between Egypt and Israel. I suggested the strengthening of the United Nations Truce Supervision Organisation (UNTSO). Nasser had not much hope of improvement from that. There must be territorial concessions by Israel and the transfer of southern Negev to Egypt; Eilat and perhaps Haifa could become free ports. He did not think internationalisation of Jerusalem was possible any longer, but he had no strong views. He had been surprised by the violence of the feeling amongst

Palestinian refugees against being resettled. He did not expect
a major attack by Israel; and Egypt's intentions were solely
pacific. When the Tripartite Declaration was raised, he said
that it 'gave no rights and created no obligations'. I got the
impression that he would as soon have had a scorpion in his
bed as the re-entry of Western troops on to Egyptian soil, and
that he would never ask for help under the Declaration. He
complained more than once that we were trying to worsen
relations between Egypt and the Sudan.

The real argument, however, was about the Baghdad Pact.
He repeated what Fawzi had already said. Iraqi membership
was the trouble. It divided the Arab world. He was not opposed
to bilateral treaties between the United Kingdom and Iraq,
or Jordan, or Libya, but the Pact had ruined any benefit to our
relations which might have followed from the Base Agreement.
I repeated that the Pact looked north and not south. It was to
prevent Soviet infiltration and to protect the oil. For that
reason we had also to maintain our position in the Gulf, but
we had no interest in old-fashioned domination.

Nasser said that there was no chance of improvement in
Anglo-Egyptian relations unless we gave an undertaking that
there should be no new Arab members. Iraq could remain a
member, although, as he said that, I had the impression that
he meant to have Iraq out by fair means or foul. I said that the
trouble was Egypt's propaganda against Britain everywhere in
the Middle East, the Sudan, Libya and East Africa. Radio
Cairo's broadcasts in Swahili were just incitements to murder.
Nasser admitted that this propaganda was put over on his
directions. I then said that I was prepared to put to my colleagues the proposition that we would undertake not to try to
persuade any other Arab country to join the Pact, provided he
would stop his propaganda. He said that he was prepared to
agree to that and we should talk more about it when we met
again the following morning.

Towards the end of our conversation a message arrived for
Trevelyan. He went outside to take it.

My recollection is that later Nasser also received a message, which he put in his pocket. Trevelyan also remembers noticing this.

The dinner had been excellent; the conversations were good-tempered, although there was some very plain speaking on both sides.

On the way to the Embassy, Trevelyan told me that Glubb had been dismissed and ordered to leave Jordan at 7 a.m. the next day.

When we returned to the Embassy I got in touch with London at once. The Prime Minister suggested that I should fly to Amman to reason with King Hussein. It was doubtful, however, where I could arrive before Glubb left. For me to fly in either after he had left or with not enough time to delay his departure would have been a further humiliation. I decided not to go to Amman but to continue my journey as planned.

This meant that after only an hour or two's sleep I had to meet Nasser again. The meeting was polite but not cordial. Nasser began by congratulating me on having arranged for Glubb's dismissal in order to improve relations between Egypt and Britain. It was very wise of us. In spite of what he had said the night before about having been a conspirator from 1942 onwards, and having always thought as a conspirator, this pretence seemed to me to be outrageous and I showed and said what I thought of it. We then went over the Baghdad Pact ground again, together with our complaints about Egyptian propaganda. He confirmed his agreement to stop the latter, at all events until I had reported to my Cabinet colleagues. In due course I went off to catch the aircraft.

So ended my second and last meeting with Nasser. Perhaps had I not had a long flight, some hours of talks requiring concentration, the shock of Glubb's dismissal, and only an hour or two's sleep, I might have been more amused by Nasser's pretence that he thought that the British had agreed to remove Glubb in order to improve relations with Egypt.

I left with mixed feelings. I thought that he had deteriorated since our meeting three years before. He smiled a great deal more, for no apparent reason. He had lost the simplicity which I had rather liked in 1953. He did not exactly condescend, but he gave the impression that he thought he had better cards in his hand or, to put it another way, with the Base agreement in his pocket and Communist arms in the hands of his troops, he could do more harm to us than we could do to him.

I did not believe him when he said that he had no objection to our bilateral treaties with Iraq or Jordan or Libya, nor when he said that he had no intention of attacking Israel. I had, however, the faint hope that he would carry out his promise to stop at once the hostile broadcasts. If that did happen, if only for a few weeks, perhaps something might be salved. I very soon heard that, far from stopping them, they were stepped up as soon as I left until, as Trevelyan wrote, they amounted to a flood of abuse.

It was sad about Glubb. Later King Hussein made generous financial amends to him and, I believe, regretted what he had done and particularly the way he had done it. I was the more distressed because when the King was in London in the autumn of 1955 I had spoken to him about Glubb. We knew that Glubb was nearly sixty. He had been in Jordan for a very long time. We suspected that he irritated the King. It was obvious that the time for his retirement could not be long delayed. I asked whether relations between him and Glubb were still very good. The King said that he was completely satisfied with the existing state of affairs. There is no doubt, however, that after that conversation Glubb's position had been further undermined by Nasser's propaganda. Any magazine or newspaper saying that Glubb was the real ruler of Jordan was imported into Amman in large numbers by the agents of Nasser or the Saudis. Steps were taken to ensure that the King saw them all over the place. I thought that the King had reacted in a fit of temper to one of these newspaper articles, but I read afterwards that this was not Glubb's own opinion.

We reached Bahrain on the afternoon of 2nd March. I was met by the Ruler, members of his family and the Resident, Bernard Burrows. I drove off to the Residency with Burrows and Caccia heading the motorcade, except for a police car in front. At one point where the road was narrow, and opposite the house of a man who had recently served a prison sentence for dangerous driving, there were shouts from the crowd. They did not seem particularly hostile. I was told afterwards that they were shouting, 'Go home, Belgrave'. Belgrave was the Ruler's principal adviser. He had been in Bahrain for a long time and had served the Ruler and his people faithfully and well. I was later told that there were also shouts mentioning Nasser's name. One handful of sand was thrown at my car, some of which came through an open window and alighted on Caccia's knees. Later cars in the procession were treated rather more roughly; a window was broken in one, but all got through.

At the Residency, I had a press conference. I said that the British Government believed in the gradual evolution of representative institutions and in the maintenance of law and order and social stability. The speed of progress must vary, country by country. I repeated more than once that we had great confidence in the Ruler.

The Ruler's banquet for me was the next engagement. I had had some experience of the extent and scope of Arab hospitality. I hoped therefore that I would be able to do full justice to what was laid before me and not cause any offence to my host. I had an agreeable conversation with him. He began it by saying that he wanted to have no relations with any Government, other than the British, in the Middle East or anywhere else. He did not appear to be particularly perturbed about what had happened coming from the airport. His son sat on the other side of the table listening carefully but not saying a word throughout the meal.

As soon as dinner was over I was told that a crowd was still waiting in the street, intending to demonstrate again when I left for the airport to continue my journey. The Chief of Police said that he thought he could get me through to the airport. I asked if there would be any risk of casualties; there had been some in a disturbance not very long before. The Chief of Police replied that there certainly might be some casualties but his men could handle the situation. I replied that I had no intention of having a way cleared for me through the crowds by force. I did not want a single Bahraini injured, much less killed, in that process. I would stay, after the banquet, at the Residency until the streets were cleared. By about 1.30 a.m. the crowd had gone home to bed and the street was clear. I was driven without incident to the airport.

I knew well enough what a meal the papers would make of this. Sure enough, the stories were that I had been stoned and had had to take refuge in a neighbouring house; I had been rescued by the police; I had stayed, fearful for my life, besieged in the Residency; I had then had to be smuggled out at dead of night. To add insult to injury, after I had arrived at Delhi later that day, Nehru had said to someone that my experience in Bahrain had made me jittery.

Even if I myself was not suffering from the jitters, quite a lot of people at home were so about Jordan. The papers were in full cry. Conservative and Labour Members were calling for action. One senior Labour backbencher asked when the Government was going to stop 'dithering and grovelling'. The withdrawal of all British officers from the Arab Legion was ordered. A debate took place in the House of Commons on 7th March. During it, the usefulness of the Baghdad Pact was called in question. When signed in January 1955, Herbert Morrison had welcomed it on behalf of the Labour Party. Gordon Walker had described it as good and to be approved. Now, in 1956, Robens, the Shadow Foreign Secretary, had his doubts about it, calling it a source of danger to peace in the Middle East. On the other hand, Gaitskell said that the Government were rightly basing their policy on the Baghdad Pact. Shinwell strongly supported it in the existing conditions. Gaitskell added that Glubb's dismissal had been a blow to our

1   President Nasser uses the radio for his propaganda to undermine the stability of the Middle East. 'Nasser possessed a propaganda machine which even Dr Gobbels would have envied.' (p. 34)

2 Eden meets Nasser, Cairo, February 1955.

3 Selwyn Lloyd and Nasser, March 1956.

4 Public adulation of Nasser, after evacuation of the British military base in the Suez Canal Zone in June.

5 Selwyn Lloyd and Ben-Gurion, the Israeli Prime Minister, in Tel Aviv, March 1956.

6   26th July, 1956. Under the watchful eye of armed troops 50,000
people gather in Manchia Square, Alexandria, to hear Nasser's speech
announcing seizure of the British and French owned Suez Canal.

7   Pineau, the French Minister of Foreign Affairs, Lloyd and
Murphy, American Deputy Under-Secretary of State, meet in
London for talks following nationalisation of the Suez Canal.

prestige and to the Pact. What were we going to do about it?

With hindsight, I think that Eden made a tactical mistake in not opening the debate himself. He could have attributed Glubb's fall to Nasser's undermining of the position, spoken of the menace of Egyptian propaganda and Saud's money, said that we would continue steadfast support for the Baghdad Pact, but meanwhile we should re-examine our relations with Egypt. Opening the debate, he need not have said more; but, as he had decided to wind up, expectation grew that he would have some striking statement to make at the end.

In the event, his speech was strongly criticised. He was accused of losing his temper, and he himself in his book *Full Circle** is extremely critical of his own performance. I have read his speech several times since and each time I have thought it perfectly adequate and indeed a good speech. Perhaps it read better than it sounded. This can be a recurring factor in House of Commons speaking. The content may be good but out of tune with the atmosphere of the House. In February 1958, I made a speech in a Foreign Affairs debate which was so badly received and seemed to be so bad that I felt that I ought to offer to resign. The next day a Conservative Member, who was not a personal friend, came up and asked what the fuss was about. He had not heard me but he had read the speech and it had seemed a very good one. The same sort of thing happened in a debate in March 1960. Macmillan opened and his speech was described as a flop. I wound up rather pugnaciously and was generally praised. When I read the speeches afterwards, Macmillan's was an excellent statement of our case. My own had little in it except a few jibes at the Opposition.

At New Delhi I stayed with Nehru, the Prime Minister, in his official residence. His sister, Mrs Pandit, then Indian High Commissioner in London, was also there. I liked her very much. Knowing that it was a teetotal house and that I would miss my

* Cassell, 1960, p. 352.

5

whisky and soda in the evening, she had arranged for me to find in my room two bottles of Johnnie Walker, which was typically thoughtful, and after some very dry talks a considerable comfort to me.

She was most anxious that the visit should be a success. The only other person staying in the house was Nehru's daughter, Mrs Indira Gandhi, later herself to become Prime Minister. It was obvious that Mrs Pandit did not care for her niece, and I was not at all surprised that in the 1977 election Mrs Pandit should have come out in opposition and helped to turn Mrs Gandhi out of office.

Nehru, I think, although a little patronising, meant to be friendly. He was relaxed about Anglo-Indian relations. We discussed a wide variety of topics; military alliances, which he was against, believing they did more harm than good; Kashmir; Goa; Soviet thinking; relations with China; Cyprus; Indo-China; Antarctica. On the Arab-Israeli problem, Nehru had little to suggest. Soviet actions, like the supply of arms to Egypt, were moves in a bigger game. The Russians, he said, were not much interested in the Arabs or Israelis as such.

I had two hours with him on the Saturday evening, three hours on the Sunday afternoon, and then another two hours that evening after dinner. At no time was an official there with me. That involved me in one of the occupational hazards of a Foreign Secretary's life. If he has no official with him, he has to make the record of the conversation himself. I spent the whole journey from Delhi to Karachi dictating records of these conversations with Nehru — seven telegrams and eight memoranda.

After Glubb's dismissal while I was in Cairo, and the Bahrain disturbance, I had been wondering what an ill wind would blow to me in Delhi. It happened at 11.30 p.m. on the last evening. Nehru said that the Indian Government were proposing to buy some Soviet IL 28 aircraft. I knew that he was leaving Delhi at 7 a.m. the next morning. Obviously he had carefully delayed telling me until further discussion was virtually impossible.

Next day, Pillai, the Permanent Under-Secretary at their Foreign Office, indicated fairly clearly to me that it had been done contrary to his advice. He thought the only hope was a personal message from Eden to Nehru.

There was to be another puff of the same wind, which may seem trivial but not to the speaker at the time. I was addressing the Indian Institute of Foreign Affairs in the open air, competing with other noises. One page of my text was missing. I had the agony of finding that after p. 22, there was no p. 23, and I had to improvise from memory a bridge to p. 24. Fortunately no one seemed to notice it but it certainly added a grey hair or two.

At Karachi I had several talks with Dulles about the Middle East. I said that I thought the situation there was serious and that no reliance could be placed on Nasser. He replied that some people in the United States administration had reached the same view; he had himself not quite reached it although he was not far off it. Unless Nasser did something definite soon, we would have to 'ditch' him. By something definite, he meant three things: the immediate cessation of propaganda against the Baghdad Pact and the West, acceptance of the Johnston plan (which dealt with water supplies in Syria, the Lebanon, Jordan and Israel), and specific steps towards a settlement of the Arab-Israeli dispute. He thought that a bargain might be made with Nasser that there should be no more Arab members of the Pact in return for these three 'definite' things.

I replied that as a matter of practical politics I did not think that, in the near future at any rate, we should obtain the accession of any new Arab members, but to try to come to an understanding about it with Nasser was quite another thing. It would have a bad effect upon the other members and on Nuri in particular.

On my return to London I was interested to find that my distrust of Nasser was shared in London, and the Foreign Office's tendency to take a pro-Arab line had not affected their judgment of him. Nutting, the Minister of State, had sent a message to me while on my tour to say that what had happened had shown that appeasement of Nasser had not paid. I was shown a minute which he had sent to the Prime Minister early in March to the effect that it did not seem that the Americans had yet hoisted in that appeasement of Nasser simply did not pay, and that Nasser would break whatever bargain we might make with him. Nutting had seen a lot of Nasser during the final stages of the negotiations about the Base, and his confirmation of my own judgment was significant. It was also clear from his minutes that the Office was getting more and more disenchanted with the Tripartite Declaration. The French would only fight if Nasser attacked Israel. The Americans had shown during our Washington visit that action under it would require Congressional approval and that would be a slow business. Eden himself endorsed emphatically the line I had taken with Dulles.

On 8th March I had another short talk with Dulles. He said that the United States were going to enter into things in the Middle East more in the future. I asked him, 'How?' He replied that he had not thought it out. I said that he might begin by joining the Baghdad Pact. He said that that was quite impossible. I never understood the real reason. He used to refer to the pro-Israel lobby and the difficulty of obtaining Congressional approval. I never knew whether there was something else at the back of his mind.

At Karachi I had my first meeting with Pineau, the French Foreign Minister. I liked him. He was a good talker. I did not get in many words that first time but he was an interesting personality. I gathered that one of his sidelines was writing fairy stories for children. I told him that his recent statement in Cairo hostile to the Baghdad Pact had hardly been that of a friend and ally. He said that it had been for local consumption. Dulles told me that he had taken a very poor view of Pineau. He could not understand what he was driving at. He was most unimpressed. I forbore to tell him I knew that the feeling was mutual between them.

The political situation in Karachi itself was a little obscure. General Iskander Mirza was in the process of moving himself up from Prime Minister to President. However, he was extremely friendly and full of distrust of Nasser. He said that Nehru and Nasser were working hand-in-glove to eradicate Western influence from Asia. He added that King Saud was beginning to be frightened of Nasser.

On 10th March I went on to Baghdad. I had a long talk with King Feisal and Nuri.

It was my first visit to Iraq, and I think the first time that I had met the King. He received me in his comparatively modest palace. I thought then how close it was to the road and how vulnerable. It would not have been too difficult to have lobbed a grenade from the road into the front rooms. It was here that two and a half years later in 1958 the King and Crown Prince, Abdul-Ilah with other members of the royal family, including women and children, were to be brutally murdered. The King was a charming young man, with plenty of ability. He was deeply interested in the development plans for Iraq and in improving standards of living. I believe that he would have been a great ruler had he lived. His uncle, the Crown Prince, had had an eventful life. He was, through many vicissitudes, a staunch and consistent friend of this country. He believed above all that it was his duty to train his nephew to be a worthy King.

Nuri was a wise and true friend of Britain dating from the time of the Arab Revolt in the First World War. But his main interest was Iraq's independence. It was due to him that first the mandate and then the 1922 treaty were ended in 1930. He was responsible for the policy of spending the oil revenues wisely. He laid the foundations on which a stable and prosperous state could have been built. Had he been twenty years younger, I do not believe the tragedy of 1958 would have taken place.

They were anxious about events in Jordan. King Hussein

had surrounded himself with bad advisers. The Egyptian/
Saudi/Syrian offer in January to Jordan to replace the British
subsidy, provided the Anglo-Jordanian treaty was terminated,
was a sinister move. We agreed that King Feisal must try to
influence King Hussein. An early meeting should be arranged.
I offered to go to Amman after that if it seemed as though such
a visit would do any good. Nuri was full of ideas about Syria.
The Government there was evil. Nuri said that he could
organise a movement against it by elements in Syria more
friendly to Iraq and the West. While it was going on it was vital
that, first, under no circumstances should the Turks invade
Syria and, second, that the Israelis should not attempt to
improve their position. I promised to speak about it to the
Turkish Ministers when I reached Ankara.

I spent that night in Tehran. The Shah was in a robust mood,
very firm in his support of the Pact. He said that it was unthinkable that we should close the door to other Arab countries
if they wished to join.

In Ankara I passed on Nuri's message and sent to him a
reassuring reply. The Turks warned me that Nasser was an
implacable enemy of Britain and the West. He was not only
trying to supplant Britain in Jordan, he had now told the
Libyans that he and his allies would guarantee Libya financial
aid if they would dispense with the help now being given by
Britain and the United States.

From Ankara I went on to Israel. I was met at Tel Aviv by
Moshe Sharett, the Foreign Minister, a friend from U.N. days
in Paris, now in uneasy partnership with Ben-Gurion. He had
been Prime Minister while Ben-Gurion was on a sabbatical
year in a kibbutz. On Ben-Gurion's return, Sharett stayed on
as Foreign Secretary for a time. Not long after my visit he
resigned on the ground that he found it impossible to work with
Ben-Gurion. It was a strange coincidence that two of the
soundest men in the Middle East, Nuri and Sharett, should
both have served in the Turkish Army in the days of the
Turkish Empire.

Ben-Gurion welcomed me as the first British Foreign Secretary to visit Israel. He said that Nasser was an imperialist. *The Philosophy of the Revolution* accurately portrayed his faith. His targets were Jordan, Iraq, Africa and, of course, Israel. He would strike against Israel soon. I asked how soon. Ben-Gurion replied that it would be in two, three or four months' time. Only the supply of adequate quantities of arms to Israel by the West would stop him. Ben-Gurion said that he had no faith in the Tripartite Declaration. I had the interesting experience of watching Israeli mounted policemen controlling a crowd of Israeli Communists trying to demonstrate in Jerusalem against my visit.

One could not but be impressed by Ben-Gurion — the diminutive figure, combative, provocative, distrustful of Britain, with the shock of white hair standing out in all directions.

Ben-Gurion referred several times to the vulnerability of Israel. The Egyptian Air Force could come in from the sea and wipe out the Israeli towns before an Israeli fighter could be got into the air. This was obvious, apart from what Ben-Gurion had said. The road from Tel Aviv to Jerusalem was within range of snipers at some point and of artillery all the way.

From Israel I flew on to Tripoli, where I spent an hour or two. Ben Halim, the Prime Minister, was fairly calm and full of pro-Western sentiments. He confirmed that Nasser was trying to subvert the Libyan Government. Ben Halim repeated the valid point, already made to me by others in the course of my journeys, that the friends of the West should be rewarded for their friendship more liberally than Nasser was rewarded for his hostility — a clear reference to the Aswan Dam.

On arrival at Tel Aviv, I had sent a personal message to Eden. It not only summed up my conclusions, it shows the terms on which we worked together. I said

(a) that my visit to Baghdad, Tehran and Ankara had been well worth while. Nuri looked well and was as firm as ever. The Shah was also quite calm;

(b) that the Turks were delighted with the visit. We had some good talks. The Cyprus developments, of course, helped the atmosphere a lot. There were certain things, however, which must be done and done quickly. The Americans must hurry up and put some reality into their solid support of the Baghdad Pact. We must also consider whether there was more that we could do. In addition to working out the new relationship with Jordan, a plan must be made about Syria;

(c) that we had to indicate our attitude to Egypt. I did not see how we could tolerate their behaviour much longer. Their offer to Libya, if accurately reported, seemed almost the last straw. Must we go on with the Dam?

(d) I was not completely exhausted, but I had a difficult day in front of me in Israel, physically and otherwise. The next day I had a long flight with talks with the Libyans at Tripoli on the way, arriving at Rome late in the evening. Unless the P.M. specially wished it, I did not propose to leave Rome very early on the following day, and would not be back in time for a morning Cabinet;

(e) that in any case, I should like to have a preliminary talk with him before reporting to the Cabinet;

(f) that I hoped his talks with Mollet went well. I was afraid that he had been having an anxious and exhausting time. I wished that I could have been at his side during it.

In his reply, he urged me to take my own time home. He agreed to all I had said. He added that he was rather troubled about Libya.

Chapter IV

Aid or Not?

Report to Cabinet—policy towards Nasser—visit of Bulganin and Khrushchev to Britain April 1956—other visitors to London—difficulties with United States over Middle Eastern policies—our withdrawal from Suez Base—withdrawal of Aswan Dam offer July 1956.

It was now mid-March 1956. There then followed four months of a kind of interregnum. Looking back, it was obviously the comparative quiet before the storm. There was the digesting of what I had learned during my tour, and the communicating of it to my Cabinet colleagues. There was the visit of the Russian leaders to Britain, by way of interlude, to be handled so that it did more good than harm. It was necessary to try to pin the United States Government down to some kind of common policy to which they would publicly subscribe. The final departure of our troops from the Suez Canal Base had to be presented as common sense rather than surrender. Above all, I had to be quite certain that, judging by the purchase of the Czech arms and what had happened since, we were right in assessing Nasser as a potential Hitler who must somehow be checked if British influence was not to be eliminated from the Middle East and East Africa, and all our friends destroyed.

After discussing with Eden the reports which I had sent back during the tour, I put my conclusions to the Cabinet on 21st March.

I said that as a result of my conversations with Nasser I was satisfied that he was unwilling to work with the Western powers in the task of securing peace in the Middle East. Our hopes that after the Base agreement he would work with the West had come to nothing. It was obvious he was aiming at leadership of the Arab world. In order to secure it he was willing to accept assistance from the Russians, and he was not prepared to work for a settlement of the Arab-Israeli dispute. Despite my conversation with him in Cairo and his promises, there had been no slackening in the Egyptian propaganda against our position in the Middle East. We could not establish a basis for friendly relations with an Egypt controlled by Nasser.

That being so, we had to realign our policy in the Middle East. Instead of seeking to conciliate or support Nasser, we should do our utmost to counter him and uphold our true friends. We should seek increased support for the Baghdad Pact and its members. We should make a further attempt to persuade the United States to join the Pact. We should seek to draw Iraq and Jordan closer together. We should try to detach Saudi Arabia from Nasser by making clear to King Saud the nature of Nasser's ambition. We should seek further support for Libya in order to prevent the extension of Egyptian or Communist influence there. We should seek to establish in Syria a Government more friendly to the West. We should counter Egypt's subversion in the Sudan and the Persian Gulf.

There were also possibilities of action more directly aimed at Nasser and his Government. For example, the withholding of military supplies, the withdrawal of financial aid for the Aswan Dam, the reduction of United States economic aid and the blocking of sterling balances. In all this, we should need the support of the United States Government. The first task, therefore, must be to seek Anglo-American agreement on a general realignment of policy towards Nasser. The Cabinet agreed.

That realignment was difficult to achieve. Our American allies were not easy to deal with; I felt all the time that inside the Administration and the State Department, there were strains and stresses, and disagreements about the situation and how to deal with it. Dulles himself said that he had almost come to the conclusion that Nasser was impossible and an enemy.

Some of his advisers in the State Department, while not disputing that, thought that any open association with colonialist, imperialist Britain would be fatal to American influence in the Middle East. The Pentagon, I felt, were much more realistic, but Dulles, as Secretary of State, was the man who called the tune.

The trouble with him was that he seemed to want to hedge every bet. He was prepared to promise military and economic aid for the Baghdad Pact countries, but on no account would he join it. He was prepared to consider ways of reducing economic support for Nasser, but he was determined to avoid any appearance of 'ganging up' with us. When I sent a minute to Eden about this, he noted, 'Even Dulles should have learnt by now that the fear of "ganging up" was the cause of so many errors in F. D. Roosevelt's wartime diplomacy.' When I told Dulles for his most private information that I did not think that Nuri could last much longer unless decisive action was taken to show that his Baghdad Pact policy was bringing results for Iraq, Dulles did not appear to take it seriously. One felt that Saudi hostility to Iraq was reflected in the State Department's advice to Dulles.

This schizophrenia was also apparent in London. Usually, I would see Winthrop Aldrich, the Ambassador, with his Minister, Barbour. Aldrich, the amateur, was enthusiastic for Anglo-American co-operation publicly avowed. Barbour, the professional State Department man, on the other hand seemed to count on Britain to follow American policy but to expect that such a close association could and should be concealed from the public.

A change from concentrating our minds upon the Middle East was provided in April by the visit of Marshal Bulganin, Chairman of the Soviet Council of Ministers, and Khrushchev, Party Secretary. Before it, Eisenhower sent a message in strong terms to Eden referring to the 'menace in the Middle East' and stating that the United States could not be 'acquiescent in any measure which would give the Bear's claws a grip on the pro-

duction or transportation of oil which is so vital to the defence
and economy of the Western world'.

There was a succession of meetings between the two Russians
and British Ministers at Downing Street and Chequers. Eden has
written that these were the longest international discussions
between two powers in which he had ever taken part. Many
topics were discussed. The positive results were hard to estimate. The visit helped to establish a personal relationship
between Khrushchev in particular and British political leaders.
But for it, I doubt whether the visit which Macmillan and I
paid to the Soviet Union in 1959 would have been as successful
as it was, if it had been possible at all. It will be remembered
that that visit came after Khrushchev's ultimatum that the
position in West Berlin could not remain as it was for more
than a further six months. As a result of the talks in Moscow,
the ultimatum faded away; there was the long series of meetings
between Foreign Secretaries in Geneva all summer and a
lessening of tension. That might all have happened in any case,
but I believe that the meetings in April 1956 helped.

During our protracted talks, there was only one occasion
when they seemed to approach a flashpoint. Talking of the
Middle East, Eden said that the oil from it was vital to our
survival and, if need be, we would fight for it. The Russians
bristled up at this and appeared angry. The same thing happened in Moscow in 1959 when Macmillan said that some
attitudes would mean war. The Russians again were angry
and seemed to lose their tempers. I have often wondered
whether there was something in the translation and whether
what seemed a simple statement of fact to us, was translated
into something offensive to their pride.

There was one very entertaining day which I spent with the
two Russians.

It had been feared that their visit would provide an opportunity for large left-wing demonstrations, and that the visitors
would be fêted by crowds wherever they went. Accordingly,
when they went out of London their schedules were carefully

planned and a Minister had to go with them to see that there were no deviations.

The programme included a visit to the atomic energy plant at Harwell, then lunch in Oxford and a tour round some of the colleges, and finally Chequers, where they were to spend the night. I was deputed to be their guide to Harwell. Almost at once a difficult problem presented itself. We were all three fairly broad in the beam. There would only be room for two of us on the back seat of a normal car; the third would have to sit on a bucket seat alongside the interpreter. It was thought that if I, Her Majesty's Principal Secretary of State for Foreign Affairs, sat on the bucket seat, it would not look good. On the other hand, if I sat on the back seat with one of them, which would it be? Bulganin was the titular senior; Khrushchev was the effective head of government. Eventually, a large and ancient Daimler was produced with room for three on the back seat.

The cavalcade moved off in due course from Claridge's, I sitting between the two Russians. It was a lovely spring day. The flowers in the gardens along the route were most attractive. Khrushchev kept saying to me what the interpreter translated as, 'How cultured the countryside is'—by that, I think he meant neat and tidy and well managed.

We came to one village. On our left, a typical British personality had taken up his stance—straight-backed, red-faced, he stood to attention. As we passed, he saluted but not in the conventional fashion. He put his fingers to his nose and, as it was described when I was a small boy, cocked a snook. I hastily directed the attention of our visitors to the other side of the road, hoping, no doubt vainly, that what had happened had gone unobserved.

At Harwell we were greeted by the management and a considerable turnout of the workers. As we began to go round the atomic energy plant, I was told that the Prime Minister wanted to speak to me on the telephone. I went and spoke to him. He merely wished to say that he thought that I ought to go on to Oxford, as a matter of courtesy, and not let them arrive unaccompanied, to be met by the Mayor and Corporation and the University authorities. I, of course, agreed. When I got back to the visitors, the worst had happened. Khrushchev was in the middle of a large crowd, talking away, no doubt spreading alarm and despondency. I hurried forward just in time to hear a man with a pronounced Scottish accent, say to Khrushchev, 'Will you tell me, Mr Khrushchev, when are you going to have free trade unions in Russia?' So much for the fears of subversion!

At Oxford we received a riotous welcome, the whole student population and most of the town turning out. A choir, several hundred strong, sang 'Poor Old Joe', a belated tribute to Stalin who had died three years earlier. There were fireworks and a lot of good-humoured barracking, which Bulganin and Khrushchev took in good part. One woman came up and spat at Khrushchev. He did not appear put out and simply said, 'I wonder why she did that; I have never done her any harm.' At length I received a message from a rather harassed Chief Constable that the crowd was becoming impossible to control in the narrow streets by the colleges, and the time had come to call it a day. So off we went to Chequers.

In addition to the visit of the Russian leaders, there were other claims on our time that summer. There was a NATO meeting in Paris in May. I attended Her Majesty on the state visit to Sweden in June. I went by air. The Queen had come by sea in the Royal Yacht *Britannia*. A company of notables gathered on the quay to go to meet her in a small boat, clad in a variety of garments: top hats, tail coats, diplomatic uniforms, cocked hats, etc. *Britannia* was late. There was a thick mist. We ventured out in our small boat, hoping not to be rammed and sunk. Some kind of radar mechanism was our only means of direction-finding. We wandered about in the fairway. Suddenly the officer in charge said, 'There she is over there.' Off we went, fastening up our uniforms, putting on our cocked hats and swords—in my case, I think, a mere top hat. A large shape loomed up. We stood to attention, prepared to pay homage to Her Majesty. A stentorian Scandinavian voice announced that it was a freighter laden with timber on the way from Helsinki to Stockholm and asking what the blazes we were doing obstructing the passage. Somewhat crestfallen, we made another cast and as the mist cleared we eventually found *Britannia* and paid our respects. We were very much behind schedule. *Britannia* swept forward at such a speed that most of the small craft on the banks were damaged by the wash. The Swedish Navy, with great gallantry and generosity, bore the cost of the considerable damage done.

The Libyan Prime Minister came for protracted talks about our aid to Libya. Important visitors came in a constant stream —von Brentano, Pearson and Martino, Foreign Ministers of West Germany, Canada and Italy respectively and Hammarskjöld, Secretary-General of the United Nations. One visitor was Sayyad Hamad Tewfiq, leading a Sudanese Parliamentary delegation. Our talks gave me some satisfaction in view of what I had said in 1954 about the British leaving the Sudan (see p. 19). He told me that British experts were very much wanted in the Sudan. Those recruited elsewhere had proved unsatisfactory. Could I help? He also asked for our help in training their Foreign Service.

A Commonwealth Prime Ministers' Conference met in London in July. That month the King of Iraq came on a state visit.

All the time, however, there was this continuing anxiety about the Middle East. The disillusionment of the Foreign Office with Nasser and my distrust of his intentions was borne out by what was happening. At the end of March I had received confirmation that he was trying to detach Libya from her alliance with Britain. He was offering to replace our aid, and trying to get them to accept Soviet offers of assistance. In April, the Egyptian/Saudi/Yemen Defence Pact was announced. It was stated that the Egyptian Government welcomed this as a blow to Britain and part of the plan to drive Britain from the Arabian Peninsula. Saudi Arabia lent $10 million to the

Yemen, and Khrushchev admitted that the Soviet were selling
arms to them. The Jordanian Ambassador told me that his
Prime Minister and Foreign Minister were under Nasser's influence and hostile to Britain. Humphrey Trevelyan, our calm
and balanced Ambassador in Cairo, who strove hard to achieve
better relations with Egypt, reported in May that in the whole
of his career he had never known such concentrated abuse of
the British as he had seen in the Egyptian press during the past
month.

Early in April I had lunch with Hammarskjöld at London
Airport when he was on his way, with the authority of the
Security Council, to survey the situation in the Middle East.
I have found in my papers a note of our conversation recorded
in a dispatch which I sent immediately afterwards to our delegation at the United Nations. Hammarskjöld told me that he
thought Nasser was comparable to Hitler in 1935; he had a
strong feeling that the Soviet did not wish Nasser to become too
powerful; he had been impressed by the general Arab resentment of Nasser's attempt to establish an Egyptian hegemony in
the Middle East. The inference clearly was that Hammarskjöld
then thought that there was a Hitlerite dictator on his way but
that he could be checked.

Looking back, I have wondered whether we should have
halted the withdrawal from the Suez Canal Base. I think that
it would have been a mistake. It would have exposed us to a
charge of breach of faith. It would have been difficult to convince Middle Eastern countries that it had been justified by the
provocation which we had received. Furthermore, I think that
at that late stage it would not have been practicable.

I knew that the withdrawal itself in June would be an important event, the departure of the last British troops from the
Base. Nasser would seek to make a great occasion of it, and he
was entitled to do so. Trevelyan handled the arrangements with
skill. General Sir Brian Robertson who had been Commander-
in-Chief Middle East Land Forces from 1950 until 1953 attended
with Trevelyan and was treated with courtesy.

8   The 22 Nation Conference opens at Lancaster House
on 16th August, 1956, under
Selwyn Lloyd's chairmanship.

9   Dulles, U.S. Secretary of State (right), and Pineau visit No. 10 Downing Street on 17th August, 1956, during the 22 Nation Conference.

10   Australian Prime Minister Menzies (left), staunch supporter of the British position and emissary from the Conference to Nasser, also called at No. 10 that day.

11 and 12 The Israeli advance into Sinai, 29th October, 1956, under the command of General Dayan (below, centre).

13 Lloyd and Head, Minister of Defence, arrive for a Cabinet meeting.

14 French Prime Minister Mollet, and Pineau come to London on 30th October to decide on action to be taken after the Israeli assault.

I had sent the following message to the Egyptian press:

> I am glad to give you this message on the occasion of the Egyptian National Day.
>
> The last British troops have left Suez under an agreement honourably and freely negotiated between our two countries. This brings to an end an association of over 70 years which, despite differences and some hard words, has brought lasting benefits to both our countries.
>
> It was always our hope and belief that the signature of the Suez Base Agreement would lead to a new era of friendship and understanding between the two countries. It has been a disappointment that this has not been so. There are no actual disputes or conflicts between Great Britain and Egypt which justify the present lack of confidence between the two countries. We have shown that we want good relations with Egypt, not only by the Canal Base Agreement but also by the Sudan Agreement, the Sterling Balances Agreement, the Cotton Futures Market Agreement and the exchange of trade missions. We wanted in these ways to show our concern for the well-being of the Egyptian people and our respect for the national position of Egypt.
>
> We are told sometimes that in our policy in the Middle East we are trying to isolate Egypt and deprive her of her legitimate place in the Arab World. That is not true at all. Some of the free countries of the Middle East have joined together on a basis of free co-operation to ensure their own defence, and we have joined them with the purpose of helping to strengthen Middle East security and to help to promote the economic development of the countries concerned. We have always hoped that Egypt would play her full part in the Middle East. We supported the foundation of the Arab League, and we have every interest in promoting unity and co-operation between Arab States. We consider that all Arab countries, great and small, have equal rights and we intend to prove loyal and reliable

6

friends to those who rely upon our support. I hope the Egyptian people will not lend too ready an ear to any attempt to foment bad relations between Arab peoples and the West.

I am sure that if we respect one another's legitimate interests and treat one another with fairness and mutual respect, the British and Egyptian people can build up a new friendship for the future. That is certainly the desire of Her Majesty's Government.

Robertson had two meetings with Nasser and told me afterwards that Nasser had thought my message 'constructive', although he had not liked a speech which Nutting, Minister of State at the Foreign Office, made in Liverpool. Robertson thought that Nasser had changed for the worse. He was rather pompous, apt to talk down to people and obviously pleased with himself.

Nasser said at the first meeting that he had no confidence in what the British said. At the second meeting, he was more relaxed, influenced perhaps by the manifestation of Egyptian democracy. He had been elected President with 5,494,555 votes, 99·84 per cent of those cast.

Throughout this time there were continuing doubts about the Aswan Dam project. I have already mentioned the view which Eugene Black, the President of the International Bank, had expressed in February. I had warned the Cabinet in March that we might have to withdraw our offer of help for the scheme, and I had sent a message to Makins in Washington at the end of that month saying that our feeling was that we should not give Nasser the money for the dam unless he genuinely changed his attitude towards Western interests in the Middle East. While attending the NATO meeting in Paris early in May, Dulles and I had come to the conclusion that it was most unlikely that agreement would be reached on Aswan, there being rumours already that Nasser was going to pledge further Egyptian resources in another arms deal with the

Soviet. We agreed to let the Aswan Dam project 'wither on the vine'.

I talked to Black about it early in June. He thought that the United States Government would have trouble with Congress, but if they really wanted to push the scheme through, they could do so. I think that that was optimistic. The China lobby had been infuriated by Nasser's recognition of Communist China in May. The cotton lobby were against the loan because of Nasser's deal with Russia over Egyptian cotton. The Israeli lobby were against it on the ground that it would strengthen one of their principal enemies. In addition, the United States was being bombarded with requests for aid from friendly countries in the Middle East. Their theme was that friendship should be better rewarded than enmity. The United States, they said, by giving aid to Egypt for the dam, was doing just the opposite.

Nevertheless, Black decided to make a final attempt. On 20th June, he saw Nasser in Cairo and made a final offer to which he believed the Western Governments would agree. Nasser riposted with a series of counter-proposals, which obviously the United States were unlikely to accept. Negotiations were halted. I am sure that well before this Nasser had made up his mind that Western aid for the dam would not materialise. An Iraqi traitor had told him after the Baghdad Pact meeting in Tehran in March that the discussions there showed that the Western powers were unlikely to support the dam. Nasser may have thought that refusal of that support by the United States would give him the pretext for a coup against the Suez Canal Company, which he had had in mind for some time, a coup to be carried out as soon as possible after the departure of British troops from the Suez Base.

Nasser was fond, as I have said, of reminding people that he had spent many years conspiring and that he still felt and thought as a conspirator. I believe that he decided about the end of May or the beginning of June to carry out his conspiracy against the Canal Company. First they had to be lulled into a

sense of false security. Accordingly, on 10th June he allowed
the protracted discussions which had been taking place with
the company to come to a conclusion. An agreement was signed
providing for certain new financial arrangements between the
company and the Egyptian Government to come into force,
and reaffirming the concession to the company, lasting until
1968. Next, it was important that Britain should have no idea
of what he planned. The tone of the Egyptian press towards
Britain improved. I acknowledged this in the House of Commons. I welcomed an Egyptian trade mission to London in the
second half of July.

The opinion that Nasser was prepared for Western refusal
of aid for the dam is confirmed by Heikal's account. He was
then very much in Nasser's confidence. He says in the Heikal
Papers (see p. 31 above) that Nasser told Ahmad Hussein, the
Egyptian Ambassador in Washington, to accept all the American conditions so long as he did not give the appearance of
being humiliated. Hussein must realise, however, that the
agreement would still fall through. The accounts given by
Eisenhower and Murphy do not tally with this. According to
them, Hussein arrived with what was—to use Murphy's words
—'in effect an ultimatum demanding from the United States
a commitment of hundreds of millions of dollars over a period
of ten years or more'. Such a commitment needed Congressional authorisation, and Congress had steadfastly refused to
make long-term pledges. Congress probably would not have
approved funds for the dam even on a year-to-year basis.
Hussein also said, according to Dulles, that if the United States
would not pay, he was sure the Soviet Union would.

Dulles promptly told him on 19th July that the United States
would not be blackmailed and the offer of help over the dam
was withdrawn. Dulles must have made up his mind at very
short notice to play it this way. Murphy says that Dulles had
not discussed with State Department officials the consequences
of an abrupt withdrawal. They had not been weighed carefully
in advance. The President had only been consulted that morn-

ing. Makins, the British Ambassador, was informed one hour
before the meeting. I had had no idea that there was going to
be this abrupt withdrawal. We had discussed it in Cabinet on
17th July without any sense of urgency, and I had promised to
circulate a memorandum on how the withdrawal of our offer
should be put to the Egyptians.

When the news broke of Dulles's abrupt action, we tried to
play it as quietly as we could. Eden said that we had been informed but not consulted. The Cabinet decided on 20th July
that Britain should also withdraw from the project. Caccia saw
the Egyptian Ambassador in London and told him that we had
come to the same conclusion as the Americans. Our decision
was taken on economic grounds. Egypt was undertaking other
commitments (industrialisation and continuing high expenditure on arms) which would prevent her giving to the dam project the degree of priority necessary to secure its success. We
still wanted good relations with Egypt. The decision did not
mean that we had lost interest in the future development of the
Nile Valley.

Dulles was asked in September by Eisenhower whether the
manner of withdrawing the offer had been undiplomatic. His
reply dated 15th September is reproduced in Eisenhower's
book *Waging Peace*.* Dulles rejects the idea of it being abrupt,
but qualifies that by adding that it was 'not abrupt, at least to
Egypt'. He says that from 'telephone conversations of which we
learned' the Egyptians knew that the reply would be negative.
He refers to Congressional opposition and asserts that if he had
not acted as he did, Congress would have imposed rejection
upon the Administration almost unanimously. He refers to
Egyptian flirtations with the Soviet Union and claims that
what happened was not a shock or a surprise to Nasser. I
believe that the real reason for Dulles's action was that he
thought that a Resolution from Congress limiting the Administration's powers to act would have been damaging in the
Presidential election campaign. However that may be, there is

* *The White House Years: Waging Peace: 1956–1961* (Heinemann, 1966), p. 33.

no doubt that Dulles was right about his reaction being no surprise to Nasser. The flying into a rage and all the theatrical performance of anger at a sudden affront was deliberately planned, leading up to the long-prepared speech of 26th July in Alexandria. But Dulles's manner of rejection was just what Nasser wanted. He gained some general sympathy. He could pretend that here was a poor country suddenly being given a raw deal by a rich one. He could claim that he had a good reason for doing something which he had in fact planned for a considerable time. Dulles later said in a letter to Eisenhower in 1957, also published in the latter's book, that Nasser had admitted that he had been planning for nearly two years to seize the Suez Canal Company.

Chapter V

Canal Takeover

*Nasser announces nationalisation of Canal 26th July 1956—
initial reactions—five phases between 26th July and 29th
October—differences in United States, French and British
approaches to Middle East problems.*

Nasser's moment had come. On 24th July, at the opening of a
new pipeline near Cairo, he made what Eisenhower later described as a vitriolic attack upon the United States, but in the
big speech on 26th July in Alexandria Britain was the principal
target. As, in the event, it had been the United States and not
Britain which had administered the rebuff, the fact that he
concentrated his venom on Britain seemed to prove that the
speech had been prepared long before. Egypt, he declared, had
had a long struggle with malevolent imperialism: imperialism's
worst defeat had been in Jordan the previous December.
Templer had 'fled' from Jordan; Arab nationalism had
triumphed; Britain's Balfour Declaration was responsible for
Israel's birth; Britain had held the mandate over Palestine;
Britain had equipped the Zionists; Britain had allowed them
to arm; Britain had turned Palestine over to the Haganah,
wishing to exterminate Palestine Arabs and install Jews instead;
Britain had tried to infuse the spirit of hatred into Egypt's
Sudanese brethren, and Britain and the United States were
aiming at the obliteration of Arab nationalism.

Then followed in his speech the reference to 'de Lesseps'
which was the code word for the occupation of the Suez Canal
Company's property, by force if necessary, the nationalisation of
the Company, the proclamation of military law in the Canal

Zone, and the order that the company's employees, including foreigners, must remain at their posts under threat of long terms of imprisonment if they failed to do so. Egyptian troops and police proceeded to take the planned action. Aneurin Bevan described it in a speech made the following year: 'if the sending of one's police and soldiers into the darkness of the night to seize somebody else's property, is nationalisation, Ali Baba used the wrong terminology.' In a broadcast after the military action in the autumn, Julian Amery described how Bevan had come up to him and said, no doubt referring to the activities of the Suez Group, 'You were right about this man.' It has been written since that we ought not to have been so surprised at Nasser's action. But the reason for the surprise was the fact that only six weeks or so before, on 10th June, Nasser had made a bargain with the Suez Canal Company to which I have referred, covering arrangements to last until the end of the concession in 1968.

I was at the dinner at No. 10 Downing Street given by Eden in honour of the King of Iraq when the news came through. Graphic accounts of the scene have been written by those who were not there. The views of the Iraqis about Nasser were very close to Eden's and mine, and we had reached the stage of complete distrust of him. I had had a word or two with Nuri. His advice was that we should hit Nasser hard and quickly. The story that the dinner broke up before it was over, in confusion and alarm, is shown to be nonsense by a curious little anecdote told in Kilmuir's book. After our Iraqi guests had left, we were to go to a meeting in the Cabinet Room. Salisbury had to go up to Kilmuir and say, 'Are you coming to the meeting?' When Kilmuir replied that he was, Salisbury said, 'You realise that no one can leave the room until the Lord Chancellor does?' Protocol rather than panic, apparently, was still the order of the day.

For the meeting, we gathered together in due course — Foster, the American Chargé d'Affaires, Chauvel, the French Ambassador, Mountbatten, the First Sea Lord, Templer, Chief of the Imperial General Staff, Boyle, the Chief of the Air Staff, who himself had been at the dinner, and the members of the Cabinet present—Eden, Salisbury, Kilmuir, Home and myself. According to my recollection, we decided that evening to concert common action with the United States and French Governments. At the Cabinet which must be called for the next morning, we would discuss what retaliatory action could be taken at once, for example against Egypt's sterling balances. The Chiefs of Staff were asked for a speedy assessment of what military action was open to us. The draft of a short statement for Eden to make in the House the next morning was considered.

Then began three months of intense pressure, extremely hard work, and each time as soon as success seemed in sight something happened to frustrate us. It was like walking up a mountain. Each time one gets to the crest of a hill it is only to find out that there is yet another one beyond it. So it was in August, September and October 1956. From my point of view at the Foreign Office, the period can be divided fairly easily into phases. In this chapter I briefly indicate the course of each phase, and the attitudes and strategies of the three Western powers which formed them.

Phase I began with the Cabinet meeting on the Friday morning to decide on the policy. There were the tripartite discussions between the Americans, the French and ourselves. Robert Murphy at first represented the United States. Phase II began when Dulles was hastily sent over as Eisenhower overreacted to some rather intemperate talk which Murphy reported. That was soon sorted out and, following some argument about membership, location and chairmanship, we reached agreement on the holding of a conference of interested countries with the objective of bringing the maximum international pressure to bear on Nasser.

Phase III was the conference itself from 16th to 23rd August, which was an outstanding success. Eighteen out of the twenty-two nations attending agreed on a resolution asserting six principles providing for international control, recognising Egypt's

sovereign rights, guaranteeing her a fair return for the use of
the Canal, and proposing the negotiation of a new convention.
This would entrust the operation of the Canal to an international board, including Egyptian membership, with other
countries chosen in the light of their maritime interests and
pattern of trade. Its object would be to secure the best possible
operating results, without political motivation in favour of, or
against, any user. Dulles played a notable part in achieving
this successful result.

Phase IV covered the Menzies mission to Cairo to put these
proposals to Nasser. Meanwhile there was a tripartite exchange
of views about referring the matter to the Security Council if the
Menzies mission failed. We were anxious to do so: Dulles was
non-committal. Then came Dulles's dream-child of an organisation of canal users to deal with the new Egyptian authority and,
to a considerable extent, manage the Canal. While this was
happening and Menzies was still in Cairo, Eisenhower suddenly
said off the cuff at a press conference that the United States
would only support a peaceful solution. As the threat of force
was one of the few good cards which Menzies held, Eisenhower's
statement made the mission futile. Nasser was off the hook and
promptly turned down the eighteen nations' proposals. That
was Tragedy No. 1.

This Phase IV was a very difficult one for us. Parliament had
been recalled for 12th September. We wished to announce a
decision that we were referring the matter to the Security
Council. But we were put in a false position by Dulles. He was
very anxious that his plan for a Suez Canal Users' Association
(SCUA) should be tried first, and strongly opposed our going to
the Security Council. We felt that we could not reveal this
difference of opinion publicly. Accordingly, Eden was manoeu-
vred into the position of having to put forward the SCUA plan
to an unenthusiastic House, almost as though it were a British
plan. That was the impression given to many. While this was
going on, Dulles himself was strangling his own brain-child. He
said at a press conference during the second day's debate in the

Commons that if an American ship sailing under the auspices of SCUA was stopped 'we do not intend to shoot our way through. It should go round the Cape'. Later he said that SCUA had never had any teeth in it anyhow. That was Tragedy No. 2. Nasser promptly said that he would regard as a hostile act any payment of dues by a shipowner to SCUA.

Phase V was the SCUA Conference and the reference to the Security Council. The former took place from 19th to 21st September in London. In spite of all the difficulties, we managed fairly effectively to preserve the unity of the eighteen nations who had endorsed the six proposals evolved at the previous London conference. Dulles made a notable speech, firmly on our side. The Security Council preparations and discussions in New York lasted from about 2nd to 13th October. We managed to make a considerable success of it, much to Dulles's surprise. When he saw how it was going and that we were carrying the Council with us, he gave valuable help. It looked as though our six principles for the operation of the Canal were going to be accepted unanimously, and there was a chance that Egypt would be called upon without opposing votes to negotiate on them or something similar as a basis. Then the day before the final crucial debate and vote, Eisenhower announced that the crisis was behind us and no one need worry any more. The Russians promptly vetoed the operative part of our resolution. That was Tragedy No. 3. Just to rub salt into the wounds, Dulles told me late that night that he did not see how we could go on avoiding, as we had done, the payment of the Canal dues to Nasser. Up to then he was only receiving about one-third of them. Dulles thought that in the future only 10 per cent could be kept back.

It is a sad and unsatisfactory story, as the later chapters of this book will show. I suppose that important factors in this tripartite disarray were the very different basic approaches held by the United States, France and ourselves to the problems of the Middle East.

The United States was genuinely anxious to stop Soviet

infiltration into the Middle East and to protect Western
supplies of oil. Eisenhower's message to Eden in April before the
visit of Bulganin and Khrushchev represented his and Dulles's
position (p. 61). The Baghdad Pact was as much their idea as
anyone's, and they encouraged us to join. They wanted to have
it both ways. They wished to show willing to Turkey, Iran and
Pakistan, then very dependent on U.S. aid. They accepted that
Iraq must be in it as the physical bridge. But it was support
short of joining, in order to avoid Zionist criticism in the United
States. Provided they could secure this anti-Soviet screen, they
did not much care what happened to British influence behind it.
At best, they were indifferent; at worst, the McGhees in Iran,
the Sweeneys in the Sudan, the Cafferys in Cairo, Aramco
in Saudi Arabia, had shown themselves openly anti-British.
Herbert Hoover Junior, the Under-Secretary of State, was
thoroughly anti-British, judging at least by what he said and
did. It was a mixture of anti-colonialism and hard-headed oil
tycoonery. The advice of a shrewd observer like Gallman, their
Ambassador in Iraq, was disregarded.

The French for their part were fighting a colonial war. Nasser
was supporting the rebels in Algeria in every way he could. His
dream of an Islamic Empire from Morocco to Muscat would be
the end of French influence in North Africa. Nasser had to be
destroyed. They attached little importance to a common front
with us in the Middle East. From 1918 to 1939 France had
exercised influence in the Middle East similar to our own, based
on her position in Syria and the Lebanon, as well as her important holdings in the Suez Canal Company and the Iraq
Petroleum Company. Then the collapse of France in 1940,
Vichy, the fight between Vichy and the Free French in the
Middle East, and French authority thereby much diminished.
They were not interested in a common Middle Eastern policy.
They strongly criticised the Baghdad Pact. They were not
prepared to back us up. French lives and property in the Middle
East were nothing like so important as French Algeria. Nasser
was Public Enemy No. 1.

Britain had a completely different approach from the United States and France, but we had not realised how little it was understood by our two principal allies.

As I have said, we had maintained our position in the Middle East from the firm base of our Indian Empire at comparatively little cost to ourselves. When the Indian sub-continent was given its independence in 1947, the situation was changed. An added complication was that a complete hash had been made at the end of the Palestinian mandate. Ernest Bevin was rightly regarded as a great Foreign Secretary for his contributions to the Marshall Plan and the creation of NATO. He maintained, except for a few left-wingers, almost complete unity in Britain against the threat of Soviet imperialism. He deserves his place in history for that. Unfortunately he also deserves a place in history for the fiasco made by the post-war Government over Palestine. To say that the Opposition might not have done much better is no answer. The blame lay with the Government and its overwhelming majority. The British troops stayed on too long in Cairo. Crossman, admittedly no admirer of Bevin, expressed the view in September 1956 that the Labour Government had sown 'the seeds in the Middle East of the harvest of hate which Sir Anthony Eden has been reaping'. This is an over-statement and over-simplification, but we had left Palestine in 1949 hated by Arab and Israeli alike.

When we were returned to office in 1951 our relations with Iran and Egypt were about as bad as they could be. We had to construct a policy. It was to preserve an anti-Soviet tier of defence, and behind it quietly and with honour and dignity reduce our commitments. This led to the settlement with Iran over the misappropriation of our oil interests, a settlement which retrieved a great deal for us. It led to the Baghdad Pact and our new defence agreement with Iraq. It led to the creation of a friendly and independent Sudan. It led to the evacuation of the Suez Canal Base on terms which were not completely one-sided. Our hope was to be able to protect our oil interests and our friends and gradually create, in Kuwait and elsewhere,

viable and, as we hoped, pro-British regimes. A military
presence would continue in the Gulf at Bahrain and in the
Trucial States but at comparatively small expense to us.

It had become obvious that Nasser was the arch enemy, with
the Soviet aiding and abetting in any way harmful to us. The
Saudis, under the influence of their feud with the Hashemites
and Aramco anti-British feeling, were unwittingly playing the
Communist game.

These differing attitudes naturally led to the adoption of
different strategies by each of the three Governments when the
crunch came. The United States, while angry with Egypt over
the Czech arms deal and her recognition of Communist China,
was not at first unduly worried by the nationalisation of the
Suez Canal Company. It is my belief that on 27th July it seemed
to many Americans just another slap at an old imperialist
institution. They were not keen on any action which would
improve our position *vis-à-vis* the Arab states, or sustain France's
position in Algeria. Even more unfortunate for us, but the
deciding factor, Eisenhower was determined to have no trouble
towards the end of his election campaign, which he was fighting
as a man of peace. He had no love for Nasser and wanted to
stop Soviet penetration if he could. His feelings for Britain were
partly affection for us because of the wartime association, and
partly a deep-seated dislike of our colonial record. He was in
favour of an Arab-Israeli settlement but nothing was to be
allowed to happen which would jeopardise his re-election. This
was not just vanity—although he was a vainer man than many
thought—it was a genuine belief that his re-election was in the
interests of the United States, the free world and peace.

France's strategy was simple. They wanted the destruction
of Nasser and the cutting off of arms and other aids from Egypt
to the Algerian rebels. They did not tell us of the extent of their
collaboration with the Israelis. This was partly because men like
Bourgès-Maunoury had been in the Resistance in the war and
were prone to secrecy, and partly because they feared that we
might try to stop it. They believed, wrongly, that Eden was

hostile to Israel. De Gaulle in his wisdom saw that the French objective was not the same as Britain's. That is why he said that he approved of the military operation at Suez but thought it wrong to put the French troops under British command.

We in Britain wished to check Nasser because we believed that what he had written in *The Philosophy of the Revolution* genuinely were his intentions. He was our enemy and the enemy of Western influence in the Middle East and Africa. We had experienced his lack of candour and untrustworthiness.

Chapter VI

What Remedies?

Phase I late July — House of Commons — Cabinet — decisions on policy and tactics — Egypt Committee — Eisenhower's first reactions — Murphy and Pineau in London — Murphy's lunch with Eden and dinner with Macmillan — the legality of Nasser's actions — Conservative Foreign Affairs Committee.

The nationalisation of the Canal was carried out on 26th July. The 27th July being a Friday, the House met at 11.00 in the morning. Gaitskell had put down a Private Notice Question asking the Prime Minister whether he had any statement to make on the reported action of the Egyptian Government with regard to the Suez Canal. Eden replied that the Egyptian Government's unilateral action in expropriating the Suez Canal Company without notice and in breach of the Concession agreements affected the rights and interests of many nations. Consultations about this serious situation were taking place with the other Governments immediately concerned. Eden was not pressed to say more. Gaitskell in a supplementary question deplored the high-handed and totally unjustifiable step which Nasser had taken, and asked about a reference to the Security Council and the blocking of Egypt's sterling balances. Paget, the Labour Member for Northampton, described it as a threat to strangle the whole industry of Europe. He asked whether the Prime Minister was aware that this weekend technique was precisely what we had got used to in Hitler's day, and also whether Eden was aware of the consequences of not answering force with force until it was too late.

The Cabinet met immediately afterwards. The unanimity

displayed in the House was also shown by the Cabinet. There was a good attendance for a Friday. In addition to Eden and myself, Salisbury (Lord President of the Council), Macmillan (Chancellor of the Exchequer), Kilmuir (Lord Chancellor), Stuart (Secretary of State for Scotland), Home (Commonwealth Secretary), Monckton (Minister of Defence), Sandys (Housing and Local Government), Thorneycroft (Board of Trade), Heathcoat-Amory (Agriculture), Eccles (Education), Macleod (Labour), Selkirk (Duchy of Lancaster) and Buchan-Hepburn (Works) were there, with Heath as Chief Whip in attendance. Of the Chiefs of Staff, Dickson (their chairman), Templer and Boyle were also present. Our reactions to what Nasser had done were quickly agreed. The nationalisation of the Suez Canal Company should be rejected. It was a breach of international law. The Canal was vital to Western Europe. Some figures were given to the Cabinet about its importance. In 1955, 14,666 ships had passed through it, one-third of them British, three-quarters of them belonging to NATO countries. Annually 70 million tons of oil came through it, of which 60 million tons was for Western Europe. That was two-thirds of Western Europe's total oil supplies, and to bring it round the Cape would require twice the tonnage of tankers. We ourselves had oil supplies sufficient for six weeks and were rather better off than our neighbours. Accordingly, to restore the international character of the Canal, we must first take economic measures against Nasser. Egypt's sterling balances should be blocked, in concert with the French authorities. The balances then amounted to about £100 million. As economic measures by themselves were unlikely to bring the desired result quickly, there should also be the maximum political pressure from those maritime and trading nations whose interests were most directly affected. It was agreed that political pressure should be backed by the threat of, and in the last resort the use of, force.

The Cabinet considered the military factors. Nasser had three infantry divisions and one armoured division. Two-thirds of his forces were in Sinai. The armoured division was straddling

7

the Canal. He had between 600 and 800 technicians from
behind the Iron Curtain: Poles, Czechs and probably Russians.
There were various geographical difficulties to be overcome if
we were to carry out a military operation. It would require
several weeks to mount it.

Nevertheless the Cabinet were unanimous that if economic
and political pressure did not lead to the desired result we
must be prepared to use force. The threat of it might be
enough. Failure to preserve the international character of the
Canal would lead to the loss one by one of all our interests and
assets in the Middle East. Even if we had to act alone, we
should not stop short of using force to protect our position if
all else failed and in the last resort. Accordingly, the Chiefs of
Staff were ordered to make the necessary military preparations.
But our first choices were economic and political pressures.

There was some discussion about referring the matter to the
Security Council. I raised it because of Gaitskell's supplementary question. Some Cabinet colleagues were very much
against on the ground that if we did so we would lose control
of the situation; and also, because of the Soviet veto, it would
be futile. I had not the slightest doubt that we must go at
some stage to the Security Council if other political pressures
failed, but I did not press it on that occasion. I was already
thinking of a Users' conference and thought that would be
much more effective than a Security Council debate over-
shadowed by the Soviet veto. In any case, in trying other ways
before recourse to the Security Council, we were acting strictly
in accordance with the Charter of the United Nations, Article
33 of which reads as follows:

(1) The parties to any dispute, the continuance of which
is likely to endanger the maintenance of international
peace and security, shall first of all seek a solution by
negotiation, enquiry, mediation, conciliation, arbitration,
judicial settlement, resort to regional agencies or arrangements, or other peaceful means of their own choice.

In addition, the mounting of a military operation would take time, but the threat of it would be a reinforcement of the political pressures.

The Cabinet also agreed that an Egypt Committee should be set up. Its members were to be Eden, Salisbury, Macmillan, Home, Monckton and myself. In practice, the membership was very fluid; Butler, Thorneycroft, Lennox-Boyd and Watkinson were frequent attenders, and towards the end Heathcoat-Amory.

The impression has been widely given that at this first Cabinet meeting we decided to use force against Nasser as quickly as possible, and it was the United States Government which hauled us back from the brink and stopped us. This is quite untrue. Our position was clearly laid down: rejection of Nasser's action, economic and political pressure, the threat of force and, in the last resort only, the use of force. Our views were sent by Eden to Eisenhower in clear and simple terms that afternoon. Eden said that the Cabinet were agreed that we could not afford to allow Nasser to seize control of the Canal in defiance of international agreement. He referred to the threat of our oil supplies and to British and American influence in the Middle East if Nasser was allowed to get away with it. The management of the Canal should be put on a firm and lasting basis as an international trust. He went on to say that economic pressure was unlikely to be effective, as no further American aid was due and no payment was to be made from the Egyptian sterling balances before January 1957. He continued:*

We ought in the first instance to bring the maximum political pressure to bear on Egypt. For this, apart from our own action, we should invoke the support of all the interested powers. My colleagues and I are convinced that we must be ready, in the last resort, to use force to bring Nasser to his senses.

* *Full Circle*, p. 428.

He added that the Chiefs of Staff had been ordered to prepare a military plan, but the first step was for the United States, France and Britain 'to exchange views, align our policies and concert together how best to bring the maximum pressure to bear upon the Egyptian Government'. I do not understand how Eisenhower could have construed this as a British decision to use force without delay. This interpretation of our position is confirmed by the messages sent that afternoon to the Prime Ministers of Canada, Australia, New Zealand and South Africa.

That evening the first meeting of the Egypt Committee took place. Orders were authorised under the Exchange Control Act, and a direction under Regulation 2(c) of the Defence (Finance) Regulations to control Egyptian assets. It was decided to ask British shipowners to continue to pay their dues in London. These British payments would account for 55 per cent of the total dues. French shipowners usually paid in Paris (another 10 per cent of the total). That meant that the maximum likely to be paid in Egypt to the new authority would be 35 per cent. It was known that the Suez Canal Company was intending to advise its employees to continue to carry out their normal functions. I thought that this was right and that the Government should not give contrary advice.

The next day, Saturday, 28th July, was my fifty-second birthday. There was a meeting of the Egypt Committee in the morning. I told it that the French Government was taking the same view of the Canal Company's employees continuing to work as we did. Eden said that he had had a reply from Eisenhower suggesting a conference of maritime nations as soon as possible. I was asked to consider its membership. The Chiefs of Staff were asked to prepare a list of preparatory measures which would advance the date at which a military operation could be undertaken if required. The rest of my birthday was spent with my daughter, then nearly four years old, at No. 1 Carlton Gardens.

Eisenhower had also told Eden that Robert Murphy, Deputy Under-Secretary of State in the State Department, was coming to London to discuss the situation. We arranged for Pineau to come from Paris to join us.

Murphy was one of the most balanced and straightforward American diplomats with whom I had to deal. He describes in his book* the discussions which took place in Washington on Friday, 27th July, after Nasser's nationalisation speech. Dulles was away in Peru attending the inauguration of their new President. Eisenhower, Herbert Hoover Junior, the Under-Secretary of State, and Murphy met to discuss what had happened. Murphy writes that Eisenhower was not greatly concerned. There was no talk of recalling Dulles. The Middle East was not regarded as of prime importance to the United States. American investment in the Suez Canal Company was negligible (I can hear Hoover saying that). It was decided that Murphy should go to London 'to see what it's all about' and 'to hold the fort'. After the previous six months of discussion with Dulles about Nasser and the dangers in the Middle East, that account of near-indifference on Eisenhower's part was enough to make one weep. On p. 34 of his own book, *Waging Peace*, published in 1966, Eisenhower gives a rather different picture. He wrote (nine years after the event itself):

> The fat was now really in the fire. Nasser had moved to take over in total the world's foremost public utility. Its loss—if it were to cease functioning—would seriously cripple Western Europe. To permit such an eventuality to occur was unthinkable.

I think that Murphy's recollection is probably more accurate.

I had a few minutes alone with Pineau before Murphy came to Carlton Gardens at about six o'clock on the Sunday evening. Pineau said that the French were ready to go with us to the end in dealing with Nasser. I said that our Chiefs of Staff had promised to produce a plan by 31st July. Pineau, rightly as I thought, emphasised that we should not seem to be fighting

* *Diplomat Among Warriors* (Collins, 1964), p. 461.

only for the shareholders of the Canal Company. It was better
to work for a new international company or authority. That
point of view was likely to be more acceptable to other underdeveloped countries.

When Murphy joined us I made that point at once. We were
not just supporting the shareholders of the company. We were
ready to contemplate new operating arrangements, but these
must be under international control. I said, and Pineau agreed
with me, that military preparations would only be carried out
in order to enable us to ensure by force, as a last resort, a
system to guarantee the free transit of vessels through the Canal.
Economic and political pressures would have no effect upon
Nasser unless he knew that there were military preparations in
the background. Murphy was cautious. He thought that the
possibility of eventual military intervention should be relegated
to the background. United States public opinion was not
prepared for the idea of using force.

The calling of an international conference was then discussed. Murphy thought that those invited should be the
signatories of the 1888 Convention or their successors, with
certain additions, including the United States. It was obvious
that this limited membership was suggested primarily with the
Panama Canal in mind, in order to make quite clear that its
status was different from that of the Suez Canal. The Americans
had built the Panama Canal and were the owners of it from the
beginning. Murphy was uncertain of the position of United
States shipowners. He thought that they paid in Egypt, and he
suggested that they might continue to do so, making it clear
that it was 'under duress'. We discussed the withdrawal of non-
Egyptian employees of the Canal Company. I think that both
Pineau and I had doubts from the beginning whether the
Company's contention that these people were essential to the
working of the Canal in the long-term was well founded, and
on this occasion the three of us concluded that the Canal could
probably continue to operate for some time without any pilots
at all. Most masters of ships were quite capable of taking their

vessels through the Canal for a time without pilots. This view was confirmed later, during the SCUA conference, when the Norwegian delegation consulted the masters of some two dozen Norwegian ships then docked in London on this point. It was their unanimous opinion that they could take their own ships through without the help of pilots, at least for a limited period.

In the course of our talks, we had to break for dinner. There had been difficulties in arranging this. At that time of year most London hotels could not arrange private dinners at short notice on a Sunday evening. We ended by having an excellent meal at the Carlton Club. Pineau, a good French Socialist, seemed quite at home.

When going through the records of this time I have been surprised to find so many discrepancies about dates of meetings and various details. Murphy in his book wrote that he had dinner on that Sunday evening at No. 11 Downing Street with Macmillan, Field-Marshal Alexander, and Barbour, the American Minister in London. He went on to say that he lunched with Eden on the following Tuesday. In fact, he dined with me, as I have said, on the Sunday, lunched with Eden on the Monday, and had his dinner at No. 11 on the Monday evening. Macmillan wrote that Andrew Foster, not Barbour, was the fourth at this dinner.

Murphy, Pineau and I resumed our talks on the Monday morning about noon. Before that the Egypt Committee had met again (Eden, Salisbury, Macmillan, Home, Butler, Head, Watkinson and myself, with Heath, Mountbatten, Templer and Boyle also present). The membership of the proposed conference was again discussed. The Chiefs of Staff reported on various preliminary moves which they thought desirable. They were authorised to make them, it being understood that they might require the call-up of 20,000 to 25,000 reservists. When Pineau, Murphy and I met after that meeting, Murphy said very little. I think Pineau did most of the talking. Then we walked across to No. 10 to have lunch with Eden. Salisbury and Macmillan were there too, and one or two others from the American Embassy.

Murphy wrote in his book that Eden seemed in top form and good health at this lunch, but he added that Eden had not adjusted himself to the altered world status of Britain; that it seemed impossible for him to keep in mind how much Britain's power had diminished in relation to the United States and Russia, and that he expected to play the diplomatic starring role which he had performed for so long between the wars and during the Second World War. This was an amazing misjudgment by a very intelligent man. If Murphy thought like that, no wonder the State Department was so unrealistic. In the discussions with Eisenhower and Dulles in January of that year, Eden had made clear beyond a peradventure the fragility of Britain's economic position (see p. 42), and Eden's role as Foreign Secretary between 1951 and 1955 eclipsed in terms of actual achievement anything that had gone before; for example, the Geneva Conference on Indo-China in 1954 and the extraction that same year of the Western European Union treaty from the ruins of the European Defence Community. Those were two post-war diplomatic triumphs due to Eden's almost single-handed efforts.

Murphy made another very revealing comment on p. 467 of his book: 'Eisenhower was determined not to have the United States used as a cat's paw to protect British oil interests.' That was the attitude which distressed us. The First World War began on 4th August 1914, a fight against Prussian militarism. The United States joined in April 1916. The Second World War against Hitler began on 3rd September 1939. The United States joined in in December 1941. We had lost countless lives and spent the accumulated wealth of more than a century to defend freedom. Here we were confronted with what we regarded as another megalomaniac dictator, leader of a less powerful nation but with much easier targets to attack, a man who if unchecked would do infinite damage to Western interest, as Eisenhower admitted when he wrote his book nine years later. At the time, however, Eisenhower was apparently more influenced by his own anti-colonialism and Hoover's prejudice against British oil interests in the Middle East.

That afternoon Eden made a short statement to a tolerant House of Commons. He referred to the order made under the Exchange Control Act, and the direction under the Defence Regulations. He said that Murphy, Pineau and I were engaged in discussions which had begun the previous day. He promised a further statement as soon as possible. We then had another meeting of the Egypt Committee. In addition to the members of the Cabinet present at the earlier meeting, Thorneycroft attended. There was a long discussion of the forthcoming conference and various other matters. The call-up notices for the reservists were delayed for twenty-four hours.

That night Murphy dined with Macmillan at No. 11 Downing Street, and it was the talk at this dinner party which led to a misunderstanding of our position, particularly by Eisenhower. Up to then, Murphy had no reason to think that we were contemplating hasty action, and the statement in Eisenhower's book that Murphy had succeeded in restraining us is untrue. At this dinner, however, Murphy describes a rather different approach.* According to him as they sipped their 'admirable after-dinner brandy' Macmillan and Alexander discussed the situation frankly. Murphy says that he was left in no doubt that the British Government believed that Suez was a test which could be met only by the use of force. He was not surprised at this reaction because it seemed to him not unjustified. He was told that the French were prepared to participate in a military operation, and it might start in August. Alexander, though now retired, was obviously in close touch with the campaign plans and approved them. Murphy went off after dinner to the American Embassy to send an account to Eisenhower. When Eisenhower received it, he decided that Dulles must come at once to London.

Macmillan recorded in his diary on 31st July 1965:

* *Diplomat Among Warriors*, p. 463.

It seems that we have succeeded in thoroughly alarming
Murphy. He must have reported in the sense which we
wanted, and Foster Dulles is now coming over post haste.
This is a very good development.*

After Macmillan had seen Dulles, he recorded on 1st August:

We must keep the Americans really frightened. They *must*
not be allowed any illusion. Then they will help us to get
what we want without the necessity for force.

The truth of course was that the Cabinet had not decided
to use force without delay, as Eisenhower thought. Macmillan's
last sentence shows that we hoped to get what we wanted without the use of force. As for Alexander approving the campaign
plans, none existed at the time of the dinner with Murphy.

During these early days I had discussed with my advisers in
the Foreign Office the legality of Nasser's actions in international law. We had little doubt about the illegality of his
action. It was a breach of the Concession and incompatible
with the 1888 Convention. It was like terminating arbitrarily
the lease of a house before its expiry day, without a legal cause.
A clause in the Concession indicating that it might be renewed
implied that it must continue at least until 1968. In reality
Nasser had not carried out an act of nationalisation. He had
expropriated a company—foreign owned, foreign financed and
foreign administered—which was not simply an Egyptian
personality. It possessed an international element which had
been recognised in the Egyptian courts. This had regulated the
dealings under the convention between the Suez Canal
Company and the Egyptian Government. For example, in 1947
when the Egyptian Government claimed that their Companies
Act requiring the engagement of a certain number of Egyptian
nationals applied to the Suez Canal Company, the Company
had disputed the matter. The Government had given way and
a separate convention had been negotiated.

* *Riding the Storm: 1956–1957* (Macmillan, 1971), p. 105.

At a Security Council Meeting on 14th October 1954, the Egyptian representatives had put it clearly:

The Suez Canal Company is an international company controlled by authorities who are neither Egyptian nor necessarily of any particular nationality. It is a universal Company. It functions and things will continue to be managed that way.

A further consideration was that the compensation proposed was inadequate and its source uncertain.

As discussions of the question whether Egypt had been guilty of a breach of international law feature largely in the chronicle of events, I have added as Appendix III parts of the speech which I made in the Security Council on 5th October 1956. I stated as fully and clearly as I could my own view and, as I understood, that of my Foreign Office advisers, that Nasser's action was clearly a breach of law. This view was shared by my Cabinet colleagues, including Kilmuir, the Lord Chancellor and Monckton, a lawyer of worldwide renown. It was supported by Menzies, Prime Minister of Australia, Spender, later to be Australian Member of the International Court, and Professor Goodhart, a well-known international jurist and Master of University College, Oxford. Many others appeared to agree: Silkin, a lawyer leading the Labour Party in the House of Lords; Jowitt, an ex-Labour Lord Chancellor; Lord Simon of Glaisdale, later to be a Lord of Appeal; Spens, with wide judicial experience; Heald, a former Attorney-General; and Clifton Webb, former Attorney-General of New Zealand. Lord McNair, too, appeared to share it. Last but not least, I was always under the impression that it was Dulles's view. It was not until I read *Waging Peace* that I learned that Eisenhower, however, did not subscribe to it. I do not remember him saying so at the time, nor do I remember Dulles saying that his view and Eisenhower's were not the same. Eisenhower's book was written nine years later.

The point with which I am dealing is whether Nasser's action was a breach of international law. Whether anyone was entitled as a consequence to use force against it is a totally different argument, with which I deal in Chapter XIV.

Tuesday, 31st July, was a day of almost continuous meetings. The Cabinet met in the morning; the Egypt Committee met three times—in the morning, the afternoon and the evening. There was a meeting between Murphy, Pineau and myself in the afternoon, and a meeting with Pineau in the evening. For good measure, I spoke to the Conservative Foreign Affairs Committee in the afternoon. Looking at the records of a day like this made me laugh at the idea subsequently canvassed that Eden, without thought or consultation with his colleagues, plunged the country into military operations against Nasser.

At the meetings of the Egypt Committee it was decided that the announcement about the recall of the reservists should be made in the House of Commons on the following day. It was reported that the French accepted British Command of the forces which might be engaged. The Chiefs of Staff intended that General Sir Hugh Stockwell should be army commander. The Egypt Committee was against inviting the signatories of the 1888 Convention to attend the proposed conference, mainly because that would include the Russians. This view was later modified. British nationals were to be advised to leave Egypt if they had no compelling reason for staying. The export of T.N.T. to Egypt was stopped. There was a discussion about the payment of dues and the position of non-Egyptians working for the new Canal authority.

At the afternoon meeting with the Conservative Foreign Affairs Committee there was a large attendance and it went well. I include a note of the remarks with which I started the discussion:

> What has happened is unacceptable. We have done every-thing possible to create conditions under which Nasser could be friendly with this country—the Sudan, the Suez

Base Agreement, sterling balances, etc. Some of you have criticised those agreements. Whatever their merits, their one advantage is that everyone in this country must feel that we have done everything possible to enable him to be friendly with us. British public opinion should be united behind us in treating what has happened as unacceptable.

The reason why it is unacceptable is that we cannot have this Canal under the control of this dictator, subject to his whims. He showed his irresponsibility by announcing this decision as a method of retaliation to something which had happened affecting the internal economy of Egypt. His threat to imprison the employees, his utter disregard for the finances of the Canal show that he cannot be trusted to manage it. He seems totally unable to realise that the Canal will need capital in the coming years, rather than be able to produce it for other projects.

If we lie down under this behaviour, he will have our oil supplies in his grasp. He will have the capacity to interfere at will with seaborne movements, troops, supplies and trade. What he has done will be an example to other countries. The pipeline will be nationalised next, then the oil companies. It will be the end of us, of Western Europe and NATO as decisive influences in world affairs. We should have to live on such dole of oil as he chose to allow us at such a price that it might destroy our export capacity.

The only acceptable solution for us is some form of international control in which we have confidence. Exactly what, it is too early to say. I do not favour a specialised agency of the United Nations. It must be an international consortium of reliable countries.

It is necessary for us to mobilise such international public opinion in favour of this idea. We want the responsible countries to support our attitude.

In the present situation it is possible that attacks may be made on British nationals in Egypt. It is possible that

those who wish to leave their employment with the Canal
Company may be imprisoned. There may be interference
with British shipping. We must therefore be ready for all
eventualities and prepared to face them. That is why certain
military arrangements are being made. You will hear
very soon the unpleasant consequences of some of them.
These preparations of course will take time. Therefore I
feel that we need to keep cool heads. There is a lot at
stake. We have to show complete firmness of purpose;
that we are not prepared to accept this situation; that we
are not prepared to compromise over this principle of free
passage through the Canal; that we are not going to be
fobbed off; that we intend to have satisfactory arrangements.

It was alleged in the debate in the House on 12th and 13th
September that this statement of mine was provocative. I do
not understand why or how. I was talking of mobilising
international opinion and not of instant hostilities.

Chapter VII

Three-power Planning

*Phase II early August — Dulles's arrival — Eisenhower and imme-
diate use of force — tripartite discussions — debates in Parliament —
Gaitskell's speech — tripartite agreement on conference in London —
communiqué — Cabinet approval — military precautions and plans —
preparing the London conference.*

During the evening of 31st July Dulles flew in. He came the
following morning to the Foreign Office and with Pineau we
resumed our tripartite discussions. But first Dulles sent across
to Eden a letter which he had brought from Eisenhower, dictated by him after he had received Murphy's message. This
letter is printed in full as Appendix B of Eisenhower's *Waging
Peace*. In it he said that he had been under the impression that
we and the Americans were approaching decisions on parallel
lines, with some important differences in detail, but he had
just received messages from Eden and Macmillan telling him
on a most secret basis of our decision 'to employ force without
delay, or attempting any intermediate and less drastic steps'.
He recognised that eventually the use of force might become
necessary in order to protect international rights, but he hoped
a conference of signatories to the 1888 Convention and other
maritime nations would bring such pressures on the Egyptians
that the efficient operation of the Canal would be assured for
the future. He stressed the unwisdom of contemplating the use
of military force 'at the moment'. If the situation continued to
deteriorate to the point where force seemed the only recourse,
Congress would have to be recalled before the United States's
military strength could be used, and it would have to be shown

that every peaceful means of resolving the difficulty had been exhausted. He added that he realised from the messages sent to him by Eden and Macmillan that the decision taken (presumably by that he meant decision to use force without delay) had already been approved by the British Government and was firm and irrevocable, but he hoped that it would be reviewed. That was why he had asked Dulles to come to London.

This was a strange letter. Eden had sent no message to the effect that we were going to use force without delay or without trying other pressures first. The Cabinet had not approved the immediate use of force. Eisenhower's reaction must have been based on the after-dinner talk at No. 11.

Dulles sent to Eden a short covering note from himself, pointing out that the letter had been dictated by Eisenhower while Dulles was making his arrangements to come—in other words, Dulles was not responsible for the drafting of it. He tried to clarify the sentence which I have quoted:

> I think it refers not to the going through the motions of an intermediate conference but to the use of intermediate steps as a genuine and sincere effort to settle the problem and avoid the use of force.

I do not believe that Dulles thought for a moment that we were going to use force at once. His approach was reasonable. He used the phrase about Nasser having to disgorge what he had swallowed. It was intolerable, moreover, that the Canal should be under the domination of any one country without any international control. Such a situation was even more unacceptable when that country was Nasser's Egypt. A way had to be found to make him give up the Canal. Force was the last method to be tried to accomplish this; and the United States Government did not exclude the use of force if all other methods failed. But force unless it was backed by world opinion would have disastrous results. Therefore, all efforts should be made to create a worldwide opinion so adverse to Nasser that he would be isolated. A genuine effort should be made to bring world opinion to favour the international operation of the Canal before force was used.

At this stage, therefore, I had no complaints at all about Dulles's own reactions to Nasser's conduct. I meant what I said about mobilising international public opinion. I wished to avoid the use of force. The idea of reoccupying Egypt was unattractive, but I told him plainly that if the conference failed and there was no settlement, we might in the end have to use force. Dulles, however, must have been a little shaken by the conversation with Macmillan to which I have referred. When we got down to discussing the details of the conference, it became clear that he was also playing for time. He thought that it would take at least three weeks to prepare for it. He did not think that it should take place in London, Paris or Washington. He was doubtful about a tripartite communiqué of any substance after our present talks. As to the membership of the conference, he was insistent that the signatories of the 1888 Convention be invited, among others.

Dulles, Pineau and I walked over from the Foreign Office to have lunch with Eden at No. 10. As we did so, the considerable crowd gathered in Downing Street loudly cheered Dulles. Obviously they felt that the wartime alliance was working again. Dulles was, or seemed to be, quite emotionally moved. He mentioned it to me more than once afterwards. Certainly, when we at last got to the subsequent conference, he was firm, strong and did earn those cheers.

Murphy wrote in his book that it was apparent at once at the lunch that Eden and Dulles were uncomfortable with each other. One reason was Eden's behaviour at the conference on Indo-China at Geneva in 1954. The atmosphere was strained. Murphy added for good measure that Hoover could not stand Eden. I do not think that that worried Eden. Murphy also said —and I repeat it for the sake of the record—that the evident strain apparent between Eden and Dulles did not appear at discussions which Dulles had with Macmillan or me. So far as my testimony is concerned, Eden and Dulles treated each other

8

with exemplary courtesy, whatever they thought. Perhaps that was part of the trouble.

I had to answer Questions in the House in the afternoon, and later Eden held a Cabinet meeting there. I reported to it on my discussions with Dulles. I told them that he had said that Nasser must be made 'to disgorge'. After discussion, he had accepted that the communiqué should include strong condemnation of Egypt and an affirmation of the need to put the Canal under international control, though not under an agency of the United Nations. The United States would deprecate the premature use of force and were ready to co-operate with Britain and France in calling a conference. But its composition must be related to the 1888 Convention. They did not want a conference so wide that it might call for the internationalisation of the Panama Canal also. It was suggested that those invited should come under three categories. First, as signatories of the 1888 Convention, Britain, Egypt, France, Holland, Italy, Russia and Spain. Second, as leading maritime powers, Denmark, Germany, Norway, Sweden and the United States. Third, countries whose trade depended to a vital extent on its passage through the Canal: Australia, Ceylon, India, Japan, New Zealand and Pakistan. These lists were not final. Our aim would be for the Conference to meet in London not later than 13th August.

I told the Cabinet that we must insist that, if we accepted Soviet membership, the United States must ensure that the conference did not drag on, and that it lasted for only a few days. Also we must have a strong communiqué.

The Cabinet reluctantly agreed. I dined with Dulles and Pineau at the Hyde Park Hotel and told them of this decision and the basis upon which it had been made. Needless to say, that basis had Pineau's enthusiastic support.

The following day, 2nd August, we had the debate in the House of Commons from sometime after noon to about 6.30 p.m. It was helpful to the Government. Eden put the case in restrained terms. He stressed the importance of the Canal. He stated the reasons why Nasser's action had been a breach of international law, basing them on a memorandum circulated by the Lord Chancellor on 31st July expressing the opinion of the Lord Chancellor, the Law Officers and the legal advisers at the Foreign Office. In their view the 1888 Convention had been entered into on the basis of a company operated by France and Britain. That Company had in the course of years acquired an international character which had been confirmed by the history of the Suez Canal Company and the various agreements it made with Egyptian Governments. To nationalise a company of such an international character was in itself a breach of international law. Eden continued that we could not accept arrangements for the future leaving the Canal in the unfettered control of a single power which could exploit it merely for the purpose of national policy. He referred to the tripartite discussions still in progress and to the military precautions being prepared. He announced the recall to the colours of certain reservists.

Gaitskell followed with one of the best speeches which I heard him make in the House. Remembering the atmosphere that day, it is astounding to recall that it was said that Anthony Eden was in a state of great excitement and had lost control of himself. In this debate, it was rather the other way round. Eden was calm, cool and collected. Gaitskell was impassioned.

Lord Stansgate, the veteran Labour peer, listened to these speeches and said in the House of Lords that afternoon:

> I went to another place [the conventional way in which Members of one House refer to the other] this morning, and I can correctly and sincerely say that I found much more reason, commonsense and conviction in the Prime Minister's speech than there was in the rather heady wine which was produced by my own Front Bench.

Gaitskell in his speech was critical of our arms policy in the Middle East and he referred to the 'vacillations' over the Aswan Dam. Then he said that he must make it abundantly plain that

anything the Government had done or not done, in no way
excused Nasser's action in seizing the Canal. The Egyptians'
case was that they were entitled to nationalise any company
they wished, provided they paid compensation. They had given
assurances that they would observe the 1888 Convention as
regards rights of transit through the Canal. Gaitskell said that
he did not dispute their right to nationalise even a foreign-
owned company provided they paid compensation; what, in
passing, he doubted was whether they would be in a position
to do that in this case. But the objection to what they had done
over the Suez Canal Company was threefold. First, it was not
an ordinary company carrying out ordinary activities. It controlled an international waterway of immense importance. It
was, therefore, a matter of international concern when it
changed hands. Up to then it had been controlled and owned
largely by the states using it, the maritime powers. The Company had had amicable relations with Nasser, as he had
admitted, and had had regard to the interests of the user
countries. Now the ownership and control had been trans-
ferred to a single power, in a position to decide even more than
before how the Canal should be run. The behaviour of the
Egyptian Government in stopping Israeli ships and defying
the United Nations Resolution of September 1951 cast doubt
on their assurances about the future.

Gaitskell's second objection was the way in which the act
of nationalisation had been carried out. It had been done without discussion or negotiation, on the excuse that this was the
way to finance the Aswan Dam. Nasser had said that he could
take $100 million a year from its revenue for that purpose.
Gaitskell asked:

How can he at one and the same time both keep the Canal
going, spend the necessary money on the repairs, extensions
and reconstruction, pay the compensation or service the
compensation loan to the shareholders, and also find money
for the Aswan Dam?

He thought that there was a threat to access, following the precedent of the Israeli ships, a warning that the Canal might not be adequately maintained and the implication of higher dues.

Gaitskell's third reason was the political background and repercussions of the whole of this episode in the Middle East. Nasser had boasted of his intention to create an Arab Empire from the Atlantic to the Persian Gulf. Mollet had rightly said that that could remind us only of one thing—Hitler's speeches before the war.

Nasser had indicated his intention to destroy the state of Israel if he could. He had attempted subversion in Jordan and other Arab countries. He wanted to raise his prestige in the Middle East. That was why he had acted as he did. It was all very familiar. It was exactly the same as we encountered from Mussolini and Hitler. We must not underestimate the effect on other Arab states.

Then Gaitskell came to the action to be taken. He welcomed our tripartite talks. He hoped there would be a conference. The signatories of the 1888 Convention should be included. It was important that Russia should be there. The conference should prepare a plan of international control. He himself hoped it would be a United Nations agency. He supported our economic measures, talked about constructing another Canal and larger tankers, and finally came to the question of force. He advised great care. There were circumstances under which we might have to use force in self-defence or as part of some collective defence measures. But we must remember that we were members of the United Nations and signatories of the Charter. We must do nothing which would involve us in being denounced as aggressors or which was a breach of international law.

Gaitskell did not actually use the phrase 'a breach of international law' but it was implicit in his condemnation. Silkin, speaking for the Labour Party in the House of Lords, said that what Nasser had done was not legal and that his manner of doing it also constituted an illegality.

Gaitskell ended by saying that we had been right to react
sharply to this move. It was important to act in co-operation
with the other nations affected. We should try to settle the
matter peacefully on the lines of an international commission.
While force could not be excluded, we must be sure that the
circumstances justified it and that it was, if used, consistent
with our belief in and our pledges to the Charter of the United
Nations and not in conflict with them.

There has been controversy about this speech. I thought it
an admirable one for the date on which it was delivered, 2nd
August. The difficulties arose later and almost entirely on the
interpretation in practical terms of that last sentence.

The Liberal leader, Clement Davies, followed very much the
same line. When he came to the action to be taken, he supported what had been done, including the precautionary
measures, but advised us to proceed carefully. He referred to
the First World War. Hinchingbrooke interrupted with the
interesting question:

> He has cited the case of the 1914 War ... but he did not
> mention 1939 in which we went to war not in defence of
> any international agreement ... but only when our own
> position, together with that of our allies throughout the
> world, was placed in a state of jeopardy. In other words, it
> was not a legalistic necessity but a political necessity.

There were robust speeches from the Labour benches by
Herbert Morrison, Paget, Jack Jones and Stanley Evans.
Morrison said:

> If our Government and France, and if possible the United
> States, should come to the conclusion that in the circum-
> stances the use of force could be justified ... it might well
> be the duty of Honourable Members, including myself, to
> say that we would give them support.

Paget intervened to say in effect that we should compel Egypt
to accept the findings of the conference, if necessary by force.

A most impressive speech came from Walter Elliot. He objected to Nasser's action on the ground that it would make it more unlikely that developed countries would finance new projects in underdeveloped countries. But he added that that was not the most important issue. It was the element of challenge in this action. He said that he spoke as a Member of an earlier Cabinet which had had a long struggle with another dictator:

Time and again we had these questions—where do we draw the line, where do we resist—and do we use force? Because to use force is undoubtedly a terrible thing, and it was a terrible thing to determine to use force against Hitler. It involved, as we have seen, the destruction of half Europe. But there is a moment at which, for all that, force has to be envisaged or else one goes under.

He was interrupted by a staunch pro-Arab, Christopher Mayhew, who asked him whether he was justifying the use of force by what Nasser had already done or by what he might do in the future.

Elliot replied that exactly the same argument was put time and time again in the case of Hitler. The two things went together, both the action and the philosophy on which it was based. They were two inseparable parts of the whole. He ended with a warning about urgency. If the matter was allowed to drag on until Christmas or next spring, Nasser would have won. His last sentence was, 'Let us not find that we have lost the peace by talking too much about it.'

I was still engaged in the tripartite talks, and the House made no objection to my intervening in the middle of the debate and speaking for only about ten minutes. I dealt with the failure of our efforts to establish better relations with Nasser, the international character of the Suez Canal Company, the danger of leaving the Canal in Nasser's sole hands, and the need for an international solution if possible.

I then went back to Dulles and Pineau. We agreed the communiqué which is printed as Appendix II. It was in terms acceptable to Pineau and myself. Dulles had gone quite a long way to meet us. The breach of international law was confirmed in appropriate terms.

At 6 p.m. there was a meeting of the Egypt Committee at which the following were present: Eden, Salisbury, Butler, Macmillan, Home, Head, Thorneycroft, Watkinson and myself. I told them about the communiqué and those who were to be invited to the conference.

The next morning, Friday, 3rd August, I reported to the Cabinet on the final results of the tripartite talks. There was to be a conference in London on 16th August which was not to last more than a week. Eden said that as it was now the Recess, there would not be regular Cabinets. The Egypt Committee, however, would continue to function, but if emergency decisions had to be taken the Cabinet would be recalled.

After lunch I saw Chauvel, the French Ambassador, and said that I thought that it would be a mistake for the French and ourselves to play up our military precautions. I also said that if there were orders to the Canal pilots to leave, the British Government would publicly disagree. We were not prepared to be accused of bringing the operation of the Canal to a halt.

Later that afternoon I saw the Crown Prince of Iraq and Nuri. I said that there were three things which Iraq could do to help: first, to avoid being drawn in as a mediator; second, to spread the word that the British Government meant business; third, to ensure that Iran and Pakistan did not take the Egyptian side at the forthcoming conference. Nuri said that there were signs that the Egyptians were nervous already—there had been approaches to Iraq to mediate. Nuri intended to be back in Baghdad by 5th August. The operation affecting Syria, which he had mentioned when I met him in Baghdad in March (see p. 56), was planned for a date not before 1st September or after 15th October. I had my doubts about it ever taking place.

Over the weekend—Bank Holiday weekend—I was left with a lot to do in connection with the conference and its membership. Nuri had wisely opted out on the ground that, if Iraq was invited, several other Arab states would demand invitation. I had to explain to the Israeli Ambassador very much the same point. If Israel was invited, every Arab state would demand to come. I explained to Spaak why Belgium did not fit into the pattern. I sent messages to Unden of Sweden and Lange of Norway, stating that we genuinely wanted a peaceful settlement to emerge from the conference. I also sent a message to Hammarskjöld saying that we by no means ruled out a link between the United Nations and the proposed international authority.

In the ten days before the conference met, there were various jobs to be done. We had to prepare for the conference itself. We agreed on tripartite proposals* for a solution, which we circulated to the Governments invited, and later also agreed that Dulles should put them forward at the conference (see p. 115). From the twenty-four invited nations there were only two refusals. Greece did not want to come for obvious reasons— the large number of Greeks living in Egypt, membership of NATO and the Cyprus problem. Greece was wise not to come. Nasser also refused. It is alleged that that was because of Eden's broadcast personal attack on him. I doubt it. He knew that the Soviet and Indian representatives could be relied upon to argue his case and he would avoid commitment.

At the same time as we prepared for the conference, the military precautions were going forward. We sent instructions to Jebb in Paris to emphasise to the French the importance of Arab opinion, and to make it clear over the military preparations that we were discussing only what would happen if the conference failed. We also told him to start discussions to agree

---

* These were the origin of the six principles put to Nasser by the Menzies mission after endorsement by eighteen participants at the London conference (Chapters VIII and IX) and of the Anglo-French proposals at the Security Council (Chapter X and Appendix IV).

the objectives of any action which we might be forced to take.
The military occupation of Egypt should not be included. The
problem of Israel should be kept separate, as we should have
to live with the Arab states afterwards. I thought that our
objective should be the security of this international waterway.
I was amused by a conversation which I had with Chauvel. He
came to see me to say that our military planning was too slow.
Could the French help in any way? I said, 'Yes, of course, we'd
like some assault craft.' He had to admit that they had not
got any.

Meanwhile the Chiefs of Staff had been working on a military plan with the force commanders. The result dated 3rd
August was put to the Egypt Committee on 10th August, another piece of evidence that we were not planning immediate
military action.

There were four different methods of aiming to secure the
Suez Canal in preparation for its return to international
control:

(a) a full-scale assault on Port Said and the capture of Abu
    Sueir airfield, fifty miles to the south, by airborne landing;
(b) a full-scale assault on Alexandria, seizing port and air-
    field, followed by an advance to the Suez Canal via the
    Cairo area;
(c) limited operations against Port Said, followed by a major
    assault on Alexandria;
(d) limited operations at Alexandria and a major assault on
    Port Said.

Methods (c) and (d) were discarded on the grounds that a sure
and early success was needed, and limited forces must be kept
concentrated. Method (a) presented difficulties. Although coast
defences were light, the beaches were shallow and unloading
facilities at Port Said were very limited — mostly by lighters —
therefore there would be a slow build-up. The beaches were
close to the town and the water supply could be cut off. The
airfield at Abu Sueir was close to the concentration area for

Egyptian tanks. The movement from Port Said had to be along a narrow causeway, twenty-five miles long. The defence of the airfield from tank attack would be difficult for our parachutists.

Method (b) was easier and safer. Although it would take longer to reach the Canal, it might deal with Nasser more quickly.

It was agreed that there should be a single command, General Keightley as Commander-in-Chief.

The point about Arab susceptibilities was borne out by a talk which I had with Muntasser Bey, the Libyan Ambassador, a fine man who had been their Prime Minister at the time of their independence. I had got to know him well in Paris in 1951. He later died a tragic death after the revolution. He said that we must understand that any government in Libya which allowed us to use Libya as a base for an attack on Egypt would be overthrown by Nasser. He added what was the opinion of most responsible Arabs: 'Nasser will not be mourned once he has disappeared.'

Our relations with the Americans were comparatively easy for a time. Eden had sent a message to Eisenhower on 5th August, trying to convince him of our attitude:

We must hope as you say, that the forthcoming Conference will bring such pressure to bear upon Nasser that the efficient operation of the Canal can be assured for the future. If so, everyone will be relieved and there will be no need of force. Our people are neither excited nor eager to use force.

The preparation of our proposals for the conference went smoothly, but Barbour surprised me when he came a few days before it was to start and said that the United States thought that I should not take the chair. I did not argue very strongly with him. They obviously had not thought of the consequences of the host country not providing the chairman. Barbour also said that, in the face of tripartite firmness, Nasser in his recent utterances appeared to have withdrawn from his more extreme position. He might have added that that was Hitler's invariable technique. After a coup, he was sweetly reasonable for a time.

There was some trouble with the Suez Canal Company directors. Lord Hankey, a great public servant in his day, and one of the British Government directors, seemed out of touch with reality. He still thought that the Canal could not possibly be operated without the expertise of the Suez Canal Company and its employees, and pressed us to base our policy upon that assumption. I did not agree.

Chapter VIII

An Offer is Made

Phase III 1st–24th August — broadcasts by Eden, Menzies and me — the twenty-two-nation conference in London 16th–23rd August — the Eighteen-Power Proposals — Spaak's letter.

Another important task was to try to keep public opinion properly informed. Gaitskell, after his tough speech, had been genuinely alarmed at the reactions in his own party to the suggestion that he had supported the use of force. He had not. He had employed the formula which satisfied many people in the middle of the road, including quite a number of Conservatives: 'We will support the use of force if agreed by the United Nations.' As the Russians would never allow agreement to any such thing, this formula was meaningless. It would have been more intellectually honest of those who shared that view to have said, 'We do not agree that Britain and France, with or without the United States, should use force unless it is approved by the United Nations. We realise that that will never happen; therefore, force must be ruled out.'

Eden made a broadcast on 8th August which was well received. Some said that it was too critical personally of Nasser, but I think that it was right to make it clear that our quarrel was not with the Egyptian people and their justified hopes of a higher standard of living. The real adversary was the new dictator who was following precedents which had had disastrous results in our lifetimes. Eden said that there was too much at risk not to take military precautions, but

> we do not seek a solution by force but by the broadest possible international agreement.

Menzies came to join in our counsels during this period and
was a notable reinforcement. He broadcast on 13th August
and dealt clearly with the legal aspect:

International law is not a precise body of jurisprudence:
it's always in the making. But if there is one thing clear
it is that national contracts with the governments or
citizens of other nations must be carried out unless there
is legal excuse for non-performance.

If at any time and for any reason of real or supposed
self-interest, a nation could claim that its sovereign rights
entitled it to set treaties aside or violate international
contracts, all talk of or reliance on international law would
become a sham.

We cannot accept the legality or the morality of what
Nasser has done.

I followed on the next evening. After agreeing with Menzies's
view of the law, I said that from the first we had sought an
international solution arrived at by international discussions.
On Sunday, 29th July, when I had had the first meetings with
representatives of France and the United States, I had put to
them our view that there should be an international conference;
it was not forced upon us. The other two had readily agreed.
I dealt with our tripartite proposals for an international
authority which would be put before the conference. After
speaking of our disappointment at failing to establish better
relations with Nasser and the efforts which we had made, I
referred to the threat and the challenge which he constituted,
and the need to check him. I ended:

The rule of law must prevail. We are not bellicose — neither
the British Government nor people. With Britain, force is
always the last resort. We shall work with all our power
for a peaceful solution, but that solution must include
some form of international control for this essential water-

way. We are not seeking British control, we are seeking international control.

And thus we proceeded to the raising of the curtain on the drama of the twenty-two-nation conference. On the way, there was a symbolic incident in the United States. Just before Dulles left he had a conversation with Roger Makins. After impressing on Makins the responsible attitude of Congressional leaders, and asking about some statement attributed to the Labour Party, Dulles laughingly added that he had just received a present of five umbrellas as a warning to avoid a 'Munich'.

On Wednesday, 15th August, the invasion of London by the conference delegations began. For me H-Hour was 10 a.m. when Krishna Menon and Pillai of India arrived to see me. Menon and I were still on friendly terms. We had worked together at the United Nations on Korea with what I thought were satisfactory results. He was a strange man, universally disliked and distrusted. But when he wanted, he had a certain charm, and his mind was acute. We never discussed any problem without my feeling in my own mind at the end of our talk that some new point had been ventilated or some light thrown upon what was up to then obscure. In spite of this, Menon afterwards usually made everything more complicated.

Menon described Nehru's views. A dispute over the repudiation of the Concession should not be allowed to develop into an international crisis. Nehru had not approved of Nasser's manner of nationalising the Canal. Menon added that Nasser had a great deal to learn, but he was calm and reasonable after his coups. I said that Hitler was just the same after his coups. The occupation of the Rhineland was a parallel. If Hitler had been checked then, he might have learned the necessity of respecting international order.

I had little doubt that Pillai agreed with all I said. He was one of the best products of the Indian Civil Service and he was very well disposed to Britain.

Then I told Menon that the Americans thought that I

should not be chairman of the conference. He professed indignation. We agreed that it would create many problems at every international conference if we did not stick to the rule that the host country should provide the chairman. Menon then, with typical ingenuity, produced an alternative suggestion which he knew the United States delegation would dislike intensely. If Britain did not provide the chairman, it must be by rotation in alphabetical order.

Later that morning I saw Dulles and he repeated his view that it was undesirable for me to take the chair. I did not advance my claims. I said that perhaps he was right, but I hoped he knew what the alternative would be, rotation day by day in alphabetical order. That was Menon's idea, and I suspected that he would carry a majority of the members with him. I hope that I suppressed what I think would have been a very legitimate chuckle when I said this. Sure enough, Dulles was horrified, as I knew he would be, and that was the end of that, except that I was worried by the fact that in putting forward the original objection to Britain providing the chairman, he and his advisers had not thought the matter through. It seemed oddly inefficient. Dulles willingly agreed at that meeting to propose the tripartite resolution.

During the rest of the day, I had preliminary talks with the Foreign Ministers of Iran (Ardalan), the U.S.S.R. (Shepilov), Spain (Artajo), Portugal (Cunha), the Netherlands (Luns) and Pakistan (Chaudhuri). Dulles, Pineau and I lunched with Eden at No. 10. Lange (Norway), Hansen (Denmark), Unden (Sweden) and Martino (Italy) came to dinner with me at No. 1 Carlton Gardens. I also saw Birgi, the Turkish Ambassador, who was representing his country at the conference. I had seen fourteen out of the twenty-two delegation leaders during that day. In due course I made personal contact with all the others.

As these talks proceeded, it became clear to me that we had a good chance of pulling off a major diplomatic success. Dulles and I were getting on well together. Menon and Shepilov

combined were having a wholly salutary effect upon him. Eden
was delighted to have Menzies in London, with his strong,
unconcealed vocal support. There was wider disapproval of
Nasser's actions from the Afro-Asians than I had dared to
hope, and a strong feeling in favour of some form of international control.

The conference began at 11 a.m. on 16th August in Lancaster
House. Eden made a brief speech of welcome to the delegates.
I was then elected chairman without opposition. There was a
tricky hour or so on procedural matters, but they accepted my
guidance that we should have no rules about voting until we
came to the possibility of there being a vote. There would be
no discussion to agree an agenda. Everyone knew why we had
assembled. If anyone wanted to challenge the chairman's ruling
on anything, that could be done. How this was to be done was
wisely left uncertain. They accepted my suggestions about when
we should sit.

Dulles made a powerful speech on that first day when we
reassembled after lunch, putting forward the tripartite proposals. He said:

On 26th July, 1956, the Egyptian Government, acting
unilaterally and without any prior international consultation of which we are aware, issued a decree purporting to
nationalise the Universal Suez Canal Company and to
take over all its property and rights pertaining thereto,
and to terminate its rights, affirmed by the 1888 Convention, to operate the Canal until 1968. The installations of
the Suez Canal Company were then physically taken over
by the Egyptian Government. Its employees were pre-
vented from leaving their work without Egyptian Government permission under penalty of imprisonment.

The United States does not believe the Egyptian
Government had the right to wipe out that Convention
establishing the rights of the Universal Suez Canal Company until 1968. This arrangement had the status of an

9

international compact; many relied upon it. The operating rights and assets of that Company were impressed with an international interest. The Government of the United States questions that the Government of Egypt had the right unilaterally to take its action of 26th July last.

Dulles went on to develop the tripartite proposals, asserting the principle of international control, recognising Egypt's sovereign rights, guaranteeing her a fair return from the Canal and suggesting the negotiation of a new Convention. Under this, the operation of the Canal would be entrusted to a board which would include Egypt, and whose membership would have regard to use, patterns of trade and geographical distribution.

We believed that Dulles was speaking for the United States Government when he said this. We had believed Eisenhower when he wrote to Eden on 31st July and said:*

We recognise the transcendent worth of the Canal to the free world, and the possibility that the use of force might become necessary in order to protect international rights.

Dulles was supported by Pineau. He referred to the Company's special status since 1856, and to the 100 agreements, conventions and contracts negotiated between the Company and the Egyptian Government. He said that it was as though the Swiss Government had tried to nationalise the Bank of International Settlement in Basle. Brentano of the Federal Republic of Germany and, somewhat surprisingly, Artajo of Spain, also came out in favour of the international character of the Canal Company.

In my own speech on 22nd August, I explained our military precautions, referring to the mob violence of 1952 in Egypt. There were 13,000 British nationals in Egypt. The Suez Canal Base was being managed by civilian contractors. We had valuable ships and cargo passing through the Canal. Nevertheless, we desired a peaceful settlement:

* *Waging Peace*, Appendix B.

As a nation we are very slow to anger, but when it is clear that vital interests are threatened by acts of deliberate hostility, we are in the habit of standing firm whatever the odds.

On the sovereignty argument, I said that a state did not suffer an infringement of its sovereignty by allowing an international authority to perform certain functions on its territory. Acceptance of an international obligation was an act of sovereignty.

While the conference continued I kept the Cabinet informed of its progress. One of their preoccupations was whether Dulles had been specific as to what would happen if the conference failed or if its proposals were not accepted by Nasser. There was an important Cabinet meeting at which Menzies was also present in the morning of 23rd August. By then it was clear that things had gone our way. I reported that after five days of discussion and speeches remarkable for their restraint, eighteen nations would probably support Dulles's resolution. It had been agreed that a committee of five of them should put the proposals to Nasser, consisting of Australia, Ethiopia, Iran, Sweden and the United States, a country from each continent. Menzies had agreed to act as chairman. I said that the Soviet delegation had been rather piano, as though they did not want to be too closely involved. Another explanation might have been the comparative inexperience of Shepilov.

About the future, I had to report that Dulles had not been at all specific, and a general discussion followed. Monckton spoke of the disadvantages of the use of force, and said that he hoped that it really would be the last resort, and that we would exhaust all other means first. Macmillan warned that if Nasser succeeded our position in the Middle East would be undermined, our oil supplies in jeopardy and the stability of our economy gravely threatened.

Salisbury was strongly in favour of a reference to the Security

Council, but the United Nations was only a means to an end; that end was not merely the preservation of peace but also the observance of the rules of law and justice. Kilmuir referred to Professor Goodhart's letter in *The Times* some days earlier, on 11th August,* in which he had argued that there was no foundation for the view that under modern international law force might be used only to repel a direct territorial attack. A state might properly use force to protect a vital national interest which had been imperilled. In such a case it was that state which had altered the *status quo* which was guilty of aggression.

While there was unanimity in the Cabinet about continuing to try to get an agreement which would frustrate Nasser's policy, there was also apparent unanimity that we should go to the Security Council, and that if that failed we should use force. Monckton, as Minister of Defence, explained the military measures which had been taken and the plans for action.

Eden and Menzies paid generous tributes to my chairmanship which were echoed in the letter written by Eisenhower to Eden on 2nd September (Appendix C in Eisenhower's book).

The final session of the conference took place that afternoon, with the expected result. Dulles had accepted amendments put forward by Iran, Pakistan and Turkey, which did not affect the substance. The Spanish Foreign Minister made the reservation that if Nasser turned down Dulles's proposals, negotiations should proceed on the basis which Artajo had earlier put forward along the lines of international participation in the Egyptian body administering the Canal. Eighteen countries said that they accepted the Resolution, and its terms became known as the Eighteen-Power Proposals (see footnote, p. 107). Of the other four, I felt that only Russia and India opposed it on the merits. The delegates of Ceylon and Indonesia felt that they must go along with India, but with what seemed to me a marked lack of enthusiasm. An unexpected event was the fact that Menon at the very end paid a handsome tribute to the chairman.

* See p. 239.

The result was better than we dared have hoped for in the firmness of Dulles's statement, the extent of the support for his Resolution and the composition of the committee of five to put the proposals to Nasser. Some hoped that Dulles might go himself, but I was not surprised when he firmly declined. His substitute, however, Loy Henderson, had our complete confidence. The fact that so prominent a neutral as Unden had agreed to serve was a plus. Ardalan and Hapte-Wold (Ethiopia) were also acceptable, and with Menzies, to our great satisfaction, having accepted the leadership, I felt that it was as good a team as we could field. It could not have been better having regard to personalities, geography and varying interests in the operation of the Canal.

After it was over, an experienced Commonwealth diplomat came up to me and said that he could not understand why we had left the Americans to make the running and shown so little leadership ourselves. That comment made me rub my eyes a little. I had been led to believe that in diplomacy the old Latin tag applied: *Ars est celare artem* (It is true art to conceal art). The facts were as follows: the conference had taken place in London, which we wanted and which the Americans did not; the membership was acceptable to us both; I was in the chair, which we wanted and the Americans did not; Dulles was induced to move the tripartite resolution: I should guess that ten days before, nothing was further from his mind; the result was a resolution completely satisfactory to us, with eighteen out of twenty-two nations supporting it.

This result was due to much preparatory effort, the careful handling of the other delegations, complete co-operation, once the conference had started, between Dulles and myself, and the full support of Eden and my Cabinet colleagues strongly reinforced by Menzies; and, throughout, a great deal of very hard work by my extremely efficient Foreign Office staff and officials from the Commonwealth Relations Office.

The next day, 24th August, might have been expected to be a day of post-conference relaxation. It depends how relaxation

is defined. It began with von Brentano coming to have breakfast with me at Carlton Gardens. After that Pineau and I
surveyed the scene. We agreed that the Israelis should be discouraged from taking advantage of the situation. I had a talk
with Dulles. The Egypt Committee met. I lunched at the
Iranian Embassy. Ardalan, the Foreign Minister, said that if
Nasser was not checked it was the end of the pro-Western
regime in Iran. I saw the Ethiopian Foreign Minister. I recorded a T.V. interview for the evening, and ended up dining
quietly with Menzies at the Turf Club. The main point which
I made in the T.V. interview was Nasser's statement in his
speech of 26th July that in future the Canal would be operated
solely in the interests of Egypt.

Eden also saw Dulles that day. Dulles emphasised the importance of avoiding the impression that there was a serious
division of opinion in the United Kingdom about the firm stand
which the Government were taking. He proposed to tell Gaitskell so. Eden yet again warned Dulles about the use of force
if there was no settlement. We could not maintain our forces
at a high state of readiness for a protracted period. Eden also
sent a message to Eisenhower* saying how helpful Dulles had
been at the conference, repeating his fears of Russian penetration of the Middle East and stating that the military preparations must continue.

I was much encouraged to receive a letter of strong support
from Spaak, the Belgian Foreign Minister. I give here the
substance of it. After explaining that he understood why
Belgium had not been invited to the conference, he said that
these events required a policy of absolute firmness: 'I do not
wish to hide from you that I am haunted by the memory of the
mistakes which were committed at the outset of the Hitler
period, mistakes which have cost us dear.' After saying that he
did not underestimate the importance of the administration of
the Canal, he stated that he believed that the psychological and
political aspects were more important. If Nasser's act of violence

* *Full Circle*, p. 452.

went unpunished, the prestige of the new dictator would be formidably increased, together with his ambitions and foolhardiness. He ended by saying that in this situation wisdom and firmness were synonymous.

I also had an interesting conversation with von Brentano. At dinner on 22nd August he said that if we had used force within forty-eight hours there would have been considerable world support. As each day passed, support for forcible action was growing less. I replied that I hoped that he realised the consequences of this. If there was no agreement, and if there was then no forcible action, Governments friendly to us in the Middle East would fall. We would lose not only our freedom to transport our oil, but the sources of the oil itself. Von Brentano did not disagree. He added that the conference had been a remarkable example of the solidarity of the Western Alliance. At that time, I certainly agreed with him.

Chapter IX

Users' Club

Phase IV 1st–13th September — Menzies mission to Nasser — message from Eisenhower — Dulles's SCUA idea — NATO meeting in Paris — Nasser rejects offer — Foreign Office views — French Ministers in London — critical Cabinet meeting 11th September — changes in military plans — debates in Parliament 12th–13th September — jurisdiction of International Court.

The Conference was over. Menzies and his colleagues were working hard on how best to present the case to Nasser. Eden had sent a message to Eisenhower, which again did not show undue bellicosity:

> The firmer the front we show together, the greater the chance that Nasser will give way without the need for any resort to force.

After Nasser had agreed to meet the Menzies mission in Cairo in September, I told Dulles that I felt strongly that if Nasser rejected our proposals we ought to go to the Security Council straight away. The danger was that if we did not, someone else — for example, the Soviet Union or Yugoslavia — might raise the concentration of our forces in the eastern Mediterranean as a threat to peace. I thought that the meeting should be at Foreign Minister level. United States support was essential. The current composition of the Council (the five permanent members — China, France, Soviet Union, United Kingdom, United States — plus Australia, Belgium, Cuba, Iran, Peru and Yugoslavia) was reasonably good from our point of view. I expressed my gratitude for his masterly handling of our case during the London conference and said, 'Under your leadership, I believe we could pull off another success.'

There then began a complicated and rather frustrating discussion by telegram with him. It was prefaced by something said to me by Dulles which is relevant to the allegation that we kept him in the dark about our military preparations. I said to him that one of the American military attachés had asked for information about our troop movements. Dulles at once replied categorically that he would prefer that information about the movement of United Kingdom troops should not be given to the United States military authorities. He said much the same to Eden.*

We discussed with Dulles the Article of the Charter under which we would go to the Security Council and the nature of the resolution which we would put forward. At first he was quite forthcoming. He agreed that we must go to the Security Council before military action, but he wanted us to understand that that did not mean that the United States was committed to the use of force. He himself would attend and support us provided it was an honest attempt to find a solution.

Meanwhile, Trevelyan on 30th August sent a revealing account of Nasser's state of mind. Nasser had very much underestimated the strength of the Western reaction against what he had done, but he was determined not to yield. He believed time to be on his side and it was ten to one against Western military intervention.

About the same time, Muntasser, the Libyan Ambassador, again warned me that Nasser would not be mourned, but that meanwhile there was general sympathy in the Arab world for Egypt.

There was to be a NATO meeting in Paris on 5th September and Pearson, the Canadian Minister for External Affairs, spent some hours in London on his way. We discussed a number of miscellaneous topics—disarmament, territorial waters, the

* *Full Circle*, p. 438.

enlargement of the Security Council, NATO, Antarctica, and finally arms for Israel. I said that I thought that the balance was turning against Israel but we did not want to give the impression of a co-ordinated Western plan to supply Israel with arms. The United States and France were continuing supplies but they did not wish any publicity. Pineau had told me that officially they were not supplying further Mystères, but in fact they might do so quietly. Pearson said that Dulles seemed to want Canada to supply some F86 aircraft to give Israel experience of them. Pearson thought that they would probably do so.

On the same day, Barbour, the United States Chargé d'Affaires, came with a copy of a message from Eisenhower to Eden, dated 2nd September. It was a reply to Eden's message (see p. 122) and is reproduced in Eisenhower's book as Appendix C. It led to a further exchange between the two men (see *Full Circle*, p. 464, and *Waging Peace*, Appendix D). The President's messages were remarkable for their length and their laboured argument. He seemed still to be under the delusion that we were impatient to use military force:

> There should be no thought of military action before the influences of the U.N. are fully explored ... American public opinion flatly rejects the thought of using force particularly when it does not seem that every possible peaceful means of protecting our vital interests has been exhausted without result ... The use of military force against Egypt under present circumstances might have consequences even more serious than causing the Arabs to support Nasser.

But his alternative suggestions contained nothing new: a semi-permanent organisation of user governments (sic) to take over technical problems, economic pressures, exploitation of Arab rivalries. Moreover, he could still say: 'I assure you we are not blind to the fact that eventually there may be no escape from the use of force.' This exchange began the day before Menzies arrived in Cairo to make the first proposals to Nasser since nationalisation, and in the midst of it Eisenhower was to make a public statement rejecting the use of force completely, which must have led Nasser to refuse to consider those proposals (see p. 129). His support for recourse to the U.N. and for organising the users was soon to seem ironic when, within a few days, Dulles was delaying reference to the Security Council, and almost immediately was to be denying the users any leverage they might have had.

I also had a message from Dulles. He thought that world opinion would be unfavourably impressed by the information which was becoming available about British and French military preparations and about evacuation plans. I replied that it was necessary to begin our evacuation plans because we had so many people to get out. There were 3,000 British subjects in Jordan, the Lebanon and Syria, and of the 13,000 in Egypt about 6,000 were United Kingdom based. We were not evacuating from the Lebanon or the Gulf. What we were doing was not inconsistent with the taking of precautions and should not be taken as indicating that we were preparing for war tomorrow. I added that I hoped, however, that there was no misunderstanding about how things might develop. The British Government were willing to give the five-nation Menzies mission a fair run and, if it failed, to go to the Security Council provided there was time; but as soon as it was clear that Nasser would not budge we would have to consider further action.

Then came one of Dulles's changes of direction. He spent the weekend of 2nd/3rd September on Duck Island. This was, and may still be, a remote, unspoiled little island in Lake Ontario about twenty miles west of the mouth of the St Lawrence. Dulles had bought it, I think, during the Second World War. It was a joy for him to go there with Janet, his wife, to get away from everybody and everything. They lived in a small log cabin, twenty-five feet square, and did everything for themselves. There was no means of communication except through the lighthouse keeper. There is a fascinating account of the island

and their way of life there in the book written by Eleanor Dulles, his sister, about him called *The Last Year** revealing an attractive side to his nature.

It was on Duck Island during this particular weekend as he did the chores and watched the birds that he conceived his brain-child, the Users' Club (later to be called the Suez Canal Users' Association—SCUA). The users of the Canal should band themselves together, hire the pilots, manage the technical features of the Canal, organise the pattern of navigation, and collect the dues from the ships of member countries. Nasser had no right to make a profit out of the Canal. He would see money slipping out of his hands, and that would be better than the threat or use of force.

The telegram containing this idea was handed to me literally as I was getting into the car to go to the airport to fly to Paris for the NATO meeting. The plan had considerable advantages if it was possible to put it into operation.

I flew to Paris with Spaak. During the morning I had a meeting with Pineau and his advisers. We talked first about going to the Security Council. Pineau was against it, but if we insisted he would agree. Anglo-French solidarity must prevail and he would go but without much pleasure. I said that the state of British public opinion was such that if force had to be used there would be very strong opposition unless the matter had first been referred to the Security Council. The Labour Party, the Trades Union Congress and the Scandinavians, apparently believed that the United Nations could solve the problem and we must give it the chance. Pineau asked whether all this would delay matters until it was too late to take military action. I agreed that this was a relevant matter, as the threat of force was an important element in the situation.

Then we discussed what other action might be taken if Nasser said 'No'. We both thought that the payment of the dues was the key matter. As little as possible should be paid to Nasser.

* *John Foster Dulles: The Last Year* (New York: Harcourt Brace, 1963).

I then told Pineau about Dulles's brain-child and what was almost a volte-face on his part. Dulles had now decided that we were in a weak position juridically. We were asking Egypt to accept a new treaty. This represented no infringement of her sovereignty. But we were threatening the use of force if she refused. The implication, Dulles said, was that we did not have adequate rights and needed to acquire them. Therefore, it was a fatal and unnecessary weakness to assume that if Egypt did not voluntarily accept our proposals we must resort to force. We ought to show Nasser that we had an alternative other than war.

This seemed to me a very tortuous argument. Egypt had broken her treaty obligations and destroyed the international character of the Canal authority. We were suggesting a new international Canal authority with greater benefits for Egypt, but our juridical rights were exactly as before. Dulles had admitted this at the London conference when he had said that the 1888 Convention gave us all the rights we required; but he did not mention its Preamble and the international system which was an integral part of the Canal convention (again, see my speech at Appendix III).

This new suggestion was that the users should form this association of their own to act as I have described. He referred to the rights granted under the convention, such as dealing with obstructions, objecting to fortifications and the stationing of warships. He was obviously unclear as to how the system would work in practice, but he was apparently firm that the dues from the shipowners of member countries should be paid to this new association. Pineau and I were in the same difficulty. There were attractions about Dulles's new plan if it was genuine. We needed United States support and a good international atmosphere and, if possible, an agreed solution. But we wanted to make certain that Dulles did not string us along with proposal after proposal until it was no longer possible for us to mount a military operation.

The discussion at the NATO meeting helped us to make up our minds. Luns of the Netherlands and Spaak took a robust line. If Nasser rejected the eighteen-power proposals, the NATO countries should refuse to recognise the seizure of the Canal; they should withhold the payment of dues, and the matter should be referred to the Security Council. Pearson also endorsed this attitude and said that, although he was averse to military sanctions, the use of force could not be excluded in the last resort. No American Minister was present, and the official representing the United States said very little.

Accordingly, Pineau and I decided that Dulles's proposal was worth examination. When I met Mollet and Pineau later in the day, it was agreed that I should try to find out when Menzies thought that his mission would finish. It was also agreed that we should instruct our Ambassador in Washington to tell Dulles of our wish to refer the matter to the Security Council, and that recourse to it would be a genuine attempt to find a peaceful solution; but that we also assumed that he, for his part, would not go back on the eighteen-power proposals, nor support any resolution which would limit our freedom of action. Meanwhile, I would try to find out more about the Users' Club idea.

When I came to read Dulles's telegram from Duck Island more carefully, I saw that he wanted me to give my reactions without discussing it with anyone else. In my reply I apologised to him for having told Pineau. I said that I thought that all the major user countries should follow the line proposed at the NATO meeting and issue a statement that they did not recognise the nationalisation of the Canal, and would not pay the dues to the new Egyptian authority. As to Dulles's scheme, I expressed my doubts about the speed with which it could be formulated, but the above proposals would be a first step towards it.

Dulles in his reply said that he understood how I had come to tell Pineau about the Users' Club. The reason he had wanted me to keep it to myself was that he did not trust French security. This brought an immediate telegram from Jebb in Paris that French security had been extremely good over the

Suez discussions, and this was the usual American unjustified excuse for not taking the French into their confidence.

There followed many telegrams from both sides of the Atlantic in which attempts were made to clarify the details of the Dulles plan. We for our part believed that Dulles was acting in good faith. Murphy in a T.V. programme some years later said:

> If Secretary Dulles was actually convinced of the possibility of organising a Canal Users' Association to operate the Suez Canal, I was not aware of this, and I am inclined to doubt it. I believe that he considered the idea useful as a negotiating device which could be helpful in delaying and avoiding a possible military operation.

While all this was in its early stages, Menzies and his colleagues had been hard at work in Cairo. Menzies has given an account in a chapter called 'My Suez Story' in his book *Afternoon Light*.* He and his colleagues travelled by air to Cairo on 2nd September and met Nasser on the following day for a preliminary meeting to establish personal conduct and arrange for procedures. The next afternoon, 4th September, Menzies presented the case on behalf of the committee. Nasser listened. Menzies had read in the press that Nasser had met his military commanders and told them that the Franco-British mobilisation moves were all bluff. Menzies asked for a private talk with Nasser and told him that it would be a great mistake on his part if he excluded the possible use of force from his reckoning. Menzies made it clear that he was not threatening Nasser, and Nasser said that he did not regard what Menzies had said as a threat and he would consider it.

Next morning, 5th September, there were flaring headlines in the newspapers: Eisenhower, questioned at a press conference about the possible use of force, had rejected it completely and unconditionally. If Nasser rejected the present proposals, others

* Robert Menzies, *Afternoon Light: Some Memories of Men and Events* (Cassell, Australia, 1967).

would have to be worked out: 'We are committed to a peaceful settlement of this dispute, nothing else.' That destroyed any chance Menzies might have had of success and made the mission futile.

Nasser rejected the eighteen-power proposals on 9th September. His alternative suggestion was that a negotiating body should be set up to consider the various views. Dulles was firm about this. He described Nasser's proposal as too vague even to be considered.

It has been suggested that Menzies was not the right man to lead this mission. I disagree. He did as well as anyone could have done. Unden said to me afterwards that Menzies had stated the case admirably in Cairo and he thought that Nasser had been impressed.

About this time, Sir Ivone Kirkpatrick, the Permanent Under-Secretary of State at the Foreign Office and therefore my principal adviser, showed me a telegram which he wished to send in my name to Makins. I remember it well. It was a first-class example of his incisiveness. It ran something like this:

> Dulles, having rejected the idea of going to the Security Council, having refused to stop paying dues to the Egyptian Authority, having decided that other economic pressure was not possible, having thought up SCUA, would very soon find out that SCUA did not work. The choice would then be force or surrender to Nasser.

The same day Kirkpatrick also responded with vigour to Eisenhower's complaint in his exchange with Eden that we were making Nasser more important than he was.

Kirkpatrick wrote to Makins that he wished the President were right but that he was convinced he was wrong. Nasser himself was not yet an important figure nor could Egypt by herself deal us a mortal blow. But if we all sat back while Nasser consolidated his position and gradually got control of the oil-bearing states, he could wreck us, and according to our information was resolved so to do. If Middle East oil were to be denied to us for a year or two our gold reserves would disappear and the sterling area would disintegrate. If the sterling area did disintegrate, we would be left with no reserves and would not be able to maintain a force in Germany or anywhere, and we should not be able to pay for the minimum defence which we required. A country which cannot provide for its defence is finished.

Kirkpatrick continued in substance as follows:

It seems to me that there is a certain analogy, as Walter Lippmann points out, between our attitude to America over China, and theirs to us over the Middle East. There is only one substantial difference. The Americans never believed that the Chinese would wreck them, at all events for a very long time. But for the reasons I have outlined very sketchily above, we, rightly or wrongly, believe that if we are denied the resources of Africa and the Middle East, we can be wrecked within a year or two.

I believe it important that my readers should be aware of the substance of this letter and telegram because it has been widely put about that ministers acted with complete disregard for the Foreign Office advice given to them.

The reason for Dulles's action in advancing his Users' Club plan is given only too clearly by Murphy on p. 467 of his book *Diplomat Among Warriors*. Dulles, operating under basic instructions to prevent military intervention, was acutely aware that a commitment to support hostilities could have a damaging effect on Eisenhower's candidacy for re-election as President. He had to think up some plan which would delay us, and in particular, at that stage, our reference of the matter to the Security Council.

We were in a quandary, particularly as Parliament was to meet again on 12th September. We decided to invite Mollet and Pineau to come to London to consider the situation.

Meanwhile, the basic purposes of the Users' Club had been more specifically defined by Dulles. It would function according to the following principles:

(a) to organise the use of the Canal by member-controlled vessels so as to promote safe, orderly, efficient and economical transit;

(b) to assure that such use will, as among member-controlled vessels, be impartial and uninfluenced for or against any ship or cargo by reason of the policies of any Government;

(c) to co-operate with Egypt in the discharge by Egypt of its obligation to take new measures for ensuring the execution of the 1888 Convention;

(d) to co-ordinate generally on behalf of the members the rights of user granted by the 1888 Convention with scrupulous regard for the sovereign right of Egypt in consonance with the 1888 Convention.

The French Ministers arrived on 11th September, and in the talks that morning with Eden and myself we came to the conclusion, not very willingly, that we should agree in principle to the Users' Club on the conditions that the United States would participate and that dues, including those from United States shipowners, should be paid to the new organisation. On that basis we would accept Dulles's view that we should not go to the Security Council at once, but we would send a letter to the President of the Council informing him of the situation. We also discussed changes in the military plans, to which I will refer later.

In the afternoon there was an important meeting of the Cabinet. I said that Nasser had flatly rejected the eighteen-power proposals put to him by Menzies. Eden reported on our talks with the French. We reviewed the three courses open to us: (a) military action — which the United States Government were strongly opposed to at this stage; (b) a reference to the

Security Council, with a resolution endorsing the eighteen-power proposals—the United States Government were not in agreement with this course; (c) to put into operation the SCUA plan, under which the users would take positive action together to assert their rights, and would call upon Egypt to give the necessary facilities. The advantages of the third course were that it would involve the United States in action designed to enforce the rights of the users; it would deprive Egypt of 80 per cent of the dues (as we then thought); if Egypt was obstructive, we had a stronger case for going to the Security Council or for the use of force. Its disadvantages were that it might simply be a delaying device on Dulles's part, and the plan depended upon Egypt's co-operation.

The Cabinet gave it very careful consideration, with the debate in the House particularly in mind. Macmillan was in favour of SCUA. It was unlikely that effective international control of the Canal would be achieved without the use of force. SCUA would be a step towards that. It would not of itself produce a solution. It could not be a permanent arrangement, but it would serve to bring the matter to a head. The discussion continued on much the same lines as at the Cabinet on 23rd August (see p. 117). Monckton was against the premature use of force. If the United States did not agree, the result would be disorder in the Middle East and the alienation of public opinion.

Kilmuir said that it was a mistake to assume that if force had ultimately to be used, it would be inconsistent with the United Nations Charter. One of the essential purposes of the Charter, as reflected in the Preamble, was to secure respect for international obligations. This was the main issue over Suez. We must do it if we could by peaceful means. SCUA would be a further effort to do it that way. But if it failed, he believed that we would be fully justified in having recourse to force and submitting the matter simultaneously to the Security Council. Salisbury believed that force would have to be used, but it must be to enforce respect for international obligations.

Butler said that the party in the country would support the use of force, if all practicable steps had been taken to try to secure a settlement by peaceful means. There were present at this Cabinet, in addition to those whom I have mentioned, Gwilym Lloyd George, Stuart, Home, Lennox-Boyd, Sandys, Thorneycroft, Heathcoat-Amory, Eccles, Macleod, Selkirk and Buchan-Hepburn. We decided to support the SCUA plan. But no one at that Cabinet can have been in any doubt that if we tried SCUA without success, and if we then went to the Security Council without success, the use of force would be the policy.

Meanwhile, it had been explained to us that changes in the military plans were necessary. Monckton told the Cabinet about them.

On 10th August the Egypt Committee had accepted the Chiefs of Staff's advice that the best plan of attack upon Egypt was a full-scale assault upon Alexandria, seizing the port and the airfield, followed by an advance to the Suez Canal through the Cairo area. This plan was called Musketeer. We had been told that the earliest feasible date for the assault was 15th September. On 22nd August, after the London conference, the date was postponed to 19th September. That would give us time to see what the Menzies mission produced, and for the reference to the Security Council which we had intended to make if the mission failed. On 28th August there was a further postponement to 26th September for the same reasons.

On 4th September, just as Dulles was about to spring upon us his SCUA plan, we were told by the Chiefs of Staff that the date had already been postponed by eleven days. The maximum future postponement possible was for another ten days until 9th October. If that did not give enough time, a new plan must be made. By 10th September we had decided to recommend to the Cabinet the acceptance of Dulles's SCUA plan, and the calling of a further conference in London of the eighteen nations who might become members. That would all take time, and we must also give ourselves time for the reference to the

Security Council. Assuming the worst and that nothing came of all this, 9th October was still too early a date. We, therefore, asked the Chiefs of Staff to prepare their new plan.

I have set this out in some detail to disprove once again the theory that we were longing for the chance to use force. We agreed to postponement after postponement in the hope that the pressure of international opinion would make Nasser see sense.

Monckton explained the new plan to the Cabinet. In it Port Said was substituted for Alexandria as the target for seaborne landing. The operation was to take place in three phases:

Stage I   The neutralisation of the Egyptian Air Force.

Stage II   A few days of aerial bombardment of selected targets, coupled with psychological warfare.

Stage III Occupation of the Canal Zone by a seaborne assault on Port Said, coupled with airborne landing as necessary.

The advantages of the new plan were that it was more flexible, fewer resources were required and there was less risk of civilian casualties. It was called Musketeer Revise and was feasible up to the end of October. It was accepted by the Cabinet.

The two Houses of Parliament met on 12th September to discuss the Middle East, the House of Commons for a two-day debate. As I have said, the decision to recall Parliament on that date had been made at a time when we thought that by then we would have had Nasser's reactions to the eighteen-power proposals and would be able to announce our decision to go to the Security Council. Owing to the Dulles's SCUA scheme, the date could not have been more unfortunate. We could not announce a reference to the Security Council because of Dulles's disagreement. We were extremely anxious to maintain a common front with the United States, and on this occasion paid dearly for it. Speaker after speaker from the Opposition benches accused us of intending to use force against Egypt without going to the Security Council. We felt that we could not announce our disagreement with the United States over reference to the Security Council—perhaps it would have been better if we had—and we were unable to be precise. The Opposition took full advantage. Eventually in the closing minutes of his final speech, Eden pointed out that Bevin had delayed three and a half months before taking to the Security Council the dispute with the Soviet Union when they stopped access by road and rail to West Berlin, and the Berlin airlift took place. Eden went on to say:

I want to deal with the question—would Her Majesty's Government give a pledge not to use force except after reference to the Security Council. If such a pledge or guarantee is to be absolute, then neither I nor any British Minister standing at this box could give it. No one can possibly tell what will be Colonel Nasser's action, either in the Canal or in Egypt. Nevertheless, I will give this reply, which is as far as any Government can go. It would certainly be our intention if circumstances allowed or, in other words, except in an emergency, to refer a matter of that kind to the Security Council. Beyond that I do not think that any Government can possibly go.

The Opposition were not satisfied and insisted on a vote. There were two. In the first, on the Opposition amendment, the figures were 321 to 251, a Government majority of 70. On the second, the Government's own Motion, the figures were 318 to 248, a Government majority of 71.

It had been an acrimonious debate but there were some notable speeches.

On the first day Edelman, Labour Member for Coventry North, spoke of the disastrous economic consequences which might result from Nasser being permitted to get away with his seizure of the Canal; he had no doubt that Nasser had been guilty of aggression; he had no doubt how Ernest Bevin would have reacted to the situation; as to the use of force, he confined himself to the belief that we must be prepared to use force under the aegis of the Security Council. He added some wise words about nationalism.

He was followed by Simon, Conservative Member for Middlesbrough West, later to become a Lord of Appeal, Lord Simon of Glaisdale. He dealt with the legal issues. Although we should not act in conflict with or in derogation of the Charter, action through the United Nations might well fail. An act of international lawlessness like Nasser's might have most serious consequences unless checked. He did not accept what a previous Labour speaker had said that 'anything was better than war'. He quoted Goodhart's letter to *The Times* of 11th August (see p. 239) about the use of force being justified wherever a vital national interest was at sake. He said that he would not agree with that as a universal proposition, but thought that one might be driven to the defence of vital national interests if the organs of international order which we had created proved incapable of performing their function.

Bob Boothby was the last speaker from the Government side on the first day. It frequently happens that a back-bencher is chosen for that task when the debate lasts two days. He made a brilliant speech which I would have liked to quote in full. Here are some extracts:

There has been much talk about Nasser. I do not think that there is any use in blinking the facts. Nasser is a dictator. I do not think that he himself would claim to be anything else.

He has established in Egypt a police state. In November last he declared that the Egyptian Government had full confidence in the attitude of the Suez Canal Company. In June he came to a new agreement with it. In July he described it as an instrument of imperialism inside

Egypt, plotting against his country's freedom and sapping
its blood. He was going to take action against 'the pirates'
who were responsible for this.

That is, whether we like it or not, the language of Hitler
and the rule of the jungle.

I do not believe that the Arab States are panting to come
under Nasser's domination. They are waiting to see how
things go. If he gets away with this, his prestige will get a
big boost. It has been asked: would he use his power,
then, to blackmail the West and bully the Middle East?
The *Daily Express* ... gave the answer this morning: 'Did
Hitler use his power after seizing the Rhineland to blackmail France and Britain while he grabbed Austria and
Czechoslovakia?'

Boothby finished his speech:

As I listened to the Prime Minister this afternoon I thought
of what Nasser had been saying about what he was going
to do to establish an Arab empire from Morocco to the
Persian Gulf, and how he was going to eliminate Israel
altogether. That is all in his speeches and in a horrible
little book called "A Philosophy of Revolution", which is
like a potted edition of "Mein Kampf". As I heard the
Prime Minister speaking I said to myself, 'Well thank
goodness, at any rate we shall not have to go through all
that again', and we shall not.

And we did not go through that again, whatever mistakes may
or may not have been made.

On the second day of the debate a speech by Lionel Heald, a
former Conservative Attorney-General, made a great impression in the House. It was referred to as having changed the
whole course of the debate. Opposition after Opposition

speaker congratulated him on his courage, by implication, in defying the Government. When one looks at what he said, I think that he would be the first to say that it was not an anti-Government speech at all. He made an appeal for national unity. He began by referring to the use of force. He specifically said that he was not one of those who said that in no circumstances should force be used. What had to be considered was what were the circumstances. He was not prepared to support any action which involved a breach of our international obligations.

After dealing with Articles 2 and 4 of the United Nations Charter and our efforts under Article 36, he said that, if all that failed, there was under Article 37 an obligation to refer the matter to the Security Council before force was used. This provoked almost ecstatic cries of support from the Opposition. Heald went on to say:

> When the tumult has subsided, I would rather continue myself. Let me make my position perfectly clear. The matter is not by any means ended when we arrive at the Security Council. In the House and in the country we must face sooner or later this position. At the present time there are no teeth in the United Nations Organisation. It may well be that a reference to the Security Council still leaves the great problem open. That is a matter which we must face and deal with, but that is no justification for breaking our own international obligations. If a reasonable and proper plan supported by 18 or 12 nations, or whatever the number may be, is put forward to the United Nations and approved there, then I will be perfectly willing to support the Government in any measure they then think it necessary to carry out.

He ended:

> What a fine thing it would be if after all this heat has been generated, we should end with the position that we all

agree that we will comply with our international obligations, [and here there were cries of approval from the
Opposition] but, and I hope that the Members opposite
will equally cheer this, that we will insist on Colonel
Nasser complying with the reasonable views of 18 nations.

This final statement, coupled with what he had said at the
beginning of his speech about the use of force, failed to leave
upon me the impression of an attack upon the Government.

The tragedy was — and it did a great deal to erode our
position for the next stage — our belief that Dulles was acting in
good faith over SCUA and not merely cooking up devices for
delay. At the back of my mind I had been uneasy about SCUA
from the beginning, but I did not put forward my doubts very
forcibly to Eden until the morning of the debate. He generously
gave me credit for this in his book. I do not think that I
deserved much credit: I had left it too late in the day.

These doubts were reinforced when I heard Gaitskell say in
his winding-up speech:

> This evening we heard that Mr Dulles has said, 'The
> United States does not intend to shoot its way through the
> Suez Canal if Egypt tries to block the passage of United
> States ships travelling under the auspices of the proposed
> new Users' Association'. He said that instead it has already
> been decided to take the United States' tankers out of
> 'moth balls' — the reserve fleet — and divert the oil and
> other traffic round the Continent of Africa if anything
> should happen to deny passage of the Canal. That seems
> to me to suggest that the name of the Association should be
> changed to the Cape Users' Association.

There was one other matter raised in this debate to which I
must refer. On 2nd August Gaitskell had asked about a
reference of Nasser's actions to the International Court of
Justice. Herbert Morrison, with our dispute with Iran over the
nationalisation of the Abadan refinery in mind, had to pour

cold water upon it, but it was raised again on 12th September. Gaitskell said that if we contended that the nationalisation of the Canal was illegal, we had a duty to refer it to the International Court. Zilliacus, a Labour specialist in Foreign Affairs, said that the International Court was the obvious body to settle the matter, as both Egypt and Britain had signed the Optional Clause relating to compulsory jurisdiction under Article 36 of its Statute.

The Optional Clause certainly had its importance here, but not in the way Zilliacus stated. All members of the United Nations can apply to the Court in the role of plaintiff, but the Court does not have jurisdiction to decide the questions raised unless the defendant state has accepted what is called the Optional Clause for that type of case (or accepts the Court's jurisdiction for that particular case).

Egypt had not signed the Optional Clause. Iran had. In our case against Iran over the nationalisation of the Anglo-Iranian Oil Company in 1951, the Court decided that although Iran had accepted the Optional Clause for disputes arising out of international treaties subsequently concluded, the company's concession was not an international treaty and the Court had no jurisdiction. This decision was made twelve months after our original application.

The position of Egypt in this matter was quite different. She had not bound herself in any way to accept the Court's jurisdiction. Zilliacus was quite wrong. Therefore, whether Nasser's action was a breach of international law or not, the Court would have held that it had no jurisdiction — unless Nasser had accepted its jurisdiction for this particular case, which was inconceivable.

This will show how ill-founded was the allegation made in that debate that we had been frightened to go to the Court because a decision that it had no jurisdiction would be a judgment for Egypt. Wedgwood Benn from the Labour backbenches, had contended:

If the Court decided that it had no jurisdiction, that would be a judgment for Egypt. That is why the Government do not take it to the International Court, because they are frightened that the Court will come out and say that this is an Egyptian matter.

At the House of Lords debate Lord McNair, who was President of the International Court, dealt with the international character of the Suez Canal Company. He quoted the Preamble of the 1888 Convention:

wishing to establish by a Conventional Act a definite system designed to guarantee at all times and for all the Powers the free use of the Suez Maritime Canal, and then to complete the system under which the navigation of the Canal has been placed by the Firman of his Imperial Majesty the Sultan, dated 22nd February, 1866.

He went on to say that that clearly indicated the international character of the Suez Canal Company. We were fully entitled to press for the negotiation of some kind of international system.

In that same debate, Kilmuir made a long and carefully argued speech explaining the Government's case. Attlee intervened briefly to say that he thought Nasser was an imperialist dictator, and he accepted the views of McNair and Kilmuir on the breach of international law. Jowitt, the former Labour Lord Chancellor, agreed.

Chapter X

Security Council at Last

*Phase V 19th September–16th October—SCUA Conference,
London—reference to Security Council—Dulles's indignation—
meetings in New York 2nd–15th October—Conservative Llandudno
Conference—review of situation on 15th October—French and
Israeli military collaboration—Challe plan—decision that Eden
and Lloyd should go to Paris on 16th October.*

However, we persevered and a conference was summoned for
19th September in London of the eighteen nations which had
endorsed the proposals put to Nasser by Menzies (p. 118). Before
setting off for it, the Scandinavian Foreign Ministers issued a
communiqué stating that in their view the time had come to
refer the matter to the Security Council. Martino, the Italian
Foreign Minister, had sent me a similar message.

The conference met at Lancaster House on the morning of
the 19th. Our friends were taking the SCUA proposals seriously,
judging by their representatives. Thirteen of the eighteen countries sent their Foreign Ministers. Australia and New Zealand
sent two redoubtable former Ministers for External Affairs in
Sir Percy Spender, later the Australian Judge of the International Court, and Sir Clifton Webb, a former Law Officer
of wide experience, who, as I have said, were firmly of the view
that there had been a breach of international law.

I was elected to the chair. I opened by saying that international control in some form was still our objective. Obviously
we wanted to proceed by peaceful means. We did not want to
settle the matter by force. I claimed that the idea of a users'
association was juridically sound. It kept the balance between

Egypt and the users. Egypt's rights were protected by the convention, and the fact that the Canal lay in Egyptian territory. The users' rights were protected by the fact that under the convention an international system was made part of it.

Dulles introduced his SCUA plan briefly and in moderate terms. In the afternoon session he spoke again. He dealt first with the view held by most that the matter should be referred to the Security Council. He admitted that at some stage this might happen, but he claimed that we were still trying to find a solution by means of our own choosing, a procedure in accordance with the Charter. He wanted the users to consolidate their position preparatory to going to the United Nations.

After answering some of the questions raised, he ended with a moving and effective plea:

> We all want a world in which force is not used. True, but that is only one side of the coin. If you have a world in which force is not used, you have also got to have a world in which a just solution of problems of this sort can be achieved. I do not care how many words are written into the Charter of the United Nations about not using force; if in fact there is not a substitute for force, and some way of getting just solutions of some of these problems, inevitably the world will fall back again into anarchy and into chaos.

He went on to define just solutions as those in conformity with the principles of justice and of international law. This was certainly the best speech which I ever heard him make. He pulled out all the stops. He spoke with emotion, apparent conviction and sincerity. It was a considerable feat of advocacy and moved us all. I felt that we were at one again.

I do not think that anyone who listened to him could have felt that if Nasser rejected the SCUA plan, and if the Security Council failed to obtain a solution, Dulles would do other than accept the use of force, even if the United States themselves did not take part.

With regard to referring the matter to the Security Council, Dulles became aware of the very strong feeling on this, and eventually said that the United States Government was coming to the view that 'we should probably move rather quickly to the United Nations', words which seemed to escape his memory very rapidly.

We had the usual protracted affair of eighteen people with at least twice that number of advisers trying to draft a resolution, and the resilience of the chairman was taxed to the full. I did get one good laugh. There had been talk of a 'declaration'. Noon of Pakistan said that he preferred the word 'resolution'. A declaration would be connected with the American Declaration of Independence and was not suitable for this meeting. After some further talk, he said that he did not mind what word was used, but 'I think the word "resolution" is better because that means that you are determined to go on with something. With a "declaration" you declare and go home.' I said that that certainly was what the British had done after the American Declaration of Independence.

Another source of considerable entertainment was the naming of Dulles's brain-child. It had first been called CASU (Co-operative Association of Suez Canal Users). That turned out to be a dirty word in Portuguese. Various other combinations were tried. Almost all of them meant something revolting, usually in Turkish. Eventually SCUA survived all tests and the Suez Canal Users' Association came into being.

After the final meeting of the conference, I had a long talk with Dulles and we went over the ground again. He began by repeating that it was imperative that Nasser should lose as a result of Suez. The question was how to achieve that. War would make Nasser a hero. It was better for him to 'wither away'. Some economic measures would hurt us more than him: for example, refusal to buy Egyptian cotton. But there were other possibilities: action over the Nile waters, discouragement of tourists, and switching purchases of oil to the Western hemisphere. Israel might help: the Jewish bankers were powerful.

Nasser, however, was having some propaganda successes in the
United States. He had made a good T.V. appearance and was
about to make another. U.S. opinion on Suez was not good
because of concentration on the elections. Dulles ended this
rather fatuous little homily about tourists and Jewish bankers
by saying that he thought that our directive to our departments
should be to get rid of Nasser in six months.

I said that I agreed that we should set up a Political Warfare
Group. This would no doubt be helpful in the long run, but
meanwhile what about referring the matter to the United
Nations? There had been the public statement by the Scandinavian Foreign Ministers on the 16th, the reiteration of those
views by them at the conference supported by many others,
and Dulles's own statement quoted above. I told him that we
had just had a luncheon party at No. 10 at which the representatives of Iran, New Zealand, Norway and Portugal had
been present. It would have been difficult to find four countries
with more different backgrounds, problems and approaches.
They had all been vehement in their argument that we must
go to the Security Council at once. The reception for SCUA,
in spite of his efforts, had not been enthusiastic and I just did not
believe that some of those at the conference would join unless
we stated that we were going to the United Nations. I also said
that our apparent reluctance had lost us ground in Britain, in
the House of Commons, among moderate opinion, members
of the United Nations Association, supporters of the United
Nations, many of whom were not identified with any political
party and some of whom were Conservatives. We could not
hold our public opinion unless there was a speedy reference.

In reply Dulles repeated his arguments against undue haste.
We ought to allow ten days for countries to decide to join
SCUA and then we should go to the United Nations. It would
take a further ten days to prepare for that. There was the letter
to the President of the Security Council and the resolution to
be drafted. The other members of the Security Council would
have to be carefully lobbied. The Panamanian attitude on

'Well, even if he is nothing but a crazy, mixed up, corporation lawyer, at least he could make up his mind exactly which river he's selling us down.'

Suez was very bad and they were influencing other Latin
American Governments. After that there would be the proceedings in the Council, which might be protracted. He talked
gloomily about counter-resolutions, etc. (The United States
elections were then six weeks away.)

I said that I much preferred an immediate reference. There
could be a preliminary meeting of the Council in the following
week (that beginning Monday, 24th September), and the first
substantive meeting could take place on the following Monday,
1st October. Dulles said that this was too soon. SCUA ought
to be in existence before we went to the United Nations. I said
that we could ask the eighteen members of the conference for a
decision by Thursday, 27th September. He thought that too
quick but he moved some way. He agreed that if we gave the
other countries ten days to decide, we could spend the next
week, beginning 24th September, on preparing our case and
have the preliminary meeting of the Council in the week beginning 1st October. He more or less agreed with me when I
emphasised again that it would be easier for the Scandinavians
and others to join if we had said that we were going to the
United Nations. I felt at the end of the talk that he would
not be unduly surprised if we and the French made the
reference to the Security Council but that it would be easier
for him if we did not ask him to join us in the reference. To
answer 'Yes' or to answer 'No' might be equally difficult for him.

During the next two days it became clear to the Prime
Minister and myself that we must act. We had wanted to go
to the United Nations since the beginning of the month. We
had been obliged to put it off because of the SCUA plan. We
had tried to play fair with Dulles by not leaking that there was
a difference of opinion between us. Another reason was the
nature of my talk with Dulles. He appeared to have understood
our difficulties at last and, provided we did not try to rush
proceedings in the Security Council, I thought that he would
not disagree provided the United States were not associated
with the reference. One thing that I was not going to do was to

continue the discussion with him by telegram. The French agreed with us. They thought that the exercise at the United Nations would be futile but they agreed to act in concert with us. The Prime Minister sent a message to Macmillan, who was in the United States attending a meeting of the International Monetary Fund, explaining our reasoning.

So we sent a letter on 23rd September to the President of the Security Council asking for a meeting on Wednesday, 26th September, to consider the following item: 'The situation created by the unilateral action of the Egyptian Government in bringing to an end the system of international operation of the Suez Canal which was confirmed and completed by the Suez Canal Convention of 1888.' On the following day Egypt countered by asking for a meeting of the Security Council to consider 'Actions against Egypt by some powers, particularly France and the United Kingdom, which constitute a danger to international peace and security and are serious violations of the Charter of the United Nations'.

Macmillan, after receiving Eden's telegram explaining what we had done, had separate talks with Eisenhower and Dulles on 25th September, which he described in his memoirs (*Riding the Storm*, pp. 133–6). He found Eisenhower in good form. The President was sure 'that we must get Nasser down'. He said nothing about our reference to the Security Council. Macmillan reported, 'He is very anxious to win the election.' With Dulles, after a general conversation in the presence of officials, Macmillan had a private talk. Dulles was full of indignation that we had decided to go to the United Nations without further consultation with him. He felt that he had been badly treated; we should get nothing but trouble in New York; we were courting disaster. Macmillan adds a typical comment: 'From the way Dulles spoke, you would have thought he was warning us against entering a bawdy house.' It is hard to believe that Dulles was being intellectually honest with himself. He had said in his T.V. interview on 13th September that we must get a programme out of the United Nations to settle the affair. He had talked at the SCUA conference about the United States Government moving rather quickly to the United Nations. He and I had talked at length and in detail, and I thought we had reached agreement about a timetable. Almost every member of SCUA was expecting a speedy reference. Dulles can only have made this fuss because Murphy's statement (p. 129) was accurate. He was acting under the policy agreed with Eisenhower and he had to prevent a reference to the Security Council. His common sense and his feel of the two London conferences told him that this line was wrong, but he felt that he had to stick to it.

The Security Council met on 26th September and both our item and Egypt's were inscribed on the agenda for a meeting to be held on 5th October. The Anglo-French item was inscribed by eleven votes to none; the Egyptian item by seven votes to none. The United States voted for the inscription of the Egyptian item as well as ours. Eisenhower wrote afterwards that he thought this had been a mistake. It was a typical example of trying to have it both ways. The only thanks Dulles got was an offensive speech later on from Fawzi about United States policy.

Eden and I felt that we must discuss with Mollet and Pineau how to manage the Security Council debate. On 26th September we flew to Paris to concert our tactics. It was not an easy meeting. After a long argument we agreed that our line should be that we were prepared to listen to any proposals put forward. If Egypt still rejected the eighteen-power proposals put forward by Menzies, she should be asked to come forward with counter-proposals, but Pineau was insistent that we should not accept anything less satisfactory than the eighteen-power proposals. We discussed SCUA, its membership, organisation, headquarters and how the dues should be paid. There was then an easier discussion about European co-operation and the clearing up of minor areas of friction between French and British policies in various parts of the world.

While we were in Paris, we received a telegram from Head,

Secretary of State for War, that the press, particularly the *Daily Herald* and the *News Chronicle*, were drawing attention to the position of the reservists, of course in critical terms. Eden sent the following message to Butler, whom he had left in charge:

> My own feeling is that the French, particularly Pineau, are in the mood to blame everyone including us if military action is not taken before the end of October. They alleged that the weather would preclude it later. I contested that. Mollet, as I believe, would like to get a settlement on reasonable terms if he could. I doubt whether Pineau wants a settlement at all.

This message also does not reveal undue bellicosity on Eden's part at that meeting.

On 27th September a report dated the previous day had been published from UNTSO (the United Nations Truce Supervision Organisation) about incidents on the Jordan/Israel borders. Between 29th July and 25th September there had been 59 complaints from Israel and 210 from Jordan; 19 Israelis had been killed and 27 wounded; 72 Jordanians had been killed and 24 wounded. Israelis had been held responsible for incidents on 1st, 19th and 21st August, and 11th and 13th September; Jordan responsible for incidents on 16th August, and 10th and 12th September. I had had a long talk on the Friday with the Israeli Ambassador, Elath, a man whom I liked and respected, but he used to get very worked up at our periodic meetings. On this occasion he said that the situation was worse for Israel than three months earlier, and in those circumstances Israel was being compelled to take the measures which she considered necessary for her self-defence. He complained about British indifference to Israel. Israel should be allowed to join SCUA. Israel ought also to be allowed to take part in the Security Council debate. I explained that we had no objection, in principle, but it did not seem to be expedient for Israel. If Israel took part in the debate, every Arab state would want to do the same.

I arrived in New York on Tuesday, 2nd October. Dulles did not exactly make my heart rejoice by his statement on that day at a press conference about differences between the United States and her European allies on Suez: 'The United States cannot be expected to identify herself 100 per cent either with colonial powers or the powers uniquely concerned with the problem of getting independence as rapidly and as fully as possible.' He went on to say that there were differences of approach and suggested that while France, the United States and the United Kingdom would always stand together in treaty relations covering the North Atlantic, any areas encroaching in some form or manner on the problem of so-called colonialism would find the United States playing a somewhat independent role. By these statements he was conceding the Egyptian case that this was a colonial problem.

He then spoke of SCUA: 'There is talk about teeth being pulled out of the plan, but I know of no teeth: there were no teeth in it so far as I am aware.'

Dulles realised the effect of all this and next day told Makins how unhappy he was about that press conference. His remarks had been given a connection which he did not intend between the colonial questions and Suez. A transcript had been handed to the press before he had seen it and that had limited his power to put the matter right. Makins replied that he thought that these press conferences were extremely hazardous. Dulles agreed but added that he thought that this was almost the only time that he had made 'a really bad blunder'.

I felt very bitter about what had happened and hoped that Dulles's penitence was sincere. It was perhaps just as well that I was not to see him face-to-face for a few days. We were to meet on the Friday morning before the Security Council met in the afternoon. I knew exactly what we must achieve in New York. The impression that we were coming to the Security Council as a formality had to be dispelled. We genuinely wanted a peaceful settlement, provided it restored the international element in the working of the Canal. We did not want to be bogged down in a long-drawn-out series of debates. We did not want a negotiating committee to be set up to mediate. We did not want to have our hands tied by a Security Council resolution forbidding the use of force. I hoped that the strength of public opinion mobilised during the proceedings would influence Nasser towards a settlement. I had always thought and said that we could not use force unless we had first tried for a settlement at the Security Council, but I certainly did not regard proceedings there just as an operation to be carried out as quickly as possible in order to clear the decks for action. The difficulties and dangers which lay in the military solution were obvious.

I began at once a series of meetings. I spoke first to Walker, who led the Australian delegation and was very helpful throughout. There has been argument about the authorship of the idea of private meetings between Pineau, Fawzi and myself, with Hammarskjöld sitting in on them. The record will show that I tried out the idea on Walker on 2nd October. He thought it a good one. The next day, Wednesday, 3rd October, I had a long talk with Hammarskjöld. He also thought my suggestion a good one. He agreed that we did not want to have a negotiation about a negotiation and that we should avoid a mediating committee. If an agreement was to be reached it would have to come from private direct talks.

I later saw Belaunde of Peru, an old friend from my times at the United Nations as Minister of State. I had to steer him tactfully away from the idea of a mediating committee, in which he clearly wanted to take part himself. I then saw Abdoh of Iran. He explained how he had been instructed to play his hand. He must make sympathetic noises about Afro-Asian unity but must end by giving us firm support.

The next day I saw Popovic of Yugoslavia. He was a member of a very wealthy family. He had turned Communist and fought with great distinction under Tito. As usual he was full of charm but I knew that he would be under orders to help Egypt as much as he could. He did, however, go so far as to say that Yugoslavia disapproved of the way in which Nasser had nationalised the Canal; but that was all.

After Popovic I saw Shepilov, the Russian. I put to him our plan for discussions — first a public session of the Council with opening speeches, then a private session, then an adjournment for two or three days for private discussions. He appeared disposed to agree to this.

On the morning of Friday, 5th October, Pineau and I confronted Dulles. He said that he felt that the United States, France and Britain had been losing touch. Eisenhower was very much against war. If war was started it would be very difficult to end. We must understand that the United States elections did not affect the issue at all. I defended our decision to go to the Security Council. It was a genuine attempt to achieve a settlement by negotiation. The situation in the Middle East was rapidly deteriorating and I dealt with it country by country once again. Nasser was planning a coup in Libya. He had stores of arms there to be used. There was a plot to kill the King. King Saud was also threatened. Nuri was still in control in Iraq but there was dissatisfaction among his younger officers, fostered by Nasser. Jordan was already deeply penetrated. Syria was virtually under Egyptian control. Nasser was actively assisting EOKA in Cyprus. Pineau joined in, giving a similar description of North Africa and justifying the military precautions. But for these precautions the mobs might have been let loose, ships not allowed through the Canal and foreign pilots detained in Egypt. Dulles repeated his objections to the actual use of force but accepted that it was right to keep its 'potential' use in being. He pointed out that there had been, for instance, a wave of relief in Cairo when the matter was referred to the Security Council, since this was taken to rule out any possibility of force being used. Dulles said that we must make it clear in the Security Council that if a real effort to get a peaceful settlement were made and failed, it would then be permissible to consider force as an alternative. This was what he had said at the second London conference and he was prepared to reaffirm it. If the United Nations could not ensure that justice was done, the United Nations would have failed; but we must try. I believed that he meant what he said about the use of force being permissible. It is true that it was quite contrary to what Eisenhower had said while Menzies was talking to Nasser in Cairo, but Dulles was not running for President. I said to him that recourse to the United Nations was a condition precedent to the use of force as far as we were concerned, but that did not mean that we regarded the Security Council proceedings just as a formality to be rushed through. Dulles ended by saying that the most important thing was that the operation of the Canal should be insulated from politics.

We then discussed tactics. I suggested that after the general debate was concluded, perhaps on Tuesday, 9th October, the Council might go into private session. After one meeting in private session, there might be an adjournment for two or three days for direct talks with the Egyptians, and the Council might reconvene on Friday, 12th October. Dulles agreed, and in answer to a direct question from me said that his general support would be forthcoming.

The following day, 6th October, the papers were full of alleged disagreements between the British and French on the one side and the United States on the other. I was told that these stories were emanating from the United States delegation. It was added that Dulles had told his inner circle of pressmen privately that the British would have to accept the Indian plan currently being devised by Khrishna Menon.

I saw Dulles on Sunday, 7th October, after he had returned from a speaking engagement away from New York. I demanded to know where we were, and showed what I thought was a well-justified loss of temper. Dulles denied that he had made the remark about the Indian plan. He was apologetic and promised to look into the behaviour of his delegation. It was untrue that there were all these differences between us; he was in full agreement with us on every point except the wisdom of the use of force. Even on that he thought that we had been absolutely

right to make our preparations, and that we were right
to maintain the threat. He did not himself rule out force at a
later stage. He proposed to make a 'powerful' speech in support
of our position. At that moment Lodge and the others came in.
We had a good meeting in a much more friendly atmosphere.
At the end of it he said to me alone that we could rely upon
him and we should win. I said that I was glad to hear it. We
discussed the future of SCUA. He wanted us to get British and
French shipowners to pay their dues to SCUA; he would then
be prepared to say that American shipowners must do the same
and try to bring United States ships under foreign registry into
line.

Meanwhile in the afternoon of 5th October the Security
Council had begun consideration in public session of our letter
and a counter-approach by Egypt. I opened the debate, and
Pineau followed. To get things moving, I succeeded in obtaining
agreement that it was unnecessary to have consecutive translation for prepared speeches, which would have doubled the
time taken by each speaker and served little purpose, since the
texts of prepared speeches were available to everyone.

In my speech I concentrated first on the history of the
development of the Canal and its administration, to show its
international character and the origin and nature of the guarantees given to users by Egyptian Governments in a series of
agreements and concessions, which were eventually confirmed
in the Suez Canal Convention of 1888. I showed how the
Egyptian Government, after formally recognising the validity
of the Company's Concession as recently as 10th June 1956, had
destroyed the balanced scheme under which the Canal was
operated. In doing so, it not only acted illegally, it had also
put at stake the economic future of many countries both east
and west of Suez. I went on to outline the eighteen-power
proposals made by the Menzies mission, which fully respected
Egyptian sovereignty. I described the formation of SCUA, and
appealed for Egypt's co-operation with it. I ended by asking the
Council to lay down a just and fair basis for negotiations, and

suggested private sessions of the Council to consider next steps in a less formal atmosphere.

I feared that a long and closely reasoned speech such as this would prove dull, but it was well received. The Peruvian Representative said I had converted him. The Security Council is not quite like the House of Commons. A lot of work had gone into the preparation, and on rereading it now I find it does present our legal case and our purposes very fully. An extract is reproduced as Appendix IV.

The public sessions continued on Monday and Tuesday, 8th and 9th October, with speeches by Fawzi (Egypt), Shepilov (U.S.S.R.), Belaunde (Peru), Abdoh (Iran), Walker (Australia), Nuñez Portuondo (Cuba), Chiang (Nationalist China) and Spaak (Belgium). The latter was particularly helpful. He said whatever the legal position might be, the method of proceeding by *fait accompli* was crude, obsolete and inadmissible. But in this case the action was also illegal. Nasser had no right to destroy international guarantees enjoyed by the Company, which represented the users. Nasser could not be trusted to manage the Canal himself even if he accepted the principles of the eighteen-power proposals.

On Tuesday, 9th October, the general debate finished with a poorish speech from Popovic of Yugoslavia and, on the whole, a good one from Dulles. Pineau, Fawzi, Hammarskjöld and I then met to discuss procedure in a private session of the Security Council. Fawzi hoped that there would be no more general speeches. I said that I was of the same opinion and hoped for a short meeting followed by a forty-eight-hour adjournment for direct talks with the Egyptians. Fawzi agreed. He said: 'We are dealing with a very difficult animal which is full of movement.' Hammarskjöld commented, 'It is a very slippery creature.'

The private session of the Security Council followed in the afternoon for just over an hour. It exposed the vagueness of the Egyptian position. Fawzi failed to answer questions from several members, was extremely evasive and showed it.

Afterwards, Hammarskjöld, Pineau, Fawzi and I met again. I said to Fawzi that I had found his speech very vague. He said that Egypt was prepared to recognise SCUA and thought that there could be joint meetings between SCUA and the Egyptian Canal authority. After that it was a very general and guarded talk but I did get one statement which seemed to be definite. I asked him whether he accepted without qualification the proposition that the Canal should be insulated from the politics of any country. He replied that he accepted that principle without qualification. I wondered. We decided to meet again the following afternoon.

When I reported back to London on this meeting, I said, 'I find the whole situation here most worrying and unpromising. I do not think that there have ever been more difficult decisions to take.'

Krishna Menon had now arrived in New York in his self-appointed role of trouble-shooter. For once, he succeeded in achieving unity: everyone, including Fawzi, Shepilov and Hammarskjöld, said to me that they regretted his interference. When he saw me he gave me a list of points which he said were part of the Indian plan which Fawzi was rejecting but he, Menon, would force Fawzi to agree. In fact, at our first meeting Fawzi had volunteered acceptance of them all.

The four of us met again in the afternoon of Wednesday, 10th October. Fawzi made some minor point affecting the previous day's discussion. I then asked him to confirm again that Egypt accepted that the Canal should be insulated from the politics of any one country. He confirmed his acceptance of that. We discussed Article 8 of the 1888 Convention about the powers of representatives of the signatories to supervise the operation of the agreement and proceed to the necessary verifications; the Canal Code; the powers of SCUA; the percentage of the dues to be set aside for development and for compensation. I think that some progress was made at this meeting, but there was still a wide gap. Pineau had developed a severe cold.

The meeting of the four in the morning of Thursday, 11th

October, began badly with some discussion of a summary prepared by Hammarskjöld. Fawzi showed signs of retreat on what insulation from the politics of one country meant, and there was a rather technical discussion of 'recourse', which had been the term for acts of enforcement. Fawzi said that he would try to produce a paper on this.

Pineau then said that he thought the time had come for a questionnaire to be put to Fawzi. The eighteen countries had produced principles and a method of implementing them. What were the Egyptian proposals? Fawzi said that he was not a defendant in the dock and objected to questionnaires.

I then suggested that the matters of principle could be defined in the following way. I did this off the cuff but, broadly speaking, they were the same six principles discussed at the first London conference and which later received unanimous approval from the Security Council

1 that there should be free and open transit through the Canal without discrimination, overt or covert;

2 that there should be respect for Egyptian sovereignty;

3 that the operation of the Canal should be insulated from the politics of any country;

4 that the level of dues should be fixed by agreement between users and owners;

5 that a fair proportion of the dues should be allotted to development;

6 that affairs between the Suez Canal Company and the Egyptian Government should be settled by arbitration, with suitable terms of reference and suitable provision for the payment of the sums found to be due.

The point was, how were these principles to be implemented? Pineau agreed with what I had said, but emphasised that the whole issue was the system. It was on that that the talks became vaguer and vaguer. We adjourned in the hope of clarification from Fawzi.

I reported to London that I was perplexed as to how to end

the Security Council discussions. I was beginning to be anxious about Pineau's position. At one moment he said agreement was impossible, and at another he seemed to favour an expression of opinion by the Security Council which would tie our hands.

At the meeting of the four of us on the morning of Friday, 12th October, Fawzi accepted my 'principles' but was still vague on implementation. Pineau and I agreed that we must have our last private meeting that afternoon. After that we should aim for a private session of the Council, and a final open session on Saturday.

Nothing fresh arose at the last private meeting. At the private session of the Council Hammarskjöld announced agreement on the six principles. I warned the Council against exaggerated optimism and said that there were wide gaps between Egypt and ourselves.

It was at this moment that Eisenhower once again cut the ground from under our feet. After Hammarskjöld had informed the Council of the six principles, Eisenhower spoke to his press conference as follows:

> I have an announcement. I have got the best announce-ment that I could possibly make to America tonight. The progress made in the settlement of the Suez dispute this afternoon at the United Nations is most gratifying. Egypt, Britain and France have met through their Foreign Ministers and agreed on a set of principles on which to negotiate, and it looks like here is a very great crisis that is behind us. I do not mean to say that we are completely out of the woods, but I talked to the Secretary of State just before I came over here tonight and I will tell you that in both his heart and mine at least there is a very great prayer of thanksgiving.

I protested strongly to Dulles. I think that even he was taken aback and murmured something about not paying too much attention to what people said in the middle of an election campaign.

When we met in public session of the Council at 5.30 p.m., I opened the debate by saying that a basis for negotiation had been established referring to the six principles. I thought that the Government of Egypt had made some advance but, as Dulles had previously said, the essence of the matter was the insulation of the Canal from the politics of any country. SCUA had apparently been accepted. I, therefore, submitted new Franco-British proposals, embodying the six principles,* and would not ask for our resolution of 5th October to be voted upon. I added that there seemed to be some need, as Spaak had pointed out, for provisional arrangements. Pineau said that the six principles were all right but the three of us had been unable to agree upon a coherent system to carry them out. He also spoke of the need for provisional arrangements. Fawzi opened and with obvious pleasure quoted verbatim Eisenhower's statement of the day before. He clearly felt that the pressure was off, and even in that speech began to hedge about the phrase 'insulation of the operation of the Canal from the politics of any country'. He said that it was a rather unfortunate as well as misleading phrase. It allowed scope for various and contradictory interpretations. The Iranian Representative put forward an amendment of an unimportant character but slightly helpful to Egypt. Shepilov said that he was prepared to vote for the first part of our resolution (including the six principles) but would vote against the second part calling on Egypt to propose a system which would conform with them. We then adjourned.

Later in the evening, when we reconvened, Dulles supported our resolution. The Chinese followed to the same effect. Popovic said that he would vote against the second part. I then made my final speech. The United Kingdom and France had acted with great restraint. We had taken the initiative throughout—in informing the Security Council about the situation, in coming there to discuss it, in suggesting private meetings of the Council and in suggesting private conversations in the presence of the

* See the extract at Appendix IV.

Secretary-General. The suggestion that we had come merely as
a formality was utterly unfounded. I said that we would accept
the Iranian amendment. I then dealt with Shepilov's suggestion
that SCUA violated the 1888 Convention. I went through the
instrument setting up SCUA paragraph by paragraph and
showed how it was completely consistent with the convention.
I believe it to have been the general opinion that this analysis
completely demolished Shepilov's argument.

Then the vote took place. Part I was voted for by all eleven
members. On Part II, nine voted for it but the Soviet Union
and Yugoslavia voted against. As the Soviet vote amounted to a
veto, that meant that Part II did not pass.

After the proceedings had finished I went to have a final talk
with Dulles to discuss with him what were the pressures
(Eisenhower's letter of 8th September had used the term)
which we could bring to bear upon Egypt to put forward
reasonable counter-proposals to those of the eighteen powers.
I started by talking about dues. To my horror I discovered
that his idea was that the dues should be paid to SCUA and
then 90 per cent of them handed on to Nasser. That would mean
that Nasser would be getting a larger proportion than he was
already receiving. I told him I was horrified by this but, it
already being very late, we did not carry the argument further.

The account in Pineau's book* seems to suggest that the
private talks with Fawzi took place after the vote on 12th
October on the Anglo-French resolution, and that I was not
present at them, having left for London disheartened. Again,
I have checked the records and am satisfied my version is
correct.

The next day I sent a telegram to Eden giving my general
conclusions with regard to the Security Council operation. On
the credit side I thought the results were better than we could
have expected. We had changed the opinion that we had come
simply as a formality. The agreed requirements in the six
principles included two that would be awkward for Egypt: the

* *1956 Suez*, Paris: Laffont, 1976, pp. 115–20.

third, about insulation from any country's politics; and the sixth, referring to disputes, which recognised the continued existence of a Suez Canal Company as a separate entity, although Nasser had purported to nationalise it. There had been no resolution against the use of force, and if we had to come to it I thought there would be a more understanding reaction at the United Nations. (I believe that if on 30th October the United States Government had paused and said in effect: 'Let us wait and see what develops,' twenty or thirty other countries would have done the same.) The eighteen-power proposals had been endorsed by nine out of eleven members of the Security Council. Egypt had been supported only by the Communists. There had been acknowledgment of SCUA.

On the debit side, however, the Egyptians would feel that the critical phase was past. They were no longer in danger of armed attack and they, therefore, had won. Whether this view was warranted would depend upon how we now played the hand. Perhaps Hammarskjöld had been given too large a role, but he was an internationalist by nature and should support an international solution.

Finally, there was the serious danger of over-optimism, as Eisenhower's extraordinarily naïve statement of 12th October had shown. I said that I would impress upon Hammarskjöld as forcefully as I could the need for Egypt to produce precise proposals as rapidly as possible.

While I was drafting this telegram matters were developing at home.

The Conservative Party Conference was held that year at Llandudno. As usual, there was a debate upon foreign affairs. Owing to my absence in New York, Salisbury was going to reply to it. Then a day or two before, he developed heart trouble. Nutting was given the task of replying and a copy of what Salisbury had proposed to say.

Nutting said to Heath on the morning of the debate that he had no intention of saying that he was just reading Salisbury's speech. It was going to be his own speech. He repeated this to Lennox-Boyd.

In it he indulged in some plain speaking. Nasser had debased the whole currency of international good faith. What he had done was not nationalisation but an act of seizure or plunder in flagrant breach of the fundamental principle of international conduct and the sanctity of treaties. He made some scathing comments on the attitude of the Opposition, and ended on the note that we were not out merely for a peaceful settlement but we demanded a just solution. If the United Nations was unable to do its duty, we should not be absolved from doing ours. If that hard test came upon us, he believed the country would not flinch from it.

This appealed to the conference. Eden spoke on much the same lines in his final speech, and the conference ended with what appeared to be complete unity in the party.

After the Llandudno Conservative conference, Eden returned to Chequers. Meanwhile, a request had come from Mollet that Eden should see Gazier, who was acting as Foreign Minister while Pineau was in New York, and General Challe, a senior French air force officer. They came to Chequers on Sunday afternoon, 14th October. Nutting was also present. According to him, a possible plan for Britain and France to gain physical control of the Canal was outlined by Challe. Israel should be invited to attack Egypt across the Sinai Peninsula. Britain and France should allow sufficient time for Israel to capture all or most of Sinai, and then order Israel and Egypt to withdraw their troops from the Canal area to allow an Anglo-French force to occupy the Canal in order to save it from damage by fighting. Eden said that he would have to think over this plan.

When the French had gone, Eden said that he thought that I should come back from New York as quickly as possible. I received a message to telephone him. My attempt to do so afforded a little light relief. The international exchange operator was requested to put a call through to Sir Anthony Eden, the

British Prime Minister, at No. 10 Downing Street, London, England. The operator's comment was, 'Say, is that a hotel?' I spoke to Eden and told him that I did not want to return that day because I had arranged to see Hammarskjöld on the Monday. I agreed, however, to leave New York on the Monday evening, arriving in London on the morning of Tuesday, 16th October.

On the Sunday, 14th October, I had a talk in New York with Pineau. We discussed our tactics with regard to the inscription of an item on Algeria on the agenda for the General Assembly. With regard to the Canal, Pineau thought that we should organise SCUA into an effective bargaining instrument and await more precise proposals from the Egyptians before resuming discussions with them. He thought that Eden, Mollet, he and I should meet soon to work out a common policy so that 'we can speak clearly to Israel'. He seemed satisfied with the way that we had worked together in the Security Council.

Later that day I saw Azzam Pasha of Saudi Arabia. He said that King Saud thought that Nasser was gambling over the Canal and his action might well lead to a war with France and the United Kingdom. The King saw that his loyalty to a fellow Arab would then clash with his desire for friendship with Britain. That was the reason why he had reacted coolly to Nasser's action. However, the real purpose of Azzam's visit was to discuss our dispute with Saudi Arabia over the Buraimi oasis, on which we made no progress.

The next day I saw Hammarskjöld. We had a long review of the Security Council proceedings. He agreed with me on the need for precision. He said that he would do his best to get some precise proposals out of the Egyptians but that he found it very difficult to pin Fawzi down to anything definite. He hoped that we would not proceed too quickly with SCUA, particularly over the payment of dues.

Just before lunch Krishna Menon descended upon me in a very bad temper. He had attached much too much importance to his own efforts. He was exceedingly rude. I did my best to calm him down. I said that his work with Nasser had been useful, but he had been very foolish to insist on coming to New York. At 5 p.m. I took off for London. The next morning I drove straight from the airport to Downing Street. Nutting explained the French plan to me in an outer room. I thought that the idea of our inviting Israel to attack Egypt was a poor one. I joined a meeting of Ministers in the Cabinet Room. There was a general discussion of a rather indeterminate nature. Very soon, Eden said that he thought he and I should go ourselves to see Mollet and Pineau in Paris. At the Sunday meeting he had said that Nutting would bring the British answer, but now he felt that further discussion of the French plan was necessary between the Prime Ministers and Foreign Secretaries. He asked whether I would prefer to go that afternoon or the following day. I said that I would prefer to get my travelling over and done with. If we went that afternoon, I also knew that I would not be distracted by the other Foreign Office business which no doubt awaited me.

Chapter XI

Last Resort

*Taking stock 16th October — Israeli-French planning — discussion
with Mollet and Pineau — Cabinet 18th October — Hammarskjöld
and Fawzi — Sèvres meetings 22nd–24th October — Cabinets 23rd,
24th and 25th October — arguments for and against military
intervention.*

During the rest of the day, with the imminent Paris talks in
mind, I tried to sort out the various factors in the situation one
by one and produce for myself a kind of situation report. On
certain counts, as I had said in my telegram to Eden, I felt
quite pleased about the Security Council operation. Until we
came to the Soviet veto, we had gained all along the line over
friend and foe alike. We had coaxed Dulles out of his dis-
pleasure. Our tactical plan for the sittings of the Council had
been accepted and had proved itself. We had kept at one with
Pineau. We had convinced those at the United Nations (and
most of the Permanent Representatives of the member states
had listened in at all the debates) that a peaceful settlement
genuinely was our first priority. We had won over the doubters.
My definition of the six principles given off the cuff but based
largely upon the August conference in London had been
accepted even by the Soviet Union. They contained the vital
principle about insulating the operation of the Canal from the
politics of any one nation. The second part of our resolution
reaffirmed the eighteen-nation proposals, but invited the
Egyptians to put forward others of an equivalent nature. It also
affirmed the competence of SCUA to receive dues. We had
avoided a mediator or negotiating committee, and any

amendment which might have limited our future freedom of action. Fawzi had been forced into an exposed position; only the two Communist members of the Security Council had supported him. The Soviet veto had been shown to be his shield and buckler. We had avoided the proceedings becoming a slanging match between Israel and the Arab states.

On the other hand, although we had convinced those with open minds of the genuineness of our desire for a peaceful settlement, the pressures which alone could secure such a settlement were lacking. Eisenhower had given no support at all to Dulles's speeches at the two London conferences. He had made no effort to make Nasser understand that he was in for trouble if he did not agree to a reasonable settlement. Eisenhower's mind was concentrated on an election campaign, appearing as the candidate who could preserve the peace of the world. The fact was that he had twice let us down and relieved the pressure on Nasser at critical moments. That he had done it for election-eering reasons was confirmed when I read again, whilst writing this book, an opinion sent to us from Washington on 17th September by Roger Makins, our Ambassador, to the effect that three months before that date he had been confident of the re-election of Eisenhower as Republican President, the election of a Democratic Senate but perhaps of a Republican House of Representatives. At the time of his message, however, he was less confident of Eisenhower's re-election and he thought that the whole Congress would probably be Democratic. I am sure that Eisenhower himself must have feared such a trend and been desperately anxious to preserve his image as the man of peace, the great soldier who had indeed beaten his sword into a ploughshare.

Second, there was Dulles's intimation to me on 13th October that he favoured an interim system whereby Nasser would get 90 per cent of the Canal dues paid to SCUA, a good deal more than he was currently receiving. This had filled me with dismay. Dulles had been the great advocate of pressure, political and economic, upon Nasser to move him towards a satisfactory settlement and so to avoid the use of force. It was true that in September he had taken all the sting out of SCUA by saying that the United States would not try to shoot their way through the Canal and that there were no teeth in SCUA. That again I had not understood. Even Eisenhower had said that interference by the Egyptians with the shipping of other nations might well provide a *casus belli*, but Dulles had thrown that away. Now, after the Soviet veto, he had suggested to me an interim division of dues which would leave Nasser laughing at the Western powers and claiming, with some justification, complete victory. Whatever outward face I tried to put upon it, I was exceedingly worried about the future. It was clear that so far as pressure on Nasser was concerned, the United States was a broken reed, in spite of Dulles's brave words of the previous March about ditching Nasser, bringing him down in six months, and the word 'disgorging' which he had used in August.

All this is not a reconsideration based upon hindsight. Reference has been made from time to time to a statement which I made in New York, off the record to the press after the Security Council meeting, about my being handed an umbrella when I got back to Britain. I have been asked what on earth I meant by that. I was, of course, referring to Neville Chamberlain coming back from Munich and from his meeting there with Hitler. Chamberlain was carrying his umbrella and a piece of paper, an agreement between him and Hitler which proved not to be worth the paper on which it was written. I was going back with my piece of paper, the six principles, agreed to by all, a pious hope about as binding on Egypt as Chamberlain's piece of paper had proved binding upon Hitler. Any idea that I returned thinking that a settlement on reasonable terms was in the bag, is wrong. In fact, my doubts were speedily confirmed. Fawzi had begun to hedge on the third principle in his final speech to the Security Council, after Eisenhower had made his statement. He had continued to hedge with the press before he left New York. It was clear that Nasser felt as every

week passed that he was becoming more secure. He was confident that he could spin out the negotiations. Fawzi's complicated dealings with Hammarskjöld were part of the game.
His reply to Hammarskjöld's letter (p. 179), by which he
accepted a meeting in Geneva, was dated 2nd November, after
hostilities had begun and, I am sure, was written only to impress international opinion. Menon had told Nutting in London
on his way to New York that he had seen no sign of Nasser
being willing to compromise. Nasser himself told the Indian
Ambassador in Cairo some time later that he had never had
any intention of accepting the third principle, the one that
mattered, about the Canal being insulated from the politics
of one nation.

The military position was worrying. D-Day for the original
plan, Musketeer, was 15th September. That had been postponed again and again in the hope of a peaceful settlement.
Then Musketeer Revise had had to be substituted for it. This
plan was considered to be feasible up to the end of October. By
16th October it was becoming clear that it could not be
postponed further. Equipment loaded in the ships was deteriorating. Batteries were running down. Vehicles were becoming unserviceable. Equally important, the reservists were under-
standably becoming restive. They had responded willingly and
in many cases enthusiastically to the recall to the colours but,
as the weeks went by and nothing happened, they were getting
fed up.

Next there was the political situation in the Middle East. It
was grim and showed every sign of getting worse. Egypt and
Syria were collaborating. This was soon proved by the establishment of a joint military high command. Jordan was about
to have elections. There were signs also, soon to be proved
correct, that they would result in a victory for the pro-Nasser
parties. The fear that Jordan would adhere to the joint Arab
military high command then being set up was proved to be well
founded.

There was continuous trouble on the borders of Israel with

Egypt and Jordan. I could understand Israeli feelings about these incidents. The idea that it is courageous for detachments of so-called freedom fighters to cross borders and murder innocent civilians is abhorrent. In mid-September a group of Israeli archaeologists inspecting excavations near Bethlehem were machine-gunned and four were killed. A girl gathering wood was stabbed to death. A tractor driver when ploughing was killed and his body dragged across the border. On 4th October, five workers on their way to a potash plant were ambushed and killed by the same gang who had murdered three Israeli Druses three weeks before. On 9th October, two Israeli farm labourers working in an orange grove were killed. I see no reason to disbelieve these accounts. I have talked myself to some of those Israelis who, while working on their land, used to be targets for Syrian marksmen and gunners from their emplacements on the Golan Heights.

On the other hand, some of the Israeli reprisals seemed likely to exacerbate the situation rather than deter and, by their scale, to turn international opinion against Israel.

It was an explosive situation. One thing that was certain was that Nasser consistently encouraged and praised these infiltrators.

When I was reviewing these factors in my mind, I had no idea that the French and Israelis had already established a close military understanding, although I did know that the French had been supplying them with aircraft and some arms.

We now have an account of what had been happening in Moshe Dayan's *Story of My Life*,* Chapter 13. He says that on 1st September he was informed that Admiral Barjot, Commander of the French forces assigned to Musketeer, thought the Israelis should be invited to take part in the Anglo-French operation against Egypt. Prime Minister Ben-Gurion instructed Dayan (then Israeli Chief of Staff) to reply that in principle the Israelis were willing to co-operate. His Chief of Operations went to Paris for talks with French military representatives on

* Weidenfeld & Nicolson, 1976.

7th September. The French asked certain questions 'for en-lightenment' but on the assumption that Israel might take part in the operations. The next step was for Peres, Director-General of the Israeli Defence Ministry, to go to France to seek an easing of the terms of payment for the tanks and aircraft which the French had supplied. In the course of his talks with Bourgès-Maunoury, French Minister of National Defence, the possibility of a joint Franco-Israeli action against Egypt with-out the British was raised. The French had regarded the post-ponement of Musketeer on 11th September because of Dulles's SCUA plan as indicating that Britain was no longer ready to take military action against Egypt, and the French were turn-ing to Israel. After the SCUA meeting on 21st September, Pineau had come back from London gravely disappointed, particularly at American moves to prevent military action. Bourgès-Maunoury told Peres that Pineau had said to Eden that France might act alone and even be aided by Israel, and that Eden had replied that he was not against it provided Israel did not attack Jordan. The French Cabinet then decided to invite Israeli representatives to come to Paris to discuss joint military action against Egypt.

Dayan says he arrived for these talks on 29th September. Pineau reviewed the political situation. He was just off to the Security Council, from which he expected nothing. He would try to convince the British that Anglo-French military measures were the only course, but was doubtful whether he would succeed. In his view, though Eden favoured action, British Foreign Office officials preferred a policy of 'passively waiting for some miracle', Dayan relates. The Israelis agreed that there was no alternative to military action.

There followed, so we are now told, detailed discussions of the military aspects of Franco-Israeli co-operation. A list of equipment required by the Israelis was handed over.

Dayan and his party returned to Israel on 1st October with French representatives to continue the examination of the equipment needed by Israel. The French were impressed by these needs and what they saw, and cabled Paris for the supply of Bren carriers, tanks, trucks with front-wheel drive, tank trailers and fuel tankers for aircraft. There was also discussion about the French use of Israeli air bases and the supply of additional equipment for the Israeli air force. Finally, there were decisions about the operational plans of both countries when it was decided to go ahead.

I knew nothing of all this at that time. The situation as I knew it was that which I have indicated at the beginning of this chapter.

Over lunch and during our flight to Paris on 16th October, I discussed my worries with Eden. In Paris we spent several hours with the French Ministers. Eden and Mollet preferred that no officials should be present. That meant excluding Gladwyn Jebb, our Ambassador in Paris, which he obviously resented, and I had some sympathy with him.

We went over the whole ground again with Mollet and Pineau.

The first point was, what were the chances of a satisfactory settlement by negotiation? I believe that Mollet and Eden would have liked one provided that its terms were satisfactory. Pineau, in *1956 Suez*, gives an account of a last-minute effort he made in New York. I never heard Hammarskjöld's version of that. I myself would have preferred a settlement provided we could have won our point about an effective international authority controlling the Canal. But Pineau and I were doubtful about the possibility of this in view of the American failure to back us. If only one or two leading Americans had spoken to Nasser as Menzies had done in Cairo, it could have been enough for success. We were thoroughly disillusioned with SCUA. We realized that we had been double-crossed, as Murphy confirms in his book.

We then turned to Israeli intentions. Pineau said that the Israelis would not sit quietly and watch the Egyptians and Syrians assimilating more and more modern Russian weapons. He believed that they would attack soon. Mollet and Pineau said several times that the Israelis were getting desperate and they thought that, if an agreement about the Canal was not forced upon Nasser in a few days, the Israelis would act. They told us very little about the military co-operation which was already taking place between Israel and France. I still thought that it was limited to the supply of some aircraft.

The French asked us what would be our attitude if Israel attacked Egypt. Eden said that we had made it clear time after time that if Israel attacked Jordan we would honour our treaty obligations. An Israeli attack on Egypt was a different matter. Both Prime Ministers agreed that it would be a political impossibility for either country to commit troops to defend Nasser after his attitude to France and Britain. The United States Government had been very unenthusiastic in Washington about military measures under the Tripartite Declaration of 1950. Egypt had, in effect, repudiated it. Nasser had said to me (see p. 46): 'It conferred no rights or obligations.' Furthermore, in view of Nasser's deeds and words against Israel, the Israelis would be acting in self-defence. The situation was totally different from that in 1950.

We then went on to consider the consequences of such an attack. Eden thought that the Israeli forces would rapidly destroy the Egyptian bases in Sinai. After that there would be fighting for the crossing places over the Canal. The Ministers agreed, subject to the approval of their Cabinets, that if this happened Britain and France should intervene, putting into operation the plans already prepared, the object being to safeguard the Canal and stop the spread of hostilities.

It has frequently been suggested that there was something artificial about our declared intention to separate the combatants and stop the spread of hostilities. Our fear of damage to the Canal if there was fighting over the crossing places was genuine and well-founded. We later saw what happened in the Six-Day War of 1967 and the Yom Kippur War of 1973. Apart from the damage to the Canal itself, British ships were then marooned there for eight years.

As to the extension of hostilities, we did not know then or earlier the Israeli military plans, although it was a reasonable assumption that they would seek to wipe out the fedayeen bases in Sinai and neutralise the Egyptian batteries controlling the entrance to the Gulf of Aqaba. There was no certainty about the reactions of the Syrian-Egyptian-Jordanian high command. (In the event, Hakim Amer, the Egyptian head of the joint military command, ordered Syrian and Jordanian forces not to intervene.) There was a great deal of modern military equipment about and it might be operated by 'technicians' or 'volunteers' from behind the Iron Curtain. The possibility of escalation was obvious and real. Military uprisings inspired by Nasser could have happened in any Middle Eastern state. These considerations led us to fear that fighting would spread: in the event I am certain that our intervention, with its massive show of military strength, limited the area of hostilities.

The French summed up our discussions by formulating two questions. In answer to the question whether we would fight to defend Nasser, Eden said that he thought the answer was 'No'. As to the second question, whether we would intervene to safeguard the Canal and limit hostilities, he thought the answer was 'Yes', but he would have to obtain the approval of his Cabinet colleagues for both those answers.

Possibly this summary gave rise to the report which Dayan on p. 174 of his book says he received from the French about a British proposal. If so, it was embroidered on the way beyond all recognition.

The next morning we flew back to London.

Thursday, 18th October, was an important day. There was a Cabinet in the morning. Before it took place I spoke to Rab Butler outside the Cabinet Room at No. 10. He described it in his book *The Art of the Possible* as follows:*

I went straight to No. 10 where I found the Foreign Secretary, Selwyn Lloyd, in the lobby outside the Cabinet Room.

* R. A. Butler, *The Art of the Possible* (Hamish Hamilton, 1971), p. 192.

He seemed moved and, gripping my arm, described how he had got back from the U.N. early on the 16th and immediately wafted to Paris in the wake of the Prime Minister to attend a conference with Mollet and Pineau. They had discussed the ever closer line up between Jordan, Syria and Egypt and the consequences of a pre-emptive strike by Israel, and it had been suggested that, if war broke out in the Middle East between Israel and Egypt, Britain and France would jointly intervene in the canal area to stop hostilities. Selwyn Lloyd seemed anxious about my own reaction. At that moment I was summoned into the Cabinet Room.

At the Cabinet there was by no means a full attendance. In addition to Eden, Butler and myself, Macmillan, Kilmuir, Home, Monckton, Sandys, Heathcoat Amory, Eccles, Buchan-Hepburn and Head were there, with Heath in attendance as Chief Whip.

I began by reporting on the discussions at the Security Council and expressed some of my doubts about the possibility of getting the Egyptians to put forward proposals which we would find tolerable.

The general view was that we had done well in New York.

Eden then reported on our discussions in Paris. We were doing everything possible to stop Israel attacking Jordan. We had made it clear that in such an event we would have to stand by our treaty with Jordan and protect her.

Then the question had arisen of what would happen if Israel attacked Egypt, which Eden thought probable. He went through the arguments which had been used in Paris. Intervention under the Tripartite Declaration, which incidentally Egypt had repudiated, would involve British troops fighting to defend Nasser. That would not be tolerated by public opinion, particularly as the French Government had no intention of allowing French troops to defend Nasser. Egypt's defence of her breach of the Security Council's resolution about

Israeli shipping passing through the Canal was based on the fact that she was at war with Israel. Nasser had pledged Egypt to exterminate Israel. In those circumstances Israel was entitled to act in self-defence. In addition, Egypt was in breach of international law by her seizure of the Canal. Eden asked for Cabinet approval of this view. If this was given, the French would be informed and there was no reason why they should not tell the Israelis. I supported Eden. The Cabinet accepted this view.

The next question was whether, if Israel did attack Egypt, we and the French should take any action. Eden said that the French view was that in that situation Britain and France should go in to safeguard the Canal and the shipping in it. Eden said that he and I agreed with that. What did the Cabinet think? Butler describes his reaction as follows (p. 192):

> I was impressed by the audacity of the thinking behind this plan, but concerned about the public reaction. I wondered whether an agreement with the French and the Israelis, designed to free the Canal and eventually to internationalize it, would not meet our objective.

I said that I was even more concerned by the effect on Arab opinion of an agreement between France, Israel and ourselves to take military action against Egypt. Eventually it was accepted by Butler and the rest of the Cabinet that we and the French should intervene to protect the Canal, if Israel moved against Egypt. The feeling was that although we should continue to seek a negotiated settlement, it was possible or indeed probable that the issue would be brought to a head as the result of a military action by Israel against Egypt.

In the morning of Thursday, 18th October, there had been the first meeting of the SCUA council.

I welcomed those attending, and then left for the important Cabinet Meeting to which I have referred. The council went on to deal with administrative matters under the chairmanship of John Hope.

During this Thursday, news came in from Cairo and New York. Trevelyan reported that Nasser was under pressure, but there was no sign of him climbing down on what he regarded as the major point—the insulating of the Canal from the politics of any one country. That principle—the most important from our point of view—he was not prepared to accept.

Dixon reported from New York at length about his talks with Hammarskjöld since I had left. Fawzi was working on proposals but he had refused to allow Hammarskjöld to show them to Dixon. They were skilfully framed. The Egyptian Canal authority would work with representatives of the users. There would be joint meetings. The Canal Code would be reaffirmed. Different kinds of infringement of it would require different types of 'recourse'. If it was the prevention of passage through the Canal, recourse would be had to the Security Council; if it was a question of interpretation, recourse would be to the International Court; if it was something to do with the operation of the Canal, it would be to a conciliation commission. In all this there were gaps; there was nothing about tolls, verification of what was actually happening, or enforcement.

As Fawzi refused to let us and the French see the details of his plan, Hammarskjöld thought that he would have to produce his own paper. Fawzi had said that he was ready to come to a meeting in Geneva on 29th October.

On 19th October a further telegram arrived from Dixon. Hammarskjöld had given him an informal, unsigned message for me, and to the French representative a similar one for Pineau. It was to the effect that Fawzi's paper was a lengthy one and Hammarskjöld had raised a number of points on it requiring answers from Egypt. Hammarskjöld also laid down the conditions on which he was prepared to invite the Ministers concerned to the meeting at Geneva. It was clear to us that if he had found it necessary to raise a number of points on Fawzi's paper, it must be pretty vague. We also bore it in mind that Fawzi at his press conference in New York before returning to

15 British parachute troops land in the Canal Zone
in the early hours of 5th November.

16 Six helicopters carrying Marine Commandos passing landing
craft manned by Royal Marine crews in the attack on Port Said.

17   French soldiers landing on a beach near Port Said.

18   British tank in Port Said.

19 Once the Israeli army had captured Sharm al-Shaikh, an Israeli warship is free to pass the Straits of Tiran leading to the Gulf of Aqaba and the Israeli port of Eilat. The gun in the foreground had been used by the Egyptians to deny these Straits to the Israelis.

20 Port Said and Port Fuad, showing ships scuttled by Nasser to block the Canal.

21 British paratroopers dug in 23 miles along the Canal south of Port Said. Egyptian positions face them 500 yards down the road.

22 British troops examining arms captured from the Egyptian Army.

Egypt, had made further reservations about the vital third principle.

I have already referred to the allegation that I had nearly reached agreement with Hammarskjöld and Fawzi on the settlement of the Canal problem before I left New York. This is absolute nonsense. I have already described how Fawzi had spun out the discussion with Hammarskjöld and was withdrawing from the position which he had taken up at the private talks. In the letter from Hammarskjöld to Fawzi on 24th October, frequently cited as proving that an agreement was in sight, Hammarskjöld defined the position as follows:*

If I have rightly interpreted the sense of the discussions as concerns specifically the questions of verification, recourse and enforcement (Point 4(e)) and if, thus, no objection in principle is made a priori against arrangements as set down above, I would from a legal and technical point of view — without raising here the political considerations which come into play — consider the framework sufficiently wide to make further exploration of a possible basis for negotiations along the line indicated worth trying.

It would be difficult to imagine anything more indefinite. If Nasser read it, he must have congratulated Fawzi on this tangible proof of the success of his tactics. As I have said, though a date at the end of October had been mentioned for a meeting in general, the Egyptian reply to this letter was dated 2nd November, after hostilities had begun.

On Saturday, 20th October, I spoke in Liverpool to the North-Western Area Conservative Council. Richard Stanley, the area chairman and M.P. for North Fylde, was in the chair. He introduced me by saying that I had been cartooned twice that week in the *Daily Express* by Osbert Lancaster, and anybody with that record must be worth listening to.

In my speech I referred to our resolution at the Security

* U.N. Security Council S/3728, 3rd November 1956.
13

Council meeting, its terms and the voting upon it. I said that we had taken the initiative at every stage — the eighteen-nation conference, the notification to the Security Council, the request for a Security Council Meeting, the proposal for private sessions of the Council, and the private conversations. For the future, the onus was on Egypt. We had had no proposals from them yet. They must be in accordance with the six principles and no less effective than the eighteen-nation proposals. I ended:

> Our objective is an effective means of securing that this great international waterway shall not be under the unrestricted control of one government. As we have said from the very beginning, that is the principle on which we are not prepared to compromise.

Sunday, 21st October, was not a day of rest. The news from the Middle East was bad. Nasser had said that he would regard the payment by shipowners of the dues to SCUA as a hostile act. At the Jordan General Election, an anti-Western majority had been returned.

I received a summons to Chequers in the afternoon. Eden, Butler, Macmillan, Head (who had now become Minister of Defence) and, I think, Kilmuir were there and, in addition, Norman Brook (Secretary to the Cabinet), Richard Powell (Permanent Secretary at the Ministry of Defence) and General Keightley. We were told that the Israeli leaders were coming to Paris on the following day and it was important, the French thought, that we should be represented there as well. It was decided that I should join them the following day, 22nd October, travelling incognito.

Incognito has its pleasures and its pains. In this case it meant for me excusing myself from my existing engagements, on the ground that I had a cold. It meant being driven by Donald Logan, one of my Private Secretaries, in his car to an R.A.F. airfield and being flown to the French military airfield at Villacoublay. We were met by a French officer, who drove us some kilometres in a small car to a villa at Sèvres. On the way we escaped death by a hair's-breadth. A large French car emerging at lunatic speed from a side road just failed to hit us.

We arrived at the villa in the early evening and left again about midnight.

We talked first to the French. Pineau told me that Israel had decided to attack Egypt, and in his view they had good cause to do so. Egypt had committed a hostile act against Israel by refusing to allow Israeli ships and cargoes through the Canal. Egypt had denied Israel passage for Israeli ships through the Straits of Tiran to Eilat. Nasser had concentrated large forces in Sinai, so as to be able to launch an attack on Israel at short notice. Nasser had repeatedly said that a state of war existed between Israel and Egypt and that he proposed to exterminate Israel. They had every right legally and morally to attack Egypt, but they wanted French fighters and British bombers to support them.

It has been alleged that our seeing the French alone was intended as a snub to the Israelis. That is utterly untrue. The French suggested it. It seemed common sense to be brought up-to-date by them before seeing the Israelis.

Then we went in to meet the Israelis. My first impression was of a roomful of utterly exhausted people, mostly asleep. One young man was snoring loudly in an armchair. Ben-Gurion himself looked far from well. Apparently the Israeli party, which also included Dayan and Peres, had had a dreadful flight from Israel, taking over seventeen hours. On arriving over Paris they had found it impossible to land: the aircraft had been flown to Marseilles to refuel. At the second attempt to come down at Paris, the pilot had seen a break in the clouds and just managed to land them.

We soon came to brass tacks. Ben-Gurion wanted an agreement between Britain, France and Israel that we should all three attack Egypt. In particular, he wanted an undertaking from us that we would eliminate the Egyptian Air Force before Israeli ground troops moved forward. He said that otherwise

Israeli towns like Tel Aviv would be wiped out. British prior air action was a *sine qua non*.

He did not tell me, nor did I know, of the extent to which the French and the Israelis had already made joint plans. Dayan, on p. 180 of his book *Story of My Life*, wrote:

> Britain's Foreign Minister may well have been a friendly man, pleasant, charming, amiable. If so, he showed near genius in concealing these virtues. His manner could not have been more antagonistic. His whole demeanour expressed distaste—for the place, the company and the topic.

I think that a possible explanation of this rather unflattering account is that Dayan had been working at high pressure and very closely with the French, and assumed that I knew all about it, which I did not. Perhaps he was irritated by what he thought was my pretended ignorance. Although I knew that Pineau had agreed to the Israelis having rather more Mystères than had been publicly stated, I was not aware that, as Finer put it in his book,* by that time France and Israel were virtually allies in an imminent offensive against Egypt. I am not sure how much Mollet and Pineau knew. Dayan makes an interesting disclosure in his book on p. 171 when he refers to the Israeli reprisal against the Arab Legion police fort on the edge of the border town of Kalkilia:

> Forty-eight hours later, on the night of 10th October, while we were in the midst of feverish preparations for the Sinai campaign ...

On that date, 10th October, I was at the Security Council in New York working for a settlement. I had not yet enunciated the six principles which I thought should govern a settlement. I do not think that by then Mollet or Pineau had ruled out a settlement: indeed, on p. 116 of *1956 Suez* he says that at that very time he decided to stay in New York to get an agreement with Egypt on the Canal.

* Herman Finer, *Dulles Over Suez* (Chicago: Quadrangle, 1964).

Ben-Gurion himself seemed to be in a rather aggressive mood, indicating or implying that the Israelis had no reason to believe in anything that a British Minister might say. He said in his book that I treated him like a subordinate. No doubt we were both tired.

I tried to point out to Ben-Gurion the dangers inherent in a military operation of the kind he was proposing. There would be an immediate appeal to the Security Council. If the British or French vetoes were used, the Uniting for Peace procedure would possibly be invoked. The matter would be referred to the General Assembly, the majority of whose members would be hostile. Lined up against us would be the Arab states, Pakistan, Iran, the neutrals led by India, the Scandinavians and of course the Iron Curtain countries and Yugoslavia. The United States' attitude would be uncertain. Canada would probably be against. Under this kind of pressure the military operation after a few days might have to be halted. After that the outcome would be uncertain. I did not argue that these points made a military operation impossible, but I put them forward as matters for consideration.

Years later, in February 1967 in Julian Amery's house in London, Peres said to me that Ben-Gurion had subsequently remembered how I had made these points at the Sèvres meeting, and said to him that he was impressed by the accuracy of this forecast of what might happen. I gathered from Peres that Ben-Gurion then appeared to have rather more respect for my views than he had shown at the time. Certainly when I saw him at his home in Tel Aviv in 1967 I received an extremely warm welcome. He and his wife could not have been more friendly and there was no hint of past hostility.

However, to return to Sèvres. I did try to make Ben-Gurion realise that I understood his feelings of anxiety. There was no doubt that Nasser was dedicated to the destruction of Israel.

Dayan in his book wrote about the British proposals, the British plan. In fact, we had no plan for co-operation with Israel. We had said that we would not defend Egypt, and we had agreed to a French proposal that if Israel attacked Egypt we would intervene to protect the Canal. In our military plans, Musketeer and then Musketeer Revise, Israel did not figure. The object would be to prevent fighting for the crossing places over the Canal and damage to the many millions of pounds' worth of British ships and cargoes passing through it. If the combatants did not accept our military presence, we would use force. If Nasser accepted our military presence, he would lose prestige. If he did not, we would put into operation Musketeer Revise. The first element in that plan was the taking out of the Egyptian Air Force. The Egyptians had modern aircraft. It was not known whether or not they would be flown by Russian pilots, and the Chiefs of Staff had insisted that neutralisation of the Egyptian Air Force must be the first step. It would be followed by the other steps in Musketeer Revise to take control of the Canal, to preserve it and probably to restore its status as a waterway under international control.

There was a discussion as to how we would indicate our intentions to the combatants, and how soon we would move against the Egyptian Air Force if Egypt refused to accept our presence. Ben-Gurion said that he did not trust us to act as we said we would.

Throughout I tried to make it clear that an Israeli-French-British agreement to attack Egypt was impossible. We had thousands of British subjects in Arab countries with valuable property, and oil installations of great strategic importance. If there was a joint attack, there might be wholesale slaughter of British subjects and destruction of our installations. Ben-Gurion was very glum about this. This may seem far-fetched now, but we were then much closer in time to the 1952 massacres in Cairo.

I remember a meal being served, an enormous fish being the main course. It disappeared quickly. There was desultory talk, Ben-Gurion making an effort at conversation by asking Logan questions about his role and duties.

In the end it was left that I should return to London to

report to my colleagues on our conversations. I left Sèvres to do this. Nothing had been agreed except that I would report back to Pineau early the following day. Villacoublay airfield was enveloped in fog and I was told later we were the last aircraft to be allowed to take off that night. I reached Carlton Gardens very late, safe in body but perplexed in mind. My impression, as a result of our talks, was that the possibility of an immediate attack by Israel upon Egypt was hanging in the balance. I felt certain, however, that she would do so at a moment of her own choosing and probably within the next three months.

The next morning I realised quite soon that I could not give Pineau any meaningful information about my colleagues' views early in the day, as I had promised. I sent Logan back to Paris to explain this to him. I reported to my senior colleagues, in effect the Egypt Committee, and this meeting was followed by a Cabinet. All those who had been present on 18th October were there and, in addition, Salisbury, Lloyd-George, Stuart, Lennox-Boyd, Thorneycroft, Macleod and Selkirk.

I said that I was doubtful whether Israel would launch an attack against Egypt in the immediate future. Eden said that we must accordingly decide whether to continue to try for a negotiated settlement, or to take the planned military action with the French. We could not keep our forces at the present state of readiness for much longer. I was asked what I thought were the prospects of a negotiated settlement. I said that I was very doubtful about it. Fawzi was being slippery in his talks with Hammarskjöld. Nasser had said that he would not accept the vital third principle. The French were against further negotiation. The United States was not prepared to exercise any real pressure on Egypt. As we relaxed our military preparations, our negotiating position would weaken. I doubted whether the kind of settlement which we might get by negotiation would do anything to diminish Nasser's prestige or the feeling that he had triumphed.

Eden said that grave decisions would have to be taken. By

then it was known that Pineau was coming to London that evening. After some discussion, Eden said that he and I would report to the Cabinet the following day on our discussion with Pineau.

That afternoon the House of Commons met after the Recess. I made a statement about the Canal, describing what had happened at the SCUA conference and the Security Council meetings. I said that we still awaited proposals from Egypt on the way to implement the six principles. It was a holding statement, and the questions on it were not difficult.

Pineau had obviously been disappointed with my attitude at Sèvres and when he got the message from me that it would take longer than I had expected to ascertain my colleagues' views, decided to come to London himself on the evening of 23rd October. It has been suggested that he was afraid that I would give too negative a report of the Sèvres talks. Pineau came and had dinner with me at Carlton Gardens, and at 10 p.m. Eden came in. We discussed the situation for a couple of hours. The main point was greater precision about the actions which we would take if Israel attacked Egypt. It was decided that it was worthwhile having another meeting at Sèvres on the following day. I could not go myself because there were Foreign Office questions in the House. Eden and I therefore agreed that Patrick Dean, a Deputy Under-Secretary of State at the Foreign Office, should go in my place, and that Logan should go with him, as he had been present at Sèvres earlier that week.

I felt Pineau might make more of our talk than was warranted, so I wrote him a letter that evening, which he reproduced in his book. I said that I wished to make it clear that we had not asked Israel to take action. We had merely stated what would be our reactions if certain things happened.

After twenty years perhaps it is not surprising that recollections of what happened should differ. Pineau in *1956 Suez* says that the Israeli contingent arrived in Paris on 21st October. Dayan in *The Story of My Life* says it was 22nd October. Pineau says that after a meeting at Sèvres between the French and the Israelis, he was asked by Mollet and Ben-Gurion to go to London to explain the Israeli proposals. He says that he spoke to a full British Cabinet on 22nd October 'qui écouta mon exposé succinct dans le plus grand silence'. In fact, there was no British Cabinet meeting on 22nd October. He says that he proposed that I and Dean should go to Paris, and after a quick lunch with Eden and myself he left, later followed by Dean and me. He did not lunch with us on 22nd October. I was not accompanied by Dean when I went to Paris. His visit to London was after, not before, my discussions with them at Sèvres.

As to those two quite different versions, I have checked the records and I believe that I am correct.

Eden saw Dean early the next morning, 24th October, and gave him instructions that the discussions were to be about actions which might be taken in certain contingencies, and that British forces would in no circumstances act unless there was a clear military threat to the Canal.

There was another full Cabinet in the morning, which discussed the Suez problem and our talks with Pineau on the previous day. The Cabinet were told of the dilemma about our forces and their equipment, and that very soon the military plan would have to be put at longer notice. After lengthy discussion, it was agreed that the objectives of a military operation would be the same as in the summer: to obtain control of the Canal by landing an Anglo-French force after preliminary air bombardment; and to defeat Nasser, which would probably mean his downfall.

I consistently said that the operation must not involve us in the military occupation of the whole of Egypt, and the installation of a government in Cairo only maintained by British bayonets.

The question was debated whether such an operation would unite the Arab world in support of Egypt. Eden agreed that this was a serious risk, but the greater risk was that Nasser's influence would grow. He was already plotting coups in many

Arab countries. We would never have a better reason for intervention than his seizure of the Canal. Eden went on to agree
that unless our action led to the speedy collapse of Nasser its
effect in other Arab countries would be serious. International
pressures would grow. Therefore, our action must be quick and
successful. Eden emphasised repeatedly our dilemma. He concluded by saying that he thought that, in view of the Cabinet
discussion, further talks with the French were necessary. He
and I would report on them to the Cabinet.

Dayan says that when Pineau returned to Paris at 4 p.m. he
told the Israelis that he had met Eden and, as he had hoped,
found his approach far 'warmer' than mine.

When Dean and Logan arrived in the afternoon of 24th
October, there was further talk about the contingency plan.
The Israelis refused to give details of their operational plans,
except that they proposed to capture the Straits of Tiran, and
the date of 29th October was mentioned as the earliest possible
for them. The terms of the appeal which would be made to
Israel and Egypt to stop hostilities were discussed. After a time
quite unexpectedly a document was produced. It had been
typed on plain paper in a neighbouring room and recorded the
elements of the contingency plan which had been discussed,
and the actions which could be expected to follow them in
given circumstances. Dean and Logan had a word together
about this development. There had been no earlier mention
of committing anything to paper and no reason to regard the
document as anything other than a record of the discussion
on which the three delegations would report. As that, Dean
signed it.

At 11 p.m. Dean came to No. 10 and reported to a group of
Ministers, Eden, Butler, Macmillan, Head and myself. Mountbatten, First Sea Lord, was also there. We decided that we
would recommend the contingency plan to the full Cabinet.

The decisive Cabinet met at 10 a.m. on Thursday, 25th
October, the attendance being the same as on the previous day.
Eden said that on 18th October he had told the Cabinet that

he thought Israel would attack Egypt; on 23rd October he had said that he thought it less likely. Now he believed that the Israelis were advancing their military preparations with a view to attacking Egypt, and the date might be 29th October. The French felt strongly that if that happened we should both intervene, as we had agreed between us on 18th October. If we declined to do so, they might do it alone.

Eden therefore suggested that, if Israel did attack, we and the French should issue an ultimatum to both sides. If Nasser complied, his prestige would be fatally undermined. If he did not, there would be ample justification for Anglo-French action to safeguard the Canal. It was better that we should seem to hold the balance between Egypt and Israel rather than to be accepting Israeli co-operation in an attack by us on Egypt.

I supported Eden. I said that unless prompt action was taken to check Nasser's ambitions our position would be undermined throughout the Middle East. The situation in Jordan had deteriorated seriously. In Syria there was Russian equipment sufficient for two divisions. In Libya the conspiracy against the existing regime was far advanced. In Iraq Nasser was doing all he could to undermine Nuri, and our influence was gravely threatened. Israel's intervention in our dispute with Nasser had its disadvantages, but there was little prospect of any other early opportunity to bring these issues to a head.

There was a long discussion. It was generally accepted that our action was defensible in international law.

A crisis in the Middle East could not be long delayed. It was better to act now, while the Anglo-French operation was still mounted. It was considered whether our action would cause offence to the United States. It was felt that in view of their behaviour they had no reason to complain, although no doubt they would make disapproving noises. Our obligations under the Tripartite Declaration were discussed. It was asked whether the request to cease fire would appear to hold the balance evenly. On that, the point was that only by basing ourselves on the Canal could we effectively separate the combatants and deter other countries from entering the fray. As for the argument that we would not have the specific authority of the United Nations for our action, the answer, of course, was that in view of the Soviet veto we would never have authority for any action against Nasser.

Eventually it was agreed, without dissent, that if Israel attacked we would act as Eden had proposed.

It was at the meeting of senior Ministers at 11 p.m. on 24th or at this Cabinet meeting that I should have joined issue if I had thought it right to do so. I will try to recapitulate the pros and cons. In favour of what was proposed, the arguments seemed to me to be as follows:

The United Nations was powerless because of the Russian veto.

The negotiations with Egypt were unlikely to achieve anything which would appear other than a success for Nasser. He was skilfully and successfully playing for time.

Eisenhower and Dulles between them had relieved Nasser of any anxiety about strong action by the United States against him. He could go on playing them off against the Russians and vice versa in perfect safety.

Israel was certain sooner or later to break out. I believed what Pineau had told me about the Israeli decision to fight. If we and the French were about, that war was less likely to spread. We would be able to prevent it becoming a general conflagration.

Although I had my doubts about toppling Nasser and was horrified by the thought of anything like a reoccupation of the whole of Egypt or having to prop up a pro-Western regime with British troops, the idea of Nasser having the power to interfere at a moment's notice with our shipping and oil supplies was intolerable. I felt that he must be challenged and checked. The restoration of the Canal to international control would be a sufficient defeat for him.

The leaders in most Middle Eastern and near-by countries,

although they could not say it publicly, wanted Nasser cut down to size. This applied to Iraq, the Sudan, Libya, the Lebanon, King Hussein and his supporters in Jordan, Saudi Arabia, Ethiopia, the Gulf Shaikhdoms, Turkey, Iran and Pakistan.

If we now stood down our forces, we would look ridiculous in the eyes of most countries, and our prestige in the Middle East would fall still further as inconclusive negotiations dragged on. Nasser would be seen to have won.

As to the British political scene, our critics on the left would claim that it was they who had forced us to back down, but if we took no action those same people would very soon be crying 'Munich again'. We would be the 'guilty men' who had failed to stand up to Nasser, just as, according to them, the Conservatives in 1937 and 1938 had failed to stand up to Hitler. We should be accused of dithering and grovelling, as one Opposition back-bencher had put it apropos of the Government's restraint after King Hussein's dismissal of Glubb. We should also be in for a rough time from our own supporters. The brave words spoken by Nutting and Eden at Llandudno would be shown up as rhetorical verbiage and nothing else.

That these things would be said if we took no action did not matter all that much. Ministers who are guided in their decisions solely by what political friends or foes are likely to say do not deserve to rank high. The real issue was whether we were betraying our country and our Western allies.

Munich again? Was that an exaggeration or an obsession? Was it necessary to check Nasser? Well, the comparison with Hitler was made by Gaitskell, Leader of the British Labour Party, on 2nd August. About the same time it was also said in the French Chamber by Mollet, the French Socialist leader. Spaak, a leading Belgian Socialist and Foreign Minister of Belgium, had said the same in his letter to me (see p. 120). Attlee in the House of Lords had described Nasser as an imperialist dictator. Walter Elliot and Boothby, not generally regarded as being on the right wing of the Conservative Party, had compared Nasser to Hitler. The analogy was clearly in Kirkpatrick's mind when he wrote as he did to Makins early in October (see p. 130). Others preferred to compare Nasser with Mussolini. I myself thought that the comparison with Hitler was more apt, if only because Nasser's *The Philosophy of the Revolution* read like *Mein Kampf*. It has been argued since that Nasser had not behind him the German industrial base, its war potential and the backing of a martial race. That was true, but Nasser did not need them. He had Russian support. His targets, Middle East oil, the weaker Arab states, the shaikh-doms in the Gulf, were soft targets. If unchecked, Nasser could by his propaganda machine alone cause uprisings or changes of Government in his favour in most of those states, one by one.

Against action by us to check him, it was argued that we had no case for such interference. Nasser had merely nationalised an Egyptian territory, and the Company's property was mainly in Egypt. Acceptance of its nationalisation would merely be the consummation of the agreement over the Base, the agreement about the Sudan and our concessions over sterling balances. Nasser would have no further demands. In any case, he was a patriot of simple tastes, trying to restore self-confidence and pride of race to the Egyptians. He wished to relieve their poverty and improve their living standards.

Almost identical arguments had been used about Hitler and the Rhineland in 1936. The Rhine, as it was said, was a German river which ran through German territory. The Rhineland belonged to Germany. Hitler, for all his bombast, was trying to restore the self-respect of the German people. He was curing unemployment. Once one or two obvious injustices had been remedied he would settle down as the leader of a respectable member of the family of nations.

Well, we had had our lesson over Hitler. The appetite had grown with eating—the rape of Austria, Munich, the absorp-tion of Czechoslovakia, Poland and the dream of world con-quest resulting in 20 million dead.

To sum up, if Nasser was not checked, the prospect in the

Middle East was grim: the collapse of pro-Western Governments, Soviet penetration, Nasser's grip on the Canal and on the oil supplies for Western Europe, and Israeli desperation which could lead to anything. It was a strong case.

To show that I have not thought all this out twenty-one years later, Eisenhower's account of our Bermuda talks in March 1957, on p. 122 of his book makes it quite clear that my views were just the same then.

As for the arguments against action by us, I was not worried by the legal aspect. I accepted the view that we were legally entitled to act. I was not worried by the morality of it. Nasser was an enemy in a state of war with Israel and inciting people throughout the Middle East and East Africa to murder and insurrection. He had recently been responsible for two attempts to murder trusted friends of ours in Arab countries.

The argument that we ought not to offend the Americans was not conclusive. They had let us down on every occasion, when even silence from them would have helped. In addition, it would be easier for them if we did not tell them beforehand. When Macmillan and I went to Moscow in 1959 we did not tell the German Chancellor, Adenauer. We knew that if we did, he would object. We would not have accepted his objection and he would have been snubbed. If he was not told beforehand, he could grumble afterwards but not lose face. That, I thought, would apply to the Americans in October 1956. Throughout they had said that they accepted that we should use force as a last resort. The judgment that Eisenhower would have been more offended if we had told him beforehand and then acted in spite of his opposition, was confirmed in the conversation which I had in November with Allen Dulles, head of the American Central Intelligence Agency, Foster Dulles's brother, and a shrewd observer (see p. 220).

The idea that we should only act with the authority of the United Nations was utterly unrealistic. Only once had the Western world been able to act against aggression with the authority of the United Nations, and that was in the case of

Korea, when the Russians had temporarily absented themselves from the Security Council. Even if they had been there and used their veto, I have not the slightest doubt that the United States would still have intervened without the authority of the United Nations.

What did concern me was the length of time which it was going to take for our expedition to reach Port Said. The prospect of about ten days between the first Israeli attack and the landings of our forces from the air and sea was the main source of my misgivings. Even with United States neutrality or support behind the scenes, I felt that international pressures would grow, led by the anti-colonial bloc, the neutrals and — because of the Panama Canal — quite probably most of the Latin Americans. Moreover, because Israel was involved, the position of our friends in the Arab states and in Iran and Pakistan would be in jeopardy if they failed to join in the condemnations. The methods of Cairo Radio were based on those of Dr Goebbels, and its power was very great.

That we must take the risk of this delay was settled for me in my own mind by the fact that I had no better alternative to suggest. Allowing the negotiations to meander on would be a victory for Nasser. His victory would be a dangerous precedent. An alliance between France, Israel and Britain to attack Nasser would put our nationals in Arab countries and our property there in grave peril. Israel would be bound to attack sooner or later. We had not instigated it, but it was better that it should happen while we had the forces ready to intervene.

23 Lloyd and Dulles consult together at the U.N. early in October
1956. In November, the Americans opposed the Anglo-French
intervention and demanded unconditional withdrawal. Afterwards
Dulles asked Lloyd: 'Why did you stop? Why didn't you go through
with it and get Nasser down?'

24 Gaitskell, Leader of the Labour Party, had said that resort to force consistent with the U.N. Charter could not be excluded. But he vehemently opposed the British Government's intervention.

25 *Left* During the Cabinet meeting on 4th November, 'we could hear the noise of the demonstration in Trafalgar Square ... There was a steady hum of noise and then every few minutes a crescendo and an outburst of howling or booing.' (p. 206)

26 *Above* At the U.N. General Assembly on 23rd November, Selwyn Lloyd offers to withdraw British forces from Egypt as soon as a U.N. emergency force (UNEF) is able to take over.

27 Hammarskjöld, U.N. Secretary General, and Nasser.

28 'This all shows how very careful you have to be.' —
Selwyn Lloyd and his daughter Joanna.

Chapter XII

Intervention

Israeli attack 29th October — British and French reaction — Parliamentary debates — United Nations — military operations — UNEF proposal — Cabinet 4th November — Landings 5th–6th November — cease-fire.

On 27th October partial mobilisation of the Israeli reserves was ordered. On Sunday, 28th October, the Israeli Cabinet took the decision that the attack upon Egypt should go forward on the following day. At 5 p.m. on Monday, 29th October, it began. In spite of what Pineau had told me on the 22nd about the Israelis' determination to attack, I had doubts right up to the last moment as to whether the Israelis would act then or wait a little time longer. I doubted whether Ben-Gurion had made up his mind on the timing.

Meanwhile, Dulles had been speaking in Dallas, Texas, on 28th October. He reaffirmed in vehement terms his position that the Canal should not be under Egyptian control. It would be 'intolerable'.

The news of the Israeli attack was received during a dinner which Eden was giving for the Norwegian Prime Minister.

On the following day, 30th October, the Cabinet met in the morning and approved, subject to what Mollet and Pineau might have to say, the terms of the notes to be sent to Israel and Egypt, the statement to be made by Eden in the House of Commons that afternoon and the message to be sent to Eisenhower.

Mollet and Pineau arrived for the final decisions, and at 4.30 p.m. Eden made his statement in the House. It dealt with

the Israeli attack, the assurance which Nicholls, our Ambassador in Tel Aviv, had obtained that Israel would not attack
Jordan, and the danger to shipping in the Canal. The British
and French Representatives in New York had been instructed
to join the U.S. Representative in arranging an immediate
meeting of the Security Council. In the meantime, Eden continued, the two Governments had addressed notes to Egypt
and Israel calling on them to withdraw their military forces
ten miles from the Canal and to allow Anglo-French forces to
move in temporarily to separate the belligerents and to guarantee freedom of transit through the Canal. A reply within twelve
hours was requested, and it was made clear that if these
requirements were not met within that time British and French
forces would intervene to ensure compliance. There was an
immediate discussion of this statement in the House for over
an hour and again for a couple of hours later that evening.

The Anglo-French forces did have to intervene. There followed some eight or nine days of intense activity for me on
various fronts. I felt like a juggler trying to keep several balls
in the air at the same time — the House of Commons, the United
Nations, the military operation, public relations, and intensive
negotiations with other Governments.

So far as the House of Commons was concerned, we had a
strenuous time. There were debates, statements, questions
almost every day, including Saturday, 3rd November. It was a
considerable strain on Ministers, particularly Eden, Head and
myself. I thought at the time that we were subjected to unnecessary burdens and that the Leader of the House, Butler,
and the Chief Whip, Heath, were being too accommodating
to the Opposition. On reflection I think that they were
right; it acted as a safety valve; it kept the argument off
the streets and in the House of Commons. But it was hard
work.

There was one faintly amusing interlude. I had promised
some time before to speak at Watford on 1st November. It was
decided that I should keep the engagement, partly to give me a

night off from the shouting match in the Commons but, more important, to show that Ministers were not afraid to face public audiences at this time. We had a splendid meeting, the hecklers were routed, and as soon as I got back into my car I slept soundly until I was awakened in New Palace Yard. Next day I heard that I had had a motor accident on the way back, that it had required a charge of the mounted police in Parliament Square to make a way through for my car; that I had sat pale and fearful in the car. The only fact to which I can subscribe is that all this may have happened, although I doubt it, but I was fast asleep all the time. The reason why is clear from what I say later about the time factor in communicating with our delegation at the United Nations. I was desperately short of sleep.

The arguments in the House covered the same ground day after day. Was Israel an aggressor? Was our intervention an act of imperialist spleen against Egypt? Had we flouted the Charter of the United Nations? There were constant interruptions, points of argument put as points of order, and a lot of shouting. At one time the Speaker had to suspend the sitting for thirty minutes. The House does not change, nor do noisy interrupters realise that being shouted at makes things easier for Ministers. One has to pretend to be indignant, but the louder the noise the less one has to deal with the arguments of the other side. Cold, disapproving, apparently incredulous silence is a much more effective way of putting a Minister on the defensive than constant interruptions and barracking.

By and large, back-bench speeches were of a high order. I remember in particular one by Harold Lever. He courageously defended the Government's actions. He attacked in scathing terms Nasser and his junta. He supported our view that the Tripartite Declaration guaranteeing the 1949 Middle East armistice lines could not apply in this situation. But towards the end of his speech, in answer to interruptions from his own side, he said that he could not approve any action or use of force by us which was contrary to the Charter of the United

Nations. He wisely did not commit himself as to whether or not we had so acted.

Lever's speech was followed by a brilliant one from Wilfred Fienburgh, Labour Member for Islington North. From the invasion of Normandy until the end of the war in north-west Germany he had been one of my General Staff officers, Grade 2, at Second Army headquarters. All the H.Q. knew that I was standing as a Conservative at the forthcoming election. Three very competent staff officers—Kenneth Younger, Christopher Mayhew and Fienburgh—forbore to tell me that they were going to stand in the Labour interest. I never knew why they were so reticent. Afterwards, when we met in the House together, I used to tell them that they obviously were frightened that I would cast myself in the role of King David and treat them as he treated Uriah the Hittite: 'Set ye Uriah in the forefront of the hottest battle and retire ye from him that he may be smitten and die' (2 Samuel, xi).

Fienburgh made a rousing speech in reply to Lever and against the Government. He died tragically in a motor accident on his way home from a sitting of the House in May 1958. He might have had a considerable future in politics.

On the first point about Israel being an aggressor, there was not much steam in it, except for a few committed anti-Zionists, nor did the allegation that we were acting out of imperialist spleen against Egypt cut much ice. The most substantial criticism was that we had acted contrary to international law and the Charter and were defying the United Nations. This also continued to worry some Conservatives and I deal with it at length later.

In addition to the House of Commons, the United Nations was in constant session. We were very fortunate in our Permanent Representative, Pierson Dixon. I had known him at Cambridge. He had a fine intellect and a quiet manner concealed great courage and resolution. He was an outstanding public servant. His premature death just after he ceased to be our Ambassador in Paris was a serious loss to the nation. He conducted our case at the U.N. with great skill and we had complete confidence in him. I was glad to read in his son's book *Double Diploma** that whatever may have been Dixon's reservations about the actual policy of the Government, he felt that from his personal viewpoint he had received nothing but full confidence and support from his political masters.

Owing to the speed of events, our exchanges had to be by telephone. They were subject to the inconvenience of the time difference between New York and London. They were five hours behind. That meant that if a critical decision developed in a United Nations debate at 10 p.m. their time, Dixon had to ring me up for instruction about 3 a.m. our time. If after an early-morning discussion with my colleagues I wanted to talk to Dixon at 9.30 a.m. our time, it meant waking him up at 4.30 a.m. their time. This was a severe tax on stamina. A further complication was that the time in Egypt was two hours ahead of ours.

On 30th October the Security Council met in the morning, afternoon and evening. At the end of the evening session, resolutions by the United States and the Soviet Union were both vetoed by the French and ourselves. The United States resolution condemned Israel as an aggressor, demanded Israeli withdrawal and called upon all United Nations members to refrain from the use or threat of force. The Soviet one was rather milder. We would have preferred to abstain on it but the French were determined to veto it. We therefore, to maintain our solidarity with them, also voted against it.

The next day the Yugoslav representative moved a resolution invoking the Uniting for Peace procedure, to move the matter to the General Assembly. That was a device of doubtful legality invented, so I have always believed, by Dulles in November 1950 as a way to get round the Soviet veto. The Soviet Union had consistently proclaimed its view that it was illegal. Nevertheless, with their usual cynicism, the Russians voted for it on

* Piers Dixon, *Double Diploma* (Hutchinson, 1968) p. 264.

this occasion and it was carried by 7 votes to 2, Australia and Belgium abstaining. It required 7 votes to carry and, had the United States abstained, it would have been the Security Council which remained seized of the matter.

The following day, 1st November, the General Assembly was to meet at 5 p.m. New York time, 10 p.m. our time. At home, there was to be a statement by the Minister of Defence in the House, followed by another debate. I had a talk with Kirkpatrick in the morning. We were both worried by the United States's reactions, the almost ferocious way it was leading the opposition to us, and the speed with which it had allowed the matter to be taken to the General Assembly. This compared with the inevitable slowness of our seaborne expedition. I recalled my hankerings for a much-increased United Nations presence on the borders of Israel and the Arab states, which I had mentioned several times in House of Commons debates earlier in the year. We wondered whether, if we offered to hand over our peace-keeping function to the United Nations, it would improve our position. We agreed that it would be a good thing for the Prime Minister to mention this possibility in his speech that afternoon, which would be made in time for Dixon to refer to it in the General Assembly debate.

Eden willingly agreed to this. It was very much in accord with his own thoughts, as his memoirs show, and speaking at about 5.30 p.m. our time, 10.30 p.m. New York time, he said that we would welcome an international solution of the problems of the area and the participation of many other nations in bringing about and upholding a settlement. Talking about the stabilisation of the situation, he said:

If the United Nations were then willing to take over the physical task of maintaining peace in that area, no one would be better pleased than we.

About the same time, Lester Pearson of Canada had been searching for a solution. He was under attack from the

Opposition in Canada for not having given us sufficient support. Without any knowledge of what Eden was going to say
in the House of Commons, Pearson had been thinking of suggesting a United Nations force for the area.

The General Assembly debate began on a resolution introduced by Dulles urging a cease-fire, the withdrawal of Israeli,
British and French forces and the reopening of the Canal,
which by now had been blocked. Dixon in his speech referred
to what Eden had said in the House of Commons. As soon as
Pearson heard Dixon's speech he decided to propose the creation
of a United Nations Emergency Force (UNEF). He spoke to
Dulles about the possibility of amending the resolution being
debated. Dulles was unwilling to delay the vote on his resolution — another example of hostility to us. He did, however, say
that if Pearson put forward a separate resolution incorporating
the idea of UNEF, the United States would support it.

The debate continued for over twelve hours. The vote was
taken soon after 4 a.m. New York time on 2nd November. It
was carried by 65 votes to 5 (Australia, France, Israel, New
Zealand and the United Kingdom). Canada with six others
abstained. Pearson in his explanation of Canada's abstention
said that the resolution was 'inadequate to achieve the purpose
which we had in mind at the session' and referred to the
organising of a UNEF. Dulles, rather to Pearson's surprise,
immediately followed him to the rostrum and said that the
United States would be happy to support the Canadian suggestion. That was a promising start.

A clue to the reasons for Dulles's haste was given by Nixon,
then the Republican Vice-Presidential candidate, in a campaign speech on 2nd November. He claimed that the vote on
the resolution had been a world-wide vote of confidence in the
President. He went on:*

In the past the nations of Asia and Africa have always felt
we would, when the pressure was on, side with the policies

* Quoted in Finer, *Dulles Over Suez*, p. 397.

of the British and French Governments in relation to the once Colonial areas. For the first time in history we have shown independence of Anglo-French policies towards Asia and Africa which seemed to us to reflect the Colonial tradition. That declaration of independence has had an electrifying effect throughout the world.

That was a blatant piece of electioneering and showed that the American political leaders had their eyes firmly fixed on the American polls.

Early in the morning of 3rd November Dulles had some abdominal pains. He was rushed to hospital, and at 7.30 a.m. was operated on for cancer. This was a misfortune for us. After the election had been safely won, he would have seen the realities as Hoover who took over from him could not see them, and as Eisenhower refused to see them. Dulles himself frequently made this point to me during the following two years, but more on that later.

On 3rd November the Assembly met again to debate two resolutions, one sponsored by the Afro-Asian group to authorise Hammarskjöld to negotiate a cease-fire, and one by Pearson with regard to an international force (UNEF), also sponsored by Colombia and Norway.

The vote was taken at 2 a.m. New York time on the Sunday morning. The resolution about UNEF was passed with 57 votes for, and 19 abstentions — the Soviet bloc, Egypt, France, the U.K., Israel, Australia, New Zealand, South Africa, Portugal, Turkey, Laos. We abstained because it was not yet clear that it really would be an effective force, rather than a stepped-up UNTSO.

Meanwhile the military operation had been proceeding. In the late evening of 29th October an Israeli parachute battalion had been dropped near the eastern entrance to the Mitla Pass deep in Sinai and about thirty miles from the Canal. Other units of the Parachute Brigade, after a feint against Jordan, captured Kuntilla in Central Sinai. Its defenders had fled. They then captured Thamad, where there was serious fighting. The Egyptians had well-fortified and well-equipped defensive positions. Other units of the brigade took Nakhl and went on to join up with the battalion parachuted on to the Mitla Pass.

Early the following day an Israeli brigade captured the vital crossroads of Kusseima, north of Kuntilla.

Anglo-French bombing of the Egyptian Air Force began at 5 p.m. on 30th October, Nasser having refused our demand for the withdrawal of Egyptian troops ten miles from the Canal and acceptance of the landing of British and French units to safeguard the waterway. The foreign technicians from behind the Iron Curtain removed themselves speedily. The destruction of the Egyptian Air Force was carried out with great skill and almost no casualties. The Israeli ground forces continued on their victorious way. The Egyptians fought well from fixed positions already prepared but did not do so well when forced to leave their entrenchments. Israeli troops captured Abu Ageila, the Ruafa Dam, Bir Hassna and, after a bloody battle in which they sustained heavy casualties, the Mitla Pass. When El Arish fell, the Israelis captured vast quantities of military equipment.

We had no knowledge of the Israeli campaign plans but it was clear that they were carrying all before them. A brilliant stroke was directed at Egyptian positions at Sharm al-Shaikh, where on 5th November two Egyptian battalions in well-fortified positions and prepared for a long siege were overcome.

While this was going on, our invasion fleet was sailing towards Port Said. Its speed was limited by the fact that the tank landing craft could only do five knots an hour. On 3rd November it was decided that the Minister of Defence should go to Keightley's headquarters in Cyprus to see whether the landings could be made sooner than planned. He returned with the news that it would be possible for the airborne landings to take place at first light on Monday 5th November, with the seaborne assault the following day.

Meanwhile, Nutting, one of the Ministers of State at the Foreign Office had resigned. He had told me during the week beginning 22nd October that he could not support the action which we proposed to take and would resign. He had been a close personal friend. We had worked together well when he was Under-Secretary and I was Minister of State. When I went to the Ministry of Supply in October 1954, I had strongly recommended that he should succeed me.

When he said that he must resign, I tried to dissuade him. I was, to say the least of it, somewhat surprised to find him taking this attitude after what he had said in March (see p. 54) about appeasement not working and that Nasser would break any agreement made with him. I also remembered his strong language at the party conference (pp. 163–4). I suggested that he should go away for a time and take no part in the debates about Suez. He could have a diplomatic illness. He said that that was impossible. Sooner or later he would have to defend the Government's actions, which he could not do. I saw the force of that. With Eden's approval, I asked Lennox-Boyd whether he would take Nutting as a Minister of State at the Colonial Office if we could arrange it. Lennox-Boyd was a staunch and helpful colleague and agreed. I put it to Nutting but, to my regret, he refused. He agreed to defer the public announcement of his resignation for a day or two until 2nd November.

I was also very sorry when I heard that he intended to resign his seat in Parliament. That was quite unnecessary. Others who disagreed with the policy, like Edward Boyle, had no difficulty in their constituencies as events developed up to the 1959 Election.

Nutting's decision to resign was of course politically embarrassing to me, but I much more regretted the loss of one whose friendship I had valued and whose abilities as a colleague I had admired.

On the Sunday afternoon, 4th November, the UN General Assembly debated the Russian invasion of Hungary. Dixon recorded that this was a classic example of double standards. It took seven days — from 28th October to 4th November — for the U.N. to denounce the Soviet Union over Hungary; and only three days — from 30th October to 2nd November — to denounce Britain over Suez.

Meanwhile in London Sunday, 4th November, was one of the most dramatic days in the whole period of the Suez crisis. The Egypt Committee was summoned to meet at 12.30 p.m. on that day. Some time before the meeting was due to begin I walked across from Carlton Gardens to No. 10 to have a preliminary talk with Eden. He was tired but very calm. We were both aware of the gravity of the decisions which we had to ask our colleagues to make, and I believe that we were in complete agreement that having got thus far, it would be wrong to call off the operation. The consequences of that would be dreadful.

Head had flown to Cyprus to General Keightley's headquarters on the previous day. We had to consider his account of what was happening, and also developments at the United Nations. He told the Egypt Committee that the Israeli military operations were being brilliantly successful. The Egyptian Air Force had been eliminated without loss to us. The seaborne expedition was sailing steadily towards Port Said. The Egyptian forces were withdrawing on Cairo. There were two possible reasons for that. It was known that we were not attacking civilian targets and, therefore, the troops would be safer in a city area. The second possibility was that Nasser was taking no risks about his personal position. Whatever the reason, their withdrawal meant that the allied commanders agreed that it would be possible for the airborne attack to take place at first light on the following day, the Monday, 5th November, twenty-four hours sooner than planned.

We also considered the situation at the United Nations. Two further resolutions were before the General Assembly. The first was a Canadian one asking Hammarskjöld to prepare a plan within forty-eight hours for a UNEF. The second, sponsored by Afro-Asians, called upon him to secure a cease-fire within twelve hours.

We decided to take our stand upon the Canadian resolution, even though we could not vote for it exactly as it was framed. We must do everything within our power to stop one recommending sanctions against us France and Israel.

We broke up for lunch pending further news from New York, where it was now breakfast time. I stayed on at No. 10 and someone kindly produced some sandwiches.

The committee met again at 2.30 p.m. The same Ministers attended and the only additional person was Marshal of the Royal Air Force Sir William Dickson, Chairman of the Chiefs of Staff Committee. A message had come from the Secretary-General asking us to comply with the Afro-Asian resolution and cease fire from 8 p.m. that day (Greenwich Mean time). We were also told that inclusion of Anglo-French troops in the UNEF was unacceptable. It was added that the Israeli representative at the United Nations had said that Israel would accept the cease-fire if Egypt agreed to do so, and the Egyptians had so agreed. After further enquiry it appeared that this was not as simple as it seemed. The Israelis had not agreed to withdraw behind the former border, the armistice lines, nor had they agreed to the introduction of a UNEF.

The committee decided that we should press again for the inclusion of Anglo-French troops in the UNEF. We did not see how otherwise it would ever come into being. In the event, it was only our logistic support which did make it capable of functioning. The question was then raised of postponing the Anglo-French airborne landing for twenty-four hours, to give time for an answer on this point. This led to a further question, whether if there were this twenty-four-hour postponement, it would be possible for it ever to take place.

It was at this meeting that a report came in from Dixon that there had been some discussion in New York about oil sanctions. Macmillan threw his arms in the air and said, 'Oil sanctions! That finishes it.' Two of those present remember this.

It was obvious that the full Cabinet must take the crucial decisions. It met at 6.30 p.m. During this time we could hear the noise of the demonstration in Trafalgar Square at which Bevan was speaking. There was a steady hum of noise and then every few minutes a crescendo and an outburst of howling or booing.

Eden said that there were three courses open to us:

(1) to proceed with the initial phase of occupation, while saying that we were willing to transfer responsibility for keeping the peace to the United Nations force; we should make it a condition that Anglo-French detachments must not be excluded from a UNEF; or

(2) to suspend the parachute landings for twenty-four hours to give Egypt and Israel a chance to accept a UNEF, and the U.N. time to decide whether Anglo-French troops should form part of the UNEF and land as an advance guard; or

(3) to defer military action indefinitely.

After some discussion in which I had not taken part, Monckton turned towards me and asked what was the Foreign Secretary's view. I said that I was in favour of the first course. Unless we had some troops on the ground, I did not think that a UNEF would ever come into existence, or, if it did, be allowed by Nasser to set foot on Egyptian soil.

The Cabinet decided on the first course. Three or four members were for the second course—a twenty-four-hour delay to give time for consultations with the Americans about the two points mentioned above—and a couple more were for deferring the landing indefinitely. With one exception, all said that they would support whatever course the majority agreed. Monckton reserved his position. I went back to No. 1 Carlton Gardens at about 9 p.m., having been at No. 10 for nearly twelve hours.

On Monday, 5th November, the parachute drops took place at first light, 7.15 a.m. Egyptian time and 5.15 a.m. our time. They were a complete success. Later in the day, Dixon and the French representative informed Hammarskjöld that we agreed to the proposal for a United Nations emergency force, and also that bombing would cease. Parliament was being prorogued, but we had Question Time, and then at 3.50 p.m. I made a statement on Hungary and then one on Suez, followed by Head also on Suez. I had a stormy time. I was questioned about our abstention on the Canadian resolution. Walter Elliot from the Conservative benches doubted the wisdom of insisting on U.K. detachments in it. He was quite right ultimately, but our apparent insistence on Anglo-French participation was solely because our troops were there. In fact, without our logistic support it would have taken two or three months for UNEF to become effective. In the longer term, it was something to be given away, if only to stop Soviet troops from participating. In the course of this, Eden intervened with the news that the Governor of Port Said was discussing surrender terms with Brigadier Butler, who commanded the 16th Parachute Brigade. Later in the day, the Soviet Union tried to have the Security Council discuss an item condemning the failure of Israel, France and the United Kingdom to comply with the Assembly's Resolution of 2nd November. The item was not adopted. The Assembly called for 9 p.m. New York time met and adjourned.

Tuesday, 6th November, was another day to remember.

By now the seaborne assault had taken place, again with complete success. Brigadier Bernard Fergusson, later Lord Ballantrae and Governor-General of New Zealand, had been given the job of Director of Psychological Warfare. When appointed, his friend Peter Fleming had said that he could not think of a more certain way of bringing a promising career to an end. Through no fault of Fergusson, that enterprise had not been a great success, but he was in a position to evaluate the operational side. His comment was:

Tempers ran so high over the ethics of the Franco-British intervention at Port Said that its technical brilliance has been obscured.

He went on to say that it was the most difficult operation ever. It was planned from five centres — London, Paris, Cyprus,

Algiers and Malta—but the professional standard was first class, a verdict with which I wholeheartedly agree.

The Cabinet met at 9.30 a.m. on 6th November in the Prime Minister's Room in the Commons because the House was meeting at 11 a.m. for the Queen's Speech. Before the Cabinet meeting, Eden had spoken at 8.30 a.m. our time to Dixon, who said that he thought that he could hold on at the U.N. until the end of the week. Also before the Cabinet met, I had spoken to Macmillan, who said that in view of the financial and economic pressures we must stop.

Pineau in his book *1956 Suez* says that Eden and Mollet received messages from Eisenhower, followed up by a telephone call to Eden that there must be a cease-fire within twelve hours. Eden agreed, Pineau says, without consulting Mollet or even his colleagues. There is no confirmation of this in Eisenhower's book. The telephone conversation between Eden and Eisenhower took place at 1.43 p.m. our time, after Eden and the Cabinet had decided on the cease-fire.

Mollet was telephoned by Eden just before lunch. Pineau and Bourgès-Maunoury were for the French going on alone. Mollet refused and was supported by a majority of the French Cabinet.

According to my recollection, the first proposal was for a cease-fire at 4 p.m. that evening, 6th November. I had suggested that it should be midnight so that we could find out how much of the Canal our troops held and give them a little more time to establish themselves. When it was confirmed that we had twenty miles or so, I agreed, taking the view that that twenty miles was a substantial gauge.

Many have criticised us for the decision to stop. James Stuart, Secretary of State for Scotland, although a party to the decision, wrote in his book* that he was so sickened by it that it broke his political heart. Whether I was right in my belief that we had as good a bargaining counter with twenty-three miles of the Canal as with the whole Canal, is difficult to say. It never occurred to me that the United States would make no use at

* *Within the Fringe* (Bodley Head, 1967).

all of the counter. Whether they would have behaved differently if we had had the whole Canal, I doubt. The real damage which our decision did was to our national morale as time went on. To be stopped in the middle of a battle was much worse than being forced to give ground after the battle was over and won. If the length of time which it took the seaborne force to arrive is left out of account, and that was geography, the military operations were brilliantly successful. By that I mean the parachute drops, the landings from the sea, and the initial advance down the Canal. Also, the attacks upon the Egyptian Air Force had been most efficiently conducted. What is more, any time that had been lost was due to the extreme care taken by the Anglo-French forces to avoid civilian casualties. But the fact that we stopped in so short a time after landing has allowed the myth to grow up that there was a military failure or defeat. As usual, the British were not slow to denigrate themselves.

To return to the Cabinet decision, Eden never tried to escape responsibility for it. It was not fear of Soviet intervention. It was not that the position at the United Nations could not be handled for a few days. It was not trouble in the Parliamentary Party or with public opinion. We had the feeling that that was increasingly behind us. I think that there were two reasons. The first was that the ostensible reason which we had given for going in was to stop hostilities over the Canal and fighting between Israel and Egypt for the crossing places or along the Canal (as in fact happened in the Six-Day and Yom Kippur Wars). That fighting had stopped. Looking back, I suppose that we could have argued that in our note of 30th October to Egypt we had asked them to accept our occupation of certain places on the Canal to guarantee free passage to take place.

Eden's second reason was the financial one. Macmillan strongly advocated accepting the cease-fire both to me privately beforehand and at the Cabinet meeting. He had been a staunch supporter of our actions at every stage. He saw the dangers of a Nasser victory as clearly as any of us. But in those days the pound was on a fixed exchange rate. It was a reserve currency.

A large proportion of world trade was conducted in pounds sterling. Any Chancellor of the Exchequer must have regard to these factors. I wonder whether any of the members of the Cabinet with his responsibilities would have dared to say, 'Go on, whatever the consequences.' I believe from what I learnt of him later, when I knew him very much better, that there was another factor. I think that he was emotionally affected when he was told that the administration of his close wartime friend, Eisenhower, through the mouth of George Humphrey, the American Secretary of the Treasury whom Macmillan also regarded as a friend, was obstructing our drawing from the International Monetary Fund what was our own money. This was the first tranche. We wanted it to protect sterling from speculation against it which, it was suspected, was being stimulated by the United States Treasury.

At 5 p.m. on 6th November the Allied Commander-in-Chief was given the order to cease fire.

Chapter XIII

UNEF

My stay in the United States 12th–27th November — New York — Washington — United Nations debate — formation of U.N. Emergency Force — Pilgrims and English Speaking Union dinners — return to London — I offer to resign over withdrawal terms — withdrawal announced — Dulles at NATO — final decisions — Eden's resignation 9th January 1957.

On the following day, 7th November, the General Assembly passed a resolution calling for the immediate withdrawal of British, French and Israeli troops. I decided that I would be better employed in dealing with that situation personally in New York rather than by telegram or telephone conversation.

After attending the Remembrance Day service at the Cenotaph on 11th November I flew off to New York. Physically I felt in reasonably good shape. For that I thanked my previous experience of prolonged mental and physical strain — first in the law, practising at the Bar during busy periods, and second my time in the army, planning for D-Day and during the early operations in Normandy.

I knew that I was leaving behind a confused country. Gaitskell in his full-throated opposition thought that he was backing a winner. I was not so sure. During the previous fortnight I had realised that his followers were not unanimous. There had been a number of private assurances of support, nods and winks in private places and encouragement to 'stick it'.

As for the Government side, I knew that there would be no trouble with the Cabinet. Much has been written or said about divisions and disagreements. All I can say is that I would not ask for better colleagues. Of course there were differences of opinion on some points, as I have set out in this book. All knew that there were disadvantages in any course adopted, but their kindness, support and friendship could not have been bettered. This is not a sentimental illusion. I have kept too many notes of support from my colleagues for that to be the case. The Conservative Party in the House was more difficult to deal with. Heath, as Chief Whip, had done a superb job in keeping the party together, but there were some consistent opponents of our having gone back into the Canal Zone, and some very strong-minded opponents of our leaving it again. They would not be easy to handle.

In New York at the United Nations and elsewhere I had certain purposes in mind. First and foremost I had to come to the relief of Bob Dixon and his delegation. They had done a magnificent job in a trying situation. Dixon himself had not faltered or put a foot wrong. I felt that now I, as their political chief, must also face the music.

We had to mend our fences with the United States and our Scandinavian allies. We had to keep the Commonwealth together and in good heart. Menon would do his best to poison the atmosphere. In spite of his love-hate feelings for Britain, I knew that because he had not been allowed to influence the Security Council proceedings in early October, there would be no Menon like a Menon scorned. I hoped that I might personally be able to influence him, harking back to Korean times. There were the interests of our partners in the Baghdad Pact to be considered. We knew how they really felt, but they had to have regard to public opinion in their countries.

As for Suez itself, we had to make certain that there would be no withdrawal by the French and ourselves without an effective UNEF taking our place as we went. We had to press for the speedy clearance of the Canal. We had to try to use our possession of twenty-three miles of it as a gauge, first for agreement on the system of its future operation, and second for a positive approach to an Arab-Israeli settlement.

In some respects, we had not such a bad hand to play. Nasser had been soundly beaten. We were in limited possession. We had more friends that dared avow themselves. On the other hand, perhaps we had exposed our realisation of our weaknesses too frankly to Eisenhower and Dulles in Washington the previous January. They knew that we knew that economically we were very poorly placed. That was not a strong bargaining position.

As to personalities, I knew that Spaak among our European allies would be a redoubtable friend. In the Commonwealth Mike Pearson would prove the criticism of him by the Canadian Opposition to be absolutely wrong. Whatever he may have said publicly, he was a true friend in the private negotiations. I also pinned considerable hopes on Hammarskjöld, whose friendship for Britain has been underrated, whatever may have been said about him by our friends or enemies.

When I arrived in New York on 12th November I was delighted to find Dixon and the delegation in very good form. In a tricky situation they really had been a credit to their country and done their duty with courage and dignity.

Soon after arrival I had lunch with Pearson, the Australians Casey and Walker, and Macdonald of New Zealand. Again there was no lack of friendship and support. All of them obviously thought that I was in for a difficult time but the only thing that mattered was how they could help. They told me that the Egyptians were determined to prevent the UNEF being effective. On its composition the Egyptians would object to any Commonwealth country, or any country with which we had a treaty relationship, providing a contingent. Pearson said that he and Hammarskjöld were determined to defeat them on this.

I started at once on my theme that we must drive it into the heads of the Americans that the presence of Anglo-French forces in Port Said was the only bargaining counter we had with Nasser or the Soviet.

I was told that relations between the United States and

United Kingdom delegations were thawing, and when I received very soon after arrival an invitation from Cabot Lodge to dine with him the following evening, I realised that perhaps they were not quite as bad as reported.

That same day, 12th November, Egypt accepted the stationing of UNEF troops in Egypt. But the I.P.C. pipeline was blown up in north Jordan. This almost isolated act of retaliation did not take place until several days after the cease-fire, when its perpetrators knew that they would be safe.

I also had a long talk with Hammarskjöld. There were no recriminations. Brian Urquhart, who was a close associate of his at the United Nations, and later himself Assistant Secretary-General, wrote his account of Hammarskjöld's years at the United Nations after complete access to his private papers. In parenthesis, I add that I had first met Brian when he was a Brigade Intelligence Officer in the 43rd Wessex Division in April 1941. I was G.S.O.II. He later served with distinction in the Parachute Corps. In the copy of Brian's book about Hammarskjöld which he gave me, he wrote, 'To Selwyn Lloyd whom Hammarskjöld prized as a colleague and cherished as a friend in difficult times as well as good ones'. That I believe was the truth. I had a high regard for him, far exceeding that of many people in Britain at the time. As I have said, he was a much better friend than has been acknowledged.

At this meeting on 12th November he told me that he was determined to make a reality of the UNEF. He wanted Scandinavian and Canadian contingents in it and the Egyptians had agreed to the former. I told him that our agreement to the cease-fire was based on his report and his resolution of 2nd November. The UNEF must be effective; it must supervise the cessation of hostilities and prevent their resumption; it must see that the obstructions in the Canal were removed. I said that unless all this was assured we would not remove our troops. Hammarskjöld said that he was full of distrust of Egyptian intentions over the UNEF, but he was determined to make it a success. He was leaving for Cairo on the next day, the 13th.

That night I had a quiet dinner with the Caseys. Although
Casey differed from Menzies over Suez, he was very friendly
and anxious to help.

The 13th was a day of non-stop activities. I had two long
talks with Hammarskjöld. He had delayed his departure for
Cairo for twenty-four hours. He hoped to get Nasser to agree
to the constitution of the UNEF on the basis wished by
Hammarskjöld and including a Canadian contingent. The
emergency force should initially be based on the Canal. Its
task should be to supervise the cessation of hostilities and
prevent their recurrence. The heads of an agreement to cover
the future operation of the Canal should be negotiated forth-
with. This would cover its clearance. The emergency force
should continue in existence until the present situation had been
'liquidated'.

He admitted that he was having difficulty with the Egyptians.
There were malignant forces at work, not necessarily Soviet.
Krishna Menon was doing all he could to persuade the Egyptians not to allow the force into Egypt and to cut down
Hammarskjöld's own position. I think that I persuaded him
that the presence of Anglo-French forces in Port Said was his
strongest card. He said that officially his attitude must be that
we should withdraw in accordance with the Assembly resolution, although he acknowledged that there was a lot to be
agreed before we actually pulled out.

Lange and Engen of Norway came to lunch. They were much
more understanding of our position than I had expected.
Although disapproving of our actions, they were more concerned about the future and promised to be as helpful as they
could be in the circumstances.

Later I saw Eban, the Israeli Permanent Representative at
the United Nations. He spoke of the vast quantities of arms and
equipment captured in Sinai, and of documents found there
showing Egyptian intentions to launch a full-scale war (see the
Egyptian operation orders cited on pp. 34–5). He realised that
Israel would have to withdraw in time from Sinai. He hoped

that they would be able to retain the Gaza strip, accepting the duty to resettle perhaps half of the Arab refugees then there. I assured him of the importance which we attached to freedom of passage for Israeli ships through the Gulf of Aqaba to Eilat.

I then had a long talk with Pearson. As I reported to London at the end of the day, I felt that the project for a satisfactory UNEF was in the melting pot. The Afro-Asians were realising more and more that it would constitute a victory for us. They were trying to make its composition unsatisfactory to us, limit its functions and subject it to Egyptian authority. There were, however, strong elements including Pearson and Hammar-skjöld, fighting hard on our side.

Then came the dinner party with Lodge. He started on a high moral note. He had been deeply pained by our behaviour. It had been aggressive and was indefensible. I said that I completely disagreed with him. Protection of our national interests in the Canal was self-defence. We had certainly stopped Syria and Jordan coming into the fight, and perhaps others. As for moral guilt, what about Guatemala? Had not the United States acted there in 1954 in precisely the same way? The only difference was that then we had tried to help the United States in the Security Council in spite of the pressures on us. I then deployed the case about Russian penetration of the Middle East, the advantage to the West of Nasser's military defeat, and the opportunity to build up an effective UNEF. When he admitted his anxiety about Russian penetration, I said that I was equally worried about United States efforts to drive us out prematurely. It was not in the interests of the West for our operation to be judged a failure. I added that if the United States had not led the hunt against us in the United Nations, we would have had a brilliant success by then and Nasser would have gone. The talks after dinner lasted about two hours. Lodge's two advisers, Wadsworth and Barco, hardly said a word. Lodge was friendly but non-committal. He obviously did not like what I said about Guatemala or the United States leading the hunt against us. Dixon thought that the American attitude was improving, but we both knew that we still had a long way to go. Lodge suggested that I should go to see Dulles in Washington.

I got to bed at about 2 a.m. It had been an exhausting but not unsatisfactory day.

On the following day, 14th November, I had another long talk with Hammarskjöld. He had received the all-clear for his visit to Cairo. On clearance of the Canal, although he hoped to get an agreement with Nasser, he did not believe that Nasser would allow it to take effect until we had withdrawn, nor did he think that Nasser would negotiate about the operating of the Canal in the future until we had gone. I said that the point upon which we must be adamant was that there must be agreements about clearance and operating the Canal in the future before the UNEF was withdrawn. Hammarskjöld agreed and said it would be 'unthinkable' for the UNEF to be withdrawn before those agreements. He pressed strongly that we should improve the atmosphere by a token withdrawal. He also gave me a personal letter which added little to what he had discussed. He expected to be back on Monday, the 19th.

I decided to go to Washington at the weekend. Meanwhile, I saw Pineau, Luns and Martino, did a television programme and had a talk with Bunche, who was in charge of organising the UNEF. There had been many offers of contingents. So far, over 4,000 men had been accepted. I warned him of obstruction from Nasser. Bunche thought that Hammarskjöld and the general enthusiasm for the establishment of the force would override Nasser's objections. I also saw Mrs Golda Meir, the Israeli Foreign Minister. We covered a lot of ground in our talk. I found her the easiest Israeli with whom to deal since Sharrett's resignation. Dissatisfaction with the American attitude was our common theme. The vanguard of the UNEF had landed in Ismailia during the week. There had been signs of trouble in Port Said between the local population and British troops, stirred up by Nasser.

I flew to Washington on the Saturday morning. I had said

that I hoped to see the President, but never thought it likely to happen. There were about forty Foreign Ministers in the United States at the time. If he saw me, there were many others whom he could not refuse to see. The real reason for my going was to follow up Lodge's suggestion that I should see Dulles. I thought it politic to do this and offer my good wishes for his recovery. He had said that he would like to see me. I was to be his first visitor.

Caccia and I went to the Walter Reed Hospital. Dulles was up and dressed, with Hoover, and I think a nurse, also in the room. Dulles said at once with a kind of twinkle in his eye, 'Selwyn, why did you stop? Why didn't you go through with it and get Nasser down?' If ever there was an occasion when one could have been knocked down by the proverbial feather, this was it. Dulles was the man who had led the pack against us, supported the transfer of the matter from the Security Council to the General Assembly and pulled out every stop to defeat us. And here he was asking why we had stopped. I replied, and Caccia bears this out, 'Well, Foster, if you had so much as winked at us we might have gone on.' Dulles replied that he could not have done that. Coral Bell in her book *The Debatable Alliance** describes this incident as 'apocryphal'. Fortunately Caccia was there, too, and standing right beside me, a completely disinterested witness who had had nothing to do with the Suez operation; the story does not rest upon my unsupported testimony.

Dulles was friendly, but whenever any possible action by the United States was raised he said that he was ill and Hoover must decide. About what had happened, he said that the only difference between us had been over method and he deplored the fact that we had not brought down Nasser. He did not appear to be prepared to discuss matters like clearance of the Canal. That was for Hoover and Hammarskjöld.

While I was in Washington I saw Loy Henderson. He was friendly but said that he was without influence. He thought that we were unlikely to have peace in the Middle East while Nasser

* Chatham House Essays, R.I.I.A./O.U.P., 1964.

remained. It would be a disaster if we pulled out and were
replaced by a UNEF subject to Nasser's dictation. I next met
Allen Dulles, Foster's brother and head of the C.I.A. I asked
him point-blank whether he thought that, if we had given
Eisenhower more warning of our intention to move in, his
reactions would have been less violent. Allen Dulles doubted
this. Eisenhower would have protested vigorously, and we
would have gone ahead against his declared wishes. This would
have been worse. As it was, Allen Dulles thought that American
resentment was dying down.

The next morning I saw Bedell Smith. He said that Eisenhower had been very upset. Bedell was afraid that our action
had caused a deep wound. I stressed the importance of our
military presence in Port Said being used to influence future
events. We must not throw away our main bargaining weapon.
The United States, by insisting on our unconditional withdrawal, were doing just this. Bedell seemed to be impressed and
said that he would have a go at Eisenhower and let me know
the result.

After Bedell Smith, Air Chief Marshal William Elliot came
to see me. He had held important commands in the war and
had ended his military career as chairman of the British Joint
Services Mission in Washington and United Kingdom
Representative on the Standing Group of the NATO Military
Committee. There was a close friendship between him and
Eisenhower. He had come to tell me about an interview which
he had recently had with Eisenhower. He had found him looking extremely well. He bore no resentment at all against the
British and was determined to mend the alliance again. The real
enemy was the Soviet Union. Elliot told me that he had heard
that at a meeting of the American National Security Council,
Eisenhower was the only one to stand up for the Anglo-
American alliance. Eisenhower had talked to Elliot about his
foreknowledge of our plans. He had realised that at some time
we intended to strike against Nasser, but had not thought that
it would be so soon. He had thought that it would have been

after the American elections. Eisenhower spoke of his difficulties. He could not take sides. Elliot's conclusion was that nothing like as much harm had been done to Anglo-American relations as the pessimists made out, but the President was the only person who mattered. There was no one near him, except for Dulles, who could help. That was why Dulles's illness had been a misfortune both for him and for us.

Between these two views, the one that Eisenhower was deeply wounded and the other that he bore no resentment, lay a deep divide. In favour of the second thesis was the fact that, when Caccia presented his credentials as our new Ambassador, Eisenhower had greeted him with great affability. Nor did Dulles's reception of me look like a deep wound. Nevertheless, some of our oldest friends in the United States stuck to the theory that Eisenhower had been deeply wounded. I have no certain feelings as to where the truth lay. I suspect that he was extremely angry that, in the last days of his campaign, the commander of what he regarded as one of his subordinate units had acted contrary to his orders. When the election was over and he had won his sweeping victory, his wrath evaporated more quickly than that of certain people in the State Department.

However that may be, he would not accept our view about our withdrawal. Bedell later came to see me again in some distress. He had done his best but had made no progress with Eisenhower: it had to be an unconditional withdrawal.

My interview with Dulles and these reports of Eisenhower's attitude left me completely baffled. I decided that there was nothing for me to do but go back to New York and do my best with Hammarskjöld, using such help as I could get.

Hammarskjöld returned from Cairo on the Monday, 19th November, and Pearson was the first to give me an account of what had happened there. Hammarskjöld had found Nasser cocky and complacent, and very difficult to deal with. Hammarskjöld was worried, Pearson said, about three things: further trouble in Port Said might give Nasser an excuse for

calling in the Russians; the British and French might be so
dissatisfied with the arrangements made that they would refuse
to go; the Israelis might dig in where they were and refuse to
withdraw.

Later I saw Hammarskjöld himself. He seemed exhausted
but without doubt he had made some progress. On the UNEF
it was clear that our requirements were going to be met. Its
composition would be for him to decide, not for Nasser. It
would be based initially on the Canal. It would stay until its
tasks, as laid down, had been accomplished.

It also seemed to be assumed that there would be no gap
between the withdrawal of our troops and the arrival of the
UNEF. This was a point upon which I had been very distrustful
of Nasser. One of my principal reasons for coming down at that
Cabinet on 4th November in favour of our landing at Port
Said was my belief that, if we did not establish a presence there,
Nasser would never allow us the UNEF. I felt just the same
about our withdrawal. I told Hammarskjöld, without wanting
to be histrionic, that for every platoon of the UNEF that was
landed, we would withdraw a platoon of our troops. It soon
became clear that that was a point upon which we had
established our case.

The next matter in dispute was the clearance of the Canal.
We had an effective salvage fleet to hand. It had done yeoman
work clearing the part of the Canal under our control and Port
Said itself. Nasser refused to allow it to be used to clear the rest
of the Canal. It was cutting off his nose to spite his face, because
it was in his own financial interest to have the Canal open to
traffic as soon as possible. The weakness in our position was that
although we had the salvage fleet under our control time was
not on our side. Macmillan had told the House of Commons on
12th November that we had lost 328 million dollars from our
reserves during the three months up to the end of October.
These figures seem minuscule according to present-day
standards, but then, when rather different views were taken
about inflation and the strength of our currency, they were

'I suppose you're having to send all the No. 11's
round by the Cape!'

important. It was necessary for us to exercise our drawing rights upon the International Monetary Fund if we were to preserve the value of the pound. We had to find the best formula to clear the Canal as quickly as we could. It ended very unsatisfactorily. Some use of our salvage fleet was to be made but under some rather futile restrictions imposed by Nasser.

We had achieved reasonable arrangements about the composition of the UNEF, its area of operation, its responsibilities and its duration. The arrangement about the clearance of the Canal was thoroughly unsatisfactory but the best obtainable. Three further matters were left to be settled.

The first was the possibility of Nasser discriminating against British and French shipping once we had withdrawn and when the Canal was open again. That was later cleared up when we obtained from Nasser through Hammarskjöld a categoric statement that there would be no discrimination against us.

The second was the method of operating the Canal in the future. Nasser refused to negotiate about this until we had withdrawn, but Hammarskjöld was empowered to say to us that the Egyptian Government would not withdraw from any of the undertakings which it had been prepared to give in October. In the event, the end result was rather better than that, but we had to rely upon Hammarskjöld's influence to ensure it.

The third problem was the timing of the withdrawal. On that the Assembly was determined to take a hand. When Hammarskjöld's reports were debated on 23rd November, I spoke to the Assembly for the first time since my arrival.

It was not an unfriendly audience. I dealt with the UNEF, the withdrawal of British troops and the clearance of the Canal. I began:

> Over the past few years the United Nations, whether in the Assembly or the Security Council, has completely failed, so far as the Middle East is concerned, either to keep the peace or to procure compliance with its own

resolutions, or to pave the way for final settlement. I am not criticising, I am stating a fact. That fact is the greatest reason, the principal reason, for what took place on 29th and 30th October.

I then denied the allegation that we had instigated the Israeli attack and went on:

> Whatever may be thought of our actions or our motives, out of the painful discussions regarding them there has come the idea of a United Nations Force, the idea that the United Nations should act through an international force. The idea was first mooted by Sir Anthony Eden in his speech before the British Parliament on 1st November, when he said that if the United Nations were willing to take over the physical task of maintaining peace in the area, then no one would be better pleased than the British. That statement of the Prime Minister's was immediately repeated in the General Assembly by Sir Pierson Dixon. Mr. Pearson, the Canadian Secretary of State for External Affairs, referred to it at the same meeting and he introduced the draft resolution for establishing the Force. After that, the concept of an international force gained rapid acceptance. Many nations have offered contingents.

I referred to the untiring work of Hammarskjöld and his staff, and the start already made in bringing advance parties into Egypt. I described our help for the Norwegian-Danish unit in Port Said, and the assistance to the Yugoslav contingent in disembarkation and transit. We were ready, if needed, to provide transport for the Indian battalion and for the Norwegian medical company, and to provide medical supplies and food for the UNEF. With regard to its tasks, I asserted our confidence in Hammarskjöld and our belief that the General Assembly would in good faith see that the emergency force was effective, and competent to carry out the tasks laid upon it by the resolutions of 2nd, 5th and 7th November.

I next dealt with the withdrawal of our troops. Many representatives had said in the U.N. debate that the word 'immediate' in the resolutions' call for withdrawal did not mean instantaneous. I quoted Lodge's reference to a phased withdrawal and the connection stated by him and Pearson between the arrival of the international force and the withdrawal of our troops. I said that we had given orders for the immediate withdrawal of one battalion to show the sincerity of our intentions. I continued:

I hope that members of this Assembly will realise that in taking up this position on withdrawal, the British Government have asked the British people to endorse an act of faith. We believe—and whether you agree with us or not, we believe it sincerely—that we stopped a small war from spreading into a larger war. We believe that we have created the conditions under which a United Nations force is to be introduced into this troubled area to establish and maintain peace, and we believe that thereby we have given this Assembly and the world another opportunity to settle the problems of the area. We believe that we have brought matters to a head, to a crisis, that we have cast down a challenge to world statesmanship, the statesmanship of this Assembly to achieve results. We think that there is in this a great test for the United Nations and for the powers on whose continued support the United Nations ultimately depends. We are therefore prepared to make this act of faith because we believe that the United Nations has the will to ensure that the UNEF will effectively and honourably carry out the functions laid down for it in the Assembly resolution. But should our faith prove to have been misplaced, should all this effort and disturbance have been for nothing, should the United Nations fail to show the necessary will-power to procure the lasting settlement required, then indeed there will be cause for alarm and despondency.

I then dealt with the clearance of the Canal, expressing full support for Hammarskjöld's efforts to organise a salvage team and offering to release any salvage ships then on charter to the Admiralty. I told the Assembly how much we had already achieved. When I left the rostrum I was genuinely surprised at the warmth of the applause.

Certain delegations, however, were determined to press to a vote the resolution censuring us. Spaak drafted an amendment which called upon us to expedite the application of the resolutions of 2nd and 7th November and urged us to withdraw in the spirit in which those resolutions were adopted, particularly with regard to the functions vested in the UNEF. It omitted the censure of us.

I had a talk with Lodge, stressing the importance to us of the amendment. I said that if the amendment was carried I would vote for the resolution so amended. Lodge said that he thought that the United States could also support the amendment and vote for it. I made a second intervention in the Assembly, repeating that if the amendment was passed I would vote for the resolution as a whole.

I was followed by Menon, who delivered a vitriolic attack, full of poisonous abuse. It certainly had an emotional effect upon the audience, but it was of indirect benefit. It was too extravagant even for those most opposed to us, and it appeared to drain him of vitriol for the time being. He was not much trouble after that outburst. I think that the truth was that he had shot his bolt with almost every delegation.

When the vote was taken, Lodge abstained, much to my disappointment. The result was 23 in favour of the amendment, 37 against and 18 abstentions. If Lodge had voted for the amendment, most of the other abstainers would have done the same and the amendment would have been carried. When I saw him afterwards he said rather shamefacedly that Washington would not allow him to vote for it. When Caccia spoke to Murphy about it in Washington, Murphy said that the United States was 'the prisoner of its own policy'.

The resolution, unamended, was carried by 63 votes to 5, with 10 abstentions. The resolution dealing with the basis for the presence and functioning of the UNEF and the clearing of the Canal was then put to the vote and approved by 65 votes to nil, with 9 abstentions. The United Kingdom voted for it.

After the resolution had been voted upon, Pearson, Casey and Macdonald came to see me. Casey and Macdonald were philosophic about the voting, as I was. I thought that it indicated an improved mood in the Assembly. Pearson, however, was upset and angry with Menon. In a few minutes Hammarskjöld joined us. He felt that his hand had been greatly strengthened by the fact that no votes had been cast against the resolution dealing with the clearing of the Canal. We then discussed a possible date for our withdrawal. I thought that four weeks was about right. It would take that for the UNEF to become capable of operating. Hammarskjöld thought it was too long. But he thought that he could work something out with Fawzi.

I saw him again on the following day, 24th November. He had seen Fawzi and made progress. Work on clearing the Canal could start the day after the Anglo-French troops left. Meanwhile, all the 'desk' work could proceed—survey, planning, etc. Negotiations about the future of the Canal could begin as soon as we had gone. The next step was for us to fix a date. By 5th December there would be 4,100 United Nations troops in Egypt.

I sent a message home to the effect that I did not think that we would get better terms, and the quicker we withdrew the more credit would we get in New York. Throughout this difficult fortnight I had consistent support and encouragement from my colleagues. But I think that they were a little taken aback by a final talk which I had with Hammarskjöld, in which I took a calculated risk. I said to him that I thought that between us we might be able to fix a kind of package deal. We would agree to be out in about fifteen days' time. The UNEF must be built up certainly to twice its then size of about 4,000. Discussions on the future operation of the Canal would proceed on the basis of

Hammarskjöld's letter of 24th October and Fawzi's reply (see p. 179). Clearance would proceed *pari passu* with our withdrawal. There must be an assurance that the Egyptian expulsion order against British nationals would not be carried out. As soon as I mentioned fifteen days as a possible time for withdrawal, Hammarskjöld became quite enthusiastic about the package. I did not think that he would get all that we wanted, particularly on the clearance point, but it was an amalgam which made our withdrawal a feasible proposition to put to the Cabinet and carry our party with it.

I think that the colleagues were worried about the fifteen days, but I felt reasonably certain that it would take a good deal longer for the UNEF to be organised.

At this point I must pay my tribute to Hammarskjöld as a negotiator. Unless Dixon and I had known him so well, and his infinite resourcefulness with words, there might have been misunderstandings. My serious anxiety was that he would physically collapse under the strain. He himself said at one stage that the arrangements were becoming metaphysical in their subtlety. There had to be a combination of one-sided but interlocking declarations. Egypt's right to request the withdrawal of the force was interlocked into an undertaking from Egypt not to make such a request until the force's tasks had been completed. It all depended on good faith. The suggestion made by some that at this stage it was British policy to try to discredit the United Nations and Hammarskjöld is quite false. It was clear that he knew of my difficulties and did an excellent job as intermediary, in addition to his other responsibilities. If he or I had tried to be too specific at any one point, there might have been no agreement at all.

Though the agreement was less than we had wanted, it was not to Nasser's liking either. On p. 193 of his book, *Hammarskjöld*,* Brian Urquhart, quoting a private *aide-mémoire* of the Secretary-General, says:

* Knopf, New York, 1972.

According to Hammarskjöld, Nasser had recognised that even the 'good faith' agreement had serious implications for Egypt's freedom of action. The definition of UNEF's task was extremely loose and would, in the event of a disagreement, have to be interpreted by the General Assembly. Nasser realised that in accepting it he had agreed to 'a far-reaching and unpredictable restriction'.

More than ten years were to pass before Nasser sent his troops to take over the UNEF posts in Sinai, and then request U Thant, Hammarskjöld's successor, to withdraw the U.N. force. The UNEF Advisory Committee, to whom the question was referred in 1967, did not put it to the General Assembly: the Secretary-General concurred in the Egyptian request and was criticised for doing so.

During my last week in New York there were various happenings at home. Eden was ordered to rest, but it was hoped that after three weeks in the sun in Jamaica he would be fully restored to health. He had been fit and well until a bout of fever early in October but he had never quite recovered his strength since then. That was sad news.

On a more cheerful note. I had been touched by the widespread demonstrations of understanding and support from many individual Americans, commentators and writers. This was highlighted for me on two occasions. The Pilgrims of the United States gave a dinner for me on 20th November. Hugh Bullock was in the chair. Averell Harriman, then Governor of New York State, spoke first and critically of the United States Government's recent behaviour. I followed him and ended my speech:

I think that we have run great risks and we have made great sacrifices. We willingly accepted them because we believed that what we did was right and in the cause of ultimate peace and stability. And, you know, there comes a time when men and when Governments have to decide to act and not to talk. We decided to act. And I think the world has been shown once again that we have the will-power and the courage to take action when the need arises. I am certainly not ashamed of and I don't seek to shirk my share of responsibility in this matter. But whether you agree with what we did or not, I think you must agree that we have created a situation of great opportunity. By that I mean that war has been rapidly stopped; an international force has been created, and the Russian penetration has been unmasked. And this situation I believe can be turned to good account by the free world. It is a situation which may not recur. I would ask you and your countrymen just to ponder on the consequences of failing to take this oppor-tunity. That is why, whatever may be thought of the past, I would say to you, let us — the United States, Britain and the countries of the Commonwealth — now once again press forward together with firmness and with resolution to use that opportunity and to preserve the gains, the not inconsiderable gains.

I was also invited to speak on 26th November at a dinner given by the English Speaking Union at which General Gruenther was the guest of honour. I made a strong attack upon American anti-colonialism, pointing out that in the previous ten years or so over 600 million people had, with our support and assistance, attained independence. I referred to our objectives in the Middle East and reaffirmed our intention to co-operate with the United Nations over the withdrawal of our forces, the support of the UNEF and in seeking the objectives contained in the U.N. resolutions. I ended:

I know that that is also the policy of the United States Government. I did however read the other day some wise words:

'The United Nations cannot do everything. Its uses

are limited by its nature. It is not a substitute for United States foreign policy and its activities cannot relieve the United States of major responsibilities of its own.'

Wise words written in 1950 by Mr John Foster Dulles and even more appropriate today and applicable to all of us.

After both the speech at the Pilgrims dinner and this one, I was given standing ovations. I mention this not out of vanity but to show the warmth of feeling towards Britain by two gatherings, large in numbers but also noteworthy for those attending them.

Much more significant than anything that I could say or do was a statement by Eisenhower on 27th November reasserting the importance which he attached to the United States's friendship with Britain and France.

I flew back across the Atlantic on the night of 27th November. My aircraft was late but I was decanted safely at Heathrow on the 28th. I had no illusions about what lay before me. I had been splendidly supported by Butler acting for Eden while he was away and by the Cabinet as a whole, but I expected the worst. At the first meeting of the Cabinet that afternoon I said that I thought that I ought to offer my resignation. I had gone to the United States to try to convince them of the folly of throwing away our bargaining counter, the possession of twenty-three miles of the Canal. I had failed. Was it not better that I should resign? The expression on the faces of the colleagues needed some interpretation. One or two were clearly doubtful of my motives. All were against it. I was not surprised but I was genuine in making the offer. I reported in more detail on my latest dealings with Hammarskjöld. It was decided that I should make a holding statement to the House in the afternoon of 29th to give time for discussions with the French, and that I should inform the House of the Government's final decisions on the following Monday, 3rd December.

In my first statement I gave a brief account of the atmosphere in New York and said that Pineau was coming over the next day for consultations. I would make a further statement on the Monday to announce the definite decisions taken. I was questioned mainly about our intentions with regard to the withdrawal of our troops, and whether it was intended to keep them there until the Canal had been cleared and a settlement reached on its future operation. I was not, however, unduly pressed.

Afterwards I went to a meeting of the Conservative 1922 Committee. I have kept my notes of what I said at this meeting and one of the Foreign Affairs Committee later that evening. I tried to cover the ground as concisely as possible: why we had acted, why we had stopped, and the state of our discussions at the United Nations and with the United States Government. We were in no doubt about their strong feelings on clearance of the Canal and its future operation. I ended the first meeting by saying, 'Whatever is decided, do not let us by too much controversy among ourselves destroy the benefits of what has been achieved.' At these meetings and other private talks with Conservative Members, I said again and again that we had to decide whether our continued presence in Port Said was an asset or a liability, and that in my view it was a liability. The passage of time is bound to soften recollections and tends to make one sentimentalise situations. But my memories of this time are that, although sharp things were said about policy decisions, I was shown much personal kindness and friendship. They seemed to know that I had an extremely difficult hand to play and was doing it as best I could. From the Opposition it would have been too much to expect similar treatment, but I pay sincere tribute to Nye Bevan. He appeared to understand my difficulties better than a great many others.

The decision to withdraw was by now inevitable. George Humphrey, the United States Secretary to the Treasury, was on very friendly terms with Butler, but he made it absolutely clear to Butler that the United States Government would not move to help us financially or in any other way until we had announced our decision to withdraw. The French Government, sadly disappointed by events, agreed that there was nothing to be gained by hanging on in Port Said any longer. I announced on 3rd December the Cabinet decision that our forces would be withdrawn on a timetable to be agreed between Keightley and Burns, the UNEF commander. There was a disagreeable debate in the House on 5th and 6th December, but the Opposition's censure of the Government was defeated by 327 to 260. This debate simply went over the old areas of party dispute and recrimination. One significant contribution from my point of view was that of Patrick Spens, a lawyer of wide experience, who strongly supported Goodhart's view about the use of force.

Charles Waterhouse, leader of the 'Suez Group' in the House, which had supported the military operation and opposed the withdrawal, made a sad but moving speech explaining why he could not support the Government in the division lobby, but he was even more critical of the Opposition.

There was a NATO meeting in Paris from 9th to 15th December. Dulles, with that physical courage which he never lacked, came although he had had little time to recuperate after his operation. I had some long talks with him in private. He already seemed to be on the defensive, realising how badly matters had been handled when he was ill. However, he defended his own decisions. He did not see how, if he had acquiesced in our use of force, a world order could be established. It would be disastrous if nations thought that disputes could be settled by force. I restrained myself from reminding him of his speeches, and his constant statement that force was permissible as a last resort. He said that his actions had not been due to any love of the Egyptians. He had no confidence in Nasser.

I replied that I would not go over the old ground again. We had now to pick up the pieces. I firmly believed in Anglo-American friendship, and had been careful not to be critical of the United States Government in the statements about our withdrawal which I had recently been making in Parliament. But, before we finally withdrew, Dulles must help us to get satisfactory agreements over clearance and the future of the

Canal. He promised to do his best. He went on to say that if the United States Administration were to release us from our undertaking to withdraw, it would be a breach of faith on their part with Congress and United States public opinion. This annoyed me for two reasons. It was not true. Second, Hammarskjöld and the United Nations at this stage were doing their best to help. Dulles's remarks demonstrated the disregard for the United Nations which he showed when he was disposed to do so. However, there was no point in a violent argument with him at that time.

In the NATO Ministerial meeting, Dulles had to listen to some critical comments from some of those present. Later, he and his colleagues did their best to speed up the clearance of the Canal, with Hailsham, now First Lord of the Admiralty, making some spirited efforts to hurry things up.

On 5th December, the Anglo-French command began the first phase of withdrawal of troops from Egypt, and the last troops left on 22nd December, units of the Anglo-French salvage fleet remaining behind under U.N. authority. Clearance of the Canal began on 27th December. Meanwhile, the U.N. General Assembly continued its condemnation of the Russian invasion of Hungary two months earlier, but with no result. The double standard in international behaviour was never more clearly demonstrated.

The first four months of 1967 saw discussions about the clearance of the Canal, the establishment of the UNEF in place of Israeli troops in the Gaza Strip and in Sharm al-Shaikh, and the terms on which the Canal could be reopened. The best that can be said about the period is that it ended with some satisfactory results: the UNEF in Gaza and Sharm al-Shaikh (where it remained until the U.N. Secretary-General U Thant agreed to Nasser's request for its removal in 1967); and recognition by the United States, Britain and France that the entrance to the Gulf of Aqaba was an international waterway and therefore open to Israeli shipping. The Canal was at length cleared and

Hammarskjöld himself watched the last block ship being lifted on 25th March. The Canal was reopened on the basis of an Egyptian Declaration made on 4th April, communicated to Hammarskjöld and registered as a U.N. document. It re-affirmed Egypt's acceptance of the 1888 Convention and of co-operation between the Suez Canal authority and represen-tatives of shipping and trade. It provided that tolls should not be increased by more than 1 per cent in any period of twelve months except through negotiation. If no agreement could be reached, there should be settlement by arbitration. From all gross receipts, 25 per cent was to be set aside for development and capital expenditure. The Canal Code, covering the opera-tion of the Canal, could continue in operation. There were various provisions for disputes to be settled by arbitration, and Egypt for the first time accepted in these matters the compul-sory jurisdiction of the International Court of Justice.

Meanwhile we had suffered the shock of Eden's resignation. He had appeared to be restored to health and strength when he returned from Jamaica on 14th December and resumed his duties. He had stood up well to noisy debates in the House before the Recess.

A Cabinet was called for 8th January to consider our strategy, and was to meet throughout the day. I had done some prepara-tory work for it. My theme was that, after the serious difference of opinion with the United States, we must try to make Western Europe less dependent upon America. I did not get much sympathy from my colleagues. Most of them thought that the first priority must be the mending of our fences with the United States.

Towards the end of the morning meeting Eden said that the discussion must continue in the afternoon without him. He had to go to Sandringham. There was some barrack-room language from one of my colleagues, who thought it was unreasonable and inconsiderate to break off the discussion in this way. Neither he nor I had any idea of the reason for Eden's visit to see the Queen.

We met again at 5 p.m. on 9th January, Eden's last Cabinet. It was a sad and moving occasion.

Nothing that I have heard or read about him since January 1957 has diminished my affection or respect for him. He had a 'temperament', as Caccia put it in his tribute to Eden. He was immensely hardworking. He liked being Foreign Secretary because of the huge columns of telegrams and dispatches which he had to read. He was very sensitive to criticism; but I did not find it difficult to work for him. He could be irritated by details, but when important decisions had to be taken, he was calm and not averse to discussion and argument. To the end he believed he had been right over Suez, and his anxiety was not about his personal position or reputation but about whether he had done the right thing for the country.

Chapter XIV

Was it Wrong?
The Critics Answered

Was the use of force illegal? — Was there collusion?

In this chapter I shall deal with the two main criticisms made at the time and since of the British Government's action over Suez.

I have already dealt with the question whether the nationalisation of the Canal was illegal, in particular on pp. 92–3, 103, and 137 and in Appendix III. The non-competence of the International Court of Justice is dealt with on pp. 40 ff. We were not seriously challenged in the country on these issues. But from early in August there had been argument about our right to use force and the circumstances in which the use of force would be justified. *The Times* newspaper had begun the discussion with a forthright leading article on 1st August dealing with Nasser's actions:

> Quibbling over whether or not he was 'legally entitled' to make the grab will delight the finicky and comfort the faint-hearted, but entirely misses the real issues. If Nasser gets away with it, all the British and all Western interest in the Middle East will crumble. Compare Hitler's march into the Rhineland or the Stalinist overthrow of freedom in Czechoslovakia. Freedom of passage through the Suez Canal, in peace or war, is a prime Western interest. That freedom can be assured only if the Canal is in friendly and trustworthy hands. Nasser's actions prove that he is both

unfriendly and untrustworthy. There can be no stability and confidence in the world so long as agreements can be scrapped with impunity.

Nasser's actions were certainly in breach of international law. But was the contention right that force can only be used if approved by the United Nations? Goodhart had disputed this from the beginning. In his letter to *The Times* on 11th August he rejected the idea that force could only be used to repel a direct territorial attack. A state may take all necessary steps to protect the lives of its citizens abroad. Similarly, it may use force to protect a vital national interest which has been imperilled. In such a case it is the state which has altered the *status quo* which is guilty of aggression.

In the House of Lords debate on 12th September, McNair followed up his condemnation of Egypt for a breach of international law, to which I have already referred, by saying that during the past fifty years there had been a transformation of the law relating to the use of force. A country could still use force to protect itself or to protect its nationals when the local authorities were unable to do so. But he maintained that force was no longer a discretionary instrument of policy; its use was regulated by law. He based that, first, on the Kellogg Pact, in which the contracting parties had renounced the use of force. He admitted, however, that that did not go the whole way so far as Britain was concerned because Austen Chamberlain as Foreign Secretary had excluded from the operation of the pact those regions of the world whose welfare and integrity constituted a special and vital interest to our peace and safety. I do not see how anyone could dispute that the Canal and its operation came within that exception.

McNair also referred to Articles 2 and 4 of the U.N. Charter. The use of force was only permissible in self-defence or pursuant to some collective security act, endorsed by the Security Council, as had happened with Korea.

Kilmuir on the other hand maintained from the beginning

that we were entitled to use force under Article 51 of the Charter in self-defence. Menzies made an important contribution to the argument in a speech in the Australian House of Commons on 25th September. He put the use by us of force in proper perspective. He said that one view was that force should have been used at once, but that was out of harmony with modern thinking. Referring to the other view that force can never be employed (except presumably in self-defence) except by and pursuant to a decision of the United Nations Security Council, he added:

> This I would regard as a suicidal doctrine for, having regard to the veto, it would mean that no force could ever be exercised against any friend of the Soviet Union except with the approval of the Soviet Union, which is absurd ... The truth is that in a world not based on academic principles, a world deeply affected by enlightened self-interest and the instinct of survival, but nevertheless a world struggling to make an organisation for peace effective, force (except in self-defence) is never to be the first resort, but the right to employ it cannot be completely abandoned or made subject to impossible conditions.

He finished:

> Surely our task is not merely to prevent hostilities but to build up a firm order of law and decency in which 'smash and grab' tactics do not pay. We must avoid the use of force if we can. But we should not, by theoretical reasoning in advance of the facts and circumstances, contract ourselves out of its use, whatever those facts and circumstances may be.

Dulles himself had expressly or impliedly accepted the Menzies arguments over and over again if a reasonable interpretation is put upon his words. The United States had shown its acceptance of the Menzies doctrine by the decision to act in Korea: that decision was taken before the Security Council had approved it. The Security Council did approve it soon afterwards, but that was solely due to the fortuitous absence of the Soviet Union from the Council meeting. I and many others believe that the Soviet presence at the meeting and a Soviet veto would have made no difference to the United States's actions, and the General Assembly, where no veto applied, had no power under the Charter to authorise the use of force. The United States's actions in Guatemala in 1954 and elsewhere had shown what they thought, where their interests were concerned, of this theoretical excommunication of the use of force.

Dulles had constantly said that force should be used as a last resort. That must have meant that he regarded it as permissible in certain circumstances. For example, at the SCUA meeting on 23rd September he had said:

Peace and justice in international law are two sides of the coin, and you cannot always count on nations not using force unless there is some alternative which conforms to international peace and justice ... unless we can work out some system here which is just ... then I don't think that you can expect to go on for ever asking people not to resort to force.

In his speech at Dallas, Texas, on 28th October, he had said:*

It seemed to us in the beginning that any solution should take account of two basic facts. One is that an international waterway like the Suez Canal which has always had an international status, cannot properly be made an instrument of any government's national policies so that equal passage may depend on that government's favour.

That does not require Egypt to forgo the rights which are normal to it as the sovereign nation through whose territory this international waterway passes. It does mean that Egypt should not be in a position to exercise such

* U.S. Department of State Bulletin, 5th November 1956, pp. 695 ff.

arbitrary power, open or devious, over the operations of this international waterway that the nations dependent on the Canal would, in effect, be living under an economic sword of Damocles. That would be an intolerable state of affairs. It would be inconsistent with the United Nations Charter requirement that these situations must be dealt with in conformity with the principles of justice and international law.

No doubt the Texans listening thought at once of the Panama Canal, but they would get the point that a vital international waterway could not be subject to the likes or dislikes of the local dictator. If the Panama Canal had been seized, and if the United States had spent three months patiently seeking a peaceful settlement, I have little doubt that the Texan audience would have deduced from Dulles's language that force was permissible.

On this allegation that we had flouted the United Nations and acted in a manner inconsistent with international law, we received reassuring support from Professor Gilbert Murray. He was an outstanding Liberal thinker, an internationalist, a dedicated supporter of the League of Nations and the United Nations. At one time he was President of the United Nations Association. He wrote a letter with certain Oxford colleagues to the *Daily Telegraph* on 7th November in these terms:

The Press has already publicised a petition signed by a large number of Oxford dons in which the Government is accused of disregarding international morality and its Middle East activities condemned. We feel that in the present mood of strained emotions such a petition is inappropriate and it must not be regarded as fully representative of the views of senior members of the University.

The situation in the Middle East is so confused that there is obviously scope for marked differences of opinion about tactics. The fact remains that after years of conflicting and often cynical attempts by Russia and other nations to influence, even confuse, political affairs of the Middle East, and after the clear and repeated failures of the United Nations to act effectively in the Israeli-Egyptian dispute, a crisis was likely sooner or later to develop when one or more major Powers would feel impelled to intervene to prevent a more serious war. In their present actions the British and French Governments have chosen what seems to them the course of lesser evil, when a choice between evils was inevitable. When a fire breaks out, it must be extinguished before it spreads.

It seems improper to assume at this early stage that these Governments are acting from unscrupulous and selfish motives or that they have no regard for the ultimate objectives of the United Nations. We feel that they deserve patient but, if necessary, critical support in order to ensure that British and French forces provide an impartial police force between the Israeli and Egyptian armies until the United Nations assumes this task itself.

He defined the position even more clearly in a second letter which he wrote to *Time and Tide*, published on 10th November:

The rather wild confusion into which people have fallen about the Middle East situation is, I think, due to two main causes. First, it is strictly a question of international law, and our system of international law is not complete. The United Nations was intended to have a means of enforcing the law, and it has no such means (see Articles 43–48 of the Charter). Egypt and Israel have been breaking the law for nine years with no correction.

Secondly, the Nasser danger is much more serious and pressing than a local friction consisting of Colonel Nasser's irregular nationalisation of the Canal and the perpetual war between Egypt and Israel, with which the United Nations has been unable to deal. The real danger was that,

17

if the Nasser movement had been allowed to progress unchecked, we should have been faced by a coalition of all Arab, Muslim, Asiatic, and Anti-western States, led nominally by Egypt but really by Russia; that is, a division of the world in which the enemies of civilisation are stronger than its supporters. Such a danger, the Prime Minister saw, must be stopped instantly and, since the U.N. has no intrument, it must be stopped, however irregularly, by those nations who can act at once.

So much for the immediate present; the next step of course is the creation of a police force for the U.N. Happily this has now been done. As soon as a cessation of hostilities has been imposed, that force should proceed to discharge its functions of maintaining the law afterwards. The Russian plan has actually been revealed on 6th November.* It is frustrated and indeed shown to be absurd; but we can see now what Russia and Nasser once intended and may possibly still make a desperate attempt to renew.

The Prime Minister's policy may well prove to have been the only road to success.

The second letter expressed almost exactly my own views.
In the House of Lords debate on 8th November, Lord Coleraine (formerly Dick Law) put our dilemma with devastating clarity:

There is this strange idea that by the creation of the United Nations, the rule of law has taken the place of anarchy ...
What is the situation as a great jurist like Lord McNair outlines it? We have a complete system of international law. It is logical; it is consistent; it is ascertainable; in fact

* On p. 89 of *Waging Peace*, Eisenhower refers to the communication to him from Bulganin on 5th November 1956:

At the same time Bulganin wrote to me proposing that the United States and the Soviet Union join forces, march into Egypt, and put an end to the fighting. 'If this War is not stopped it is fraught with danger and can grow into a Third World War,' he added.

it is quite watertight. There is only one thing wrong with it—the wicked will not obey it and the righteous will not enforce it. That is not international law; that is a sham covering up international anarchy, and under that system of international law all you are doing is giving an open general licence to the criminal.

Nasser in taking over the Canal had acted in a manner fundamentally incompatible with the 1888 Convention. He could not complain if, in face of a deteriorating situation and the probability of interference with free passage through the Canal, the powers principally concerned took physical steps to see that the Canal remained open.

It was necessary for us to act. The old saying is that necessity knows no law. This is not quite true. There is a legal doctrine of necessity. International lawyers would contend that it is confined within very strict limits. The crisis must constitute a most serious danger to the state. It must place its future in jeopardy. Other means of dealing with the crisis must have been exhausted. Force must be the only effective means. These considerations are strengthened if there is grave danger to the peace of a very sensitive part of the world. It can fairly be argued that in assessing these dangers, a forward look is allowable. It certainly would have justified action in the case of the Rhineland, judging by what happened afterwards.

There are few critics of Britain's action on 4th August 1914 in deciding to go to war with Germany, although plenty of the way in which the war was waged. I read recently a book *Britain and the Origins of the First World War* by Dr Zara Steiner.* Her conclusions are that we did not go to war because the Government wanted a distraction from the turbulent domestic scene. It was not because of an anti-German bias among senior Foreign Office officials. It was not to save Belgium, although that was a good excuse. It was because with Sir Edward Grey, the Foreign Secretary, backed by Asquith, the Prime Minister,

* Macmillan, 1977.

and one or two others, a small group of Ministers had decided that it was contrary to the national interest for Germany to be allowed to subjugate France and acquire a complete hegemony in Continental Europe. It was 'necessary' to act to prevent that happening.

In accordance with these views, I believe that forcible action to preserve the safety and international character of the Canal was justified in 1956. 'Ah,' it will be said, 'but it did not keep the Canal open.' That is true. Nasser's own measures caused it to be blocked for nearly six months. After that, it remained open for ten years. After the next war, in 1967, in which we did not intervene, it remained blocked for eight years.

The other burden of criticism of the Government's action, which found expression in many debates and questions in the House in the autumn of 1956, was that there had been unacceptable collusion with the French and Israeli Governments. Indeed, the word has bedevilled all serious consideration of our actions. I have explained in the Preface why I had to delay this book so long. I much regretted it but I felt that the argument about 'collusion' had to be dealt with in the context of what actually happened, fully set out. It was ironic that I, as Leader of the House of Commons in 1964, answering Questions for the Prime Minister and on behalf of the Government, had to refuse the request for an enquiry into the Suez crisis. No doubt it was right to turn down that particular request. Enquiries of that sort would make government very difficult, and one at the time on that particular subject might have affected affairs in the Middle East and been detrimental to the public interest. On purely personal grounds, I would have welcomed an enquiry. I have the draft of a speech which I prepared for a debate on the setting up of such an enquiry. Its content is very similar to this book.

What constitutes 'collusion'? Does it apply to any confidential discussion with another Government? Does it apply to any exchange of information, explanation of intentions, or of likely reactions to what may happen in the future? If that is the appropriate definition, then almost every diplomatic exchange of views is 'collusion'.

Alternatively, is it a pejorative or abusive term? Does it denote something fraudulent or disreputable? The *Oxford Dictionary* defines it as a 'fraudulent secret understanding especially between ostensible opponents in a law suit'. I have not the slightest doubt myself that it is this second definition which is the correct one.

It is necessary to examine the circumstances to which it was sought to apply this pejorative word. I have tried to describe them in detail. The salient point is that Nasser was an enemy of this country, a public enemy. He was determined to destroy our influence and interests in the Middle East and in East Africa. By his incitements to insurrection and murder throughout the whole area, he had in effect declared war upon us. He did so in his speech of 26th July. If he got away with his seizure of the Canal and got control of it, he was in a position to do us great harm. As Dulles said, it was an 'intolerable' position, a sword of Damocles. It hung over our oil supplies. Those supplies and all other traffic passing through the Canal would be at Nasser's mercy. I have drawn the Hitler analogy. Nasser's appetite would have grown with eating.

Having regard to the proper definition of 'collusion', and the circumstances to which it was alleged to apply, our conduct has to be considered stage by stage.

I repeat that it cannot be 'collusion' merely to have confidential talks with other Governments. This was going on all the time with the United States, France and the other countries which sent representatives to the two London conferences. Talks with the Government of Israel no more constitute 'collusion' than our talks with these other Governments.

It is not collusion just to have a provisional agreement with another Government and to keep it secret. We made agreements with France, and the United States, and other Governments which were not disclosed at the time. The pages of

history are filled with examples. Edward Grey had his agreement with the French about military consultations before the
First World War. He undertook to defend the French Channel
ports from German attack. On the strength of that assurance
the French fleet moved into the Mediterranean. There was the
Sykes-Picot agreement about the future of the Middle East
after that war. There were agreements between Churchill and
Roosevelt before Pearl Harbour about United States help for
Britain which were not revealed to Congress or the American
people.

The test of 'collusion' is the motive. Was the action fraudulent or disreputable? There may have been mistaken judgments,
errors of commission or omission in carrying out our policies,
but the test is the motive. Were these things done with a
fraudulent or disreputable motive?

What were our motives? We had certain objectives which we
believed were in the national interest. First, we had a special
part to play in preventing a general conflagration in the Middle
East. Second, Nasser was a menace and must at least be checked.
Third, the Canal had to be brought back under some kind of
international control.

As to the first objective, we thought that an explosion was
inevitable. We did not believe that the Israelis would sit back
and passively watch the Egyptians and the Syrians being
equipped by the Russians with vast quantities of modern
weapons, and trained in their use. Sooner or later, hostilities
would begin. With the Anglo-French expedition mounted, we
were in the best position to intervene to control and localise
those hostilities. If we had not intervened, I doubt whether in
1956 the war would have been as confined as the Six-Day War
was in 1967 or the Yom Kippur War in 1973.

As to the second objective, the checking of Nasser, that was
shared by every friendly Government — our partners in NATO
(except perhaps Greece), our partners in the Baghdad Pact, all
the Middle East countries except Syria, and by others like the
Sudan and Ethiopia. Dulles said afterwards that the objective

of bringing down Nasser was agreed. The only difference was over method.

The third objective, the restoration of international control over the Suez Canal, was shared by all the eighteen Governments which had sent representatives to the two London conferences and by many more besides.

There was nothing fraudulent or disreputable about any of these objectives or motives. We did have discussions with the Israelis. We did say what we would do in certain circumstances. I do not myself believe that there was any binding agreement between the Israeli and British Governments. I was not certain right up to the last minute whether the Israelis would attack when they did. In fact, the Israeli Cabinet only made the decision on the morning of Sunday, 28th October, as we are now told.

It is said that 'collusion' was proved by the fact that we did not inform Nasser of the nature of our discussions with Israel. It would be a very odd doctrine that the enemy should be told what transpired in talks with potential friends. Suppose the Czechoslovakian Government, just before Hitler's seizure of Austria, had decided to make a pre-emptive strike at Hitler in order to avoid the flank of their formidable defences being turned. That is not at all a far-fetched idea. At that time, the Czechs were well equipped and might have won a short, sharp campaign. Supposing the Czechs told the French and ourselves of their intentions, would we have been expected to inform Hitler of their actions or our reactions?

Next, it is said that 'collusion' was proved by the fact that Eden denied foreknowledge of Israeli intentions in House of Commons debates throughout the autumn of 1956, though in the adjournment debate on 20th December he said there was no foreknowledge of an Israeli attack, but there was risk of an attack, and in view of that discussions took place. In my view, he was right not to be drawn into a discussion at that stage about how much we knew beforehand. It might have made the clearing up of the situation in the Middle East much more difficult, and endangered the lives of our friends and our nationals. It is never agreeable to have to refuse, in the national interest, information to the House of Commons. But it has to be done from time to time. Attlee did not tell the House that he had authorised the manufacture of the atomic bomb. Stafford Cripps told the House that he had no intention of devaluing the pound when he knew perfectly well that he was going to do so. In those cases, I think that both Attlee and Cripps were right and acted in the national interest.

If the charge is that we incited the Israelis to attack Egypt, the assumption must be that they would not have attacked otherwise. Yet their assessment of Nasser was the same as ours, and they were suffering the repeated incursions of the fedayeen. There was certainly 'a risk' that they would move against Nasser, the instigator. In fact, though we did not know it at the time, they were 'in the midst of feverish preparations for the Sinai campaign' on the night of 10th October (see p. 182) before ever the British Government was invited to enter discussions. We had by then independently made and revised our own military contingency plans and called up the reservists. In such circumstances, it would surely have been a refusal to discuss with like-minded countries when invited to do so that could have been validly criticised.

When Eden died, moving tributes were paid to him in both Houses of Parliament. All, friend and foe alike, said that whether or not they agreed with what he did, they knew that he was a man of courage and integrity, with the interests of his country first in his mind. I know that that was so, and I know that right to the end of his life he believed that the Government which he led had done what was right. Because Hitler was not checked, 20 million people had died. Eden was determined to see that it did not happen again.

Chapter XV

Balance Sheet

I have tried to describe the events of that remarkable year, 1956, as accurately as possible. It only remains to attempt a balance sheet—the pluses, the minuses, the debits, the credits. An assessment of them made more than twenty years after the event can quite fairly be aided by hindsight.

Suez, 1956, certainly stirred up political controversy. Not since the Home Rule Bill and the Parliament Act of 1911 had there been such deep feelings throughout the country. Apart from the rows in Parliament, old friends could hardly bear to speak to one another, hostesses had to be careful in their choice of guests and there were divisions within families. But how much of an event really was it? From time to time there are happenings which do affect the course of history: for example, the defeat of the Armada, Waterloo, the Battle of Britain, Stalingrad. I am sure that Suez, 1956, is not in that class.

First let me look at the debits. Without doubt it was a diplomatic defeat for Britain and France. We were condemned by an overwhelming majority as they voted at the United Nations. We knew very well that in some cases the hearts and the heads did not go with the votes, but that was little consolation when the figures were announced. We were put under strong pressure to stop military operations. We agreed to do so. When it came to the withdrawal of our forces, the United States put their whole influence into insisting that the withdrawal should be unconditional. We had to accept it. In fact, the withdrawal was not as unconditional as some critics have maintained. We withdrew on condition that a satisfactory United Nations emergency force replaced British and French troops. My friendship with Hammarskjöld stood us in good stead, and he obtained an assurance from Nasser that when the Canal reopened, there would be no discrimination against British or French ships. Nevertheless, there can be no disputing the fact that we sustained a diplomatic and political defeat.

The second item on the debit side was that our action did not result in an international regime for the Canal. The terms on which Nasser reopened it probably could have been obtained without a fight, certainly if that including Egypt's limited acceptance of the Optional Clause is not taken into account. On the other hand, it is interesting to speculate as to what would have happened if we had succeeded in establishing an international regime for the Canal. I doubt whether the Six-Day War in June 1967, or the Yom Kippur War in 1973, would have taken place. Those who point out that as a result of our Suez operation the Canal was unusable from November 1956 to May 1957 should remember the eight years it remained closed after the 1967 fighting.

The third debit was that the prospects of an Arab-Israeli settlement were not enhanced. The Arab hawks were discouraged. The UNEF reduced the border incidents. But that was all. This was a bitter disappointment to me personally. The will to make a lasting settlement was not strengthened on either side, at all events for some time.

The fourth, and to my mind the most important debit, was the psychological wound which it inflicted on so many people of British stock either at home or overseas. This result took time to develop. But Suez, 1956, became an excuse. It was the scapegoat for what was happening to Britain in the world, and for all that flowed from loss of power and economic weakness. It was in no way a cause of that loss of power or that weakness.

Some may dispute this assertion. But I do not believe that the process of decolonisation upon which we had already embarked was hastened by one day as a result of Suez. Some maintain that Suez hastened France's loss of Algeria. Others believe that it caused the Belgian Government to give in too quickly to United States pressure on Belgium to give up the

Congo. Both of these contentions may be correct. Britain, however, had already decided upon decolonisation. We were losing power and influence, but that was because of our physical and material losses in two world wars, and our consequent voluntary liquidation of the Empire. It was alleged that Suez was the watershed; the words fiasco and débâcle were on so many lips, some of them respectable lips, that they contributed to a weakening of our national will-power. We are so fond of denigrating ourselves that an excuse for this, like Suez, 1956, was eagerly adopted. A. J. P. Taylor wrote that Eden had steered the ship of state on to the rocks — a remarkable piece of hyperbole. I have often wondered whether the psychological effect would have been different if we had gone on and captured the whole Canal. We would have been forced to withdraw, the United States's attitude being what it was. We would have had to give up the fruits of victory. But it would have been better psychologically. As it was, the political decision to stop cast doubts on the military operations, brilliantly successful though they had been, given the equipment available and the geographical facts.

One very able critic said that Eden was the last Prime Minister to think that we could take independent military action, even if disapproved of by the United States, and the first to find out that we could not. In fact, Eden did not think anything of the sort. This is proved by the paper which he gave to Eisenhower on 31st January 1956 in Washington, to which I referred on p. 42. His and my misjudgments were not about that. We misjudged the American reaction to what we did. On the issue whether Suez heralded our loss of power, Pineau put it neatly on p. 188 of his book:

L'affaire de Suez, pénible pour l'amour propre britannique, n'a donc pas changé grand'chose à une situation politique de fait.*

* 'The Suez affair, painful though it was to British pride, did not greatly change the reality of the political situation.'

The reality of twentieth century international relations had made itself felt long before. Robert Rhodes James says of an earlier British and French 'close association', of 1912:

> Remorselessly the freedom to manoeuvre independently, which was at the heart of late Victorian foreign policy, was disappearing.*

Also on the debit side was its effect upon Anglo-French relations. The high hopes that it would lead to a new phase of a closer entente cordiale were dashed. The project had failed; many Frenchmen blamed us for it; close co-operation with Germany looked a better bet.

These debit items are formidable. What is there to set on the other side?

First of all, the bubble of Nasser's military might was pricked. His air force was eliminated with little or no loss to us. In spite of the vast quantities of Soviet equipment and weapons in his hands, the comparatively ill-equipped Israelis drove 45,000–50,000 Egyptian soldiers out of carefully prepared, well-fortified and well-equipped positions in three or four days. The pricking of this bubble enabled one neighbour in particular to relax — the Sudan. She had had in her mind for some time the menace of an Egyptian invasion to re-establish Egyptian rule over the Sudan. She knew that this wish lurked in many Egyptian hearts. After Suez, 1956, she felt able to relax, and when Nasser tried some strong-arm stuff a little later, he was told where to get off.

The extent of the collaboration between Nasser and the Soviet Union was exposed for all to see, and Nasser's plans against Israel were shown not just in the form of rhetoric used upon excitable crowds but in operation orders to the Egyptian Army.

The UNEF was established on the borders of Israel and

---

* *The British Revolution: British Politics 1880–1939*, vol. 2 (Hamish Hamilton, 1977) p. 7.

Egypt. As has already been said, the emergency force was not to be ordered out of Egyptian territory by Nasser without consultation with the Secretary-General and discussion in the General Assembly (though in the event the next Secretary-General quickly agreed to Nasser's request to withdraw it in 1967). I was delighted with the establishment of the principle of a UNEF. I had for some time thought that this was the way for the United Nations to move forward. With the Security Council rendered impotent by the veto, I came eventually to favour the idea of a United Nations force being constituted under the authority of the Secretary-General, which could be available to be deployed by him in circumstances which would enable him to avoid a veto. I discussed the idea at length with Hammarskjöld, and in speeches at later General Assemblies tried to prepare the way for it. Only Hammarskjöld could have worked what I had in mind. With his death the idea perished. But in his lifetime, in November 1956 a United Nations force did come into being and 'e'en the ranks of Tuscany could scarce forbear to cheer'. Bevan said in the House in December that he was prepared for us to declare a 'limited dividend' on our operation in that we had achieved a United Nations police force in the Middle East.

The Straits of Tiran were opened up so that Israeli ships and cargoes could pass through to and from the port of Eilat. It may be argued that Israel could have launched an expedition to achieve this at any time; but she did not, and the fact was that after the Suez operation she got an international guarantee of free passage as part of the consideration for her relinquishment of her conquests in Sinai. That was much better than some unilateral action.

The effect that the closing of the Canal had upon shipowners and shipbuilders was significant. They had to think of a world in which the Canal was not necessarily always open to shipping. The shipping fleets of the world became much better fitted to deal with the eight years of closure from 1967 to 1975. No doubt it will be argued that this would have happened in any case, and it would, but I doubt whether it would have been so quick or so extensive.

A further item on the credit side was the announcement of what was called the Eisenhower doctrine for the Middle East. The President asked Congress for power to use the armed forces of the United States to secure and protect the territorial integrity and political independence of any Middle Eastern nation or group of nations requesting such aid against overt armed aggression from any nation controlled by international Communism. He and his advisers realised at last that their action, official or otherwise, to diminish British influence was counter-productive. Diminishing British influence did not reduce tension. It increased it, because it resulted in a vacuum. Eisenhower told Congressional leaders that the vacuum must be filled by the United States before it was filled by Russia. He also asked for the authorisation of economic assistance. The resolution giving him these powers was passed by the House of Representatives by 355 to 61, and by the Senate 72 to 19. American aid for the Baghdad Pact was also increased.

Another item on the credit side, too often disregarded, is the fact that our actions, right or wrong, did stop a war which was inevitable. They were the catalyst which precipitated a crisis already imminent. Then followed ten years of uneasy peace between Israel and the Arab states. It may be argued that the Six-Day War ended without foreign military intervention, and so did the Yom Kippur War. It would have been the same, it is said, in 1956. I very much doubt it. Syria and Jordan certainly would have joined in, and it could very easily have escalated. When we and the French announced our intention to intervene, Hakim Amer, Commander-in-Chief of the Egyptian-Syrian-Jordanian military command, ordered the Syrian and Jordanian forces not to become involved. The ten years of uneasy peace is a fact which cannot be denied, and but for Nasser's folly in ordering out the UNEF, this uneasy peace might have lasted much longer.

There were two other rather surprising results. The failure of the Suez operation to establish international control of the Canal did not weaken our position in the Middle East to the extent expected. Eisenhower endorses this view in his book, expressing at the same time some surprise. It is true that the fall of the pro-Western regime in Iraq was a sad blow for us. But in 1964 we were certainly as powerful in the Persian Gulf as we had been in 1956. When the independence of Jordan was threatened after the revolution in Iraq, British troops were flown in at King Hussein's request to support his regime. There was not a single casualty. Similar defensive action was taken by British forces in 1961 to protect Kuwait against Iraq.

The second rather odd result was that Suez led to closer co-operation between the British and United States Governments. Macmillan deserves great credit for this. (I doubt whether Eden could have done it, because, although he got on well with Eisenhower, he and Dulles were completely out of sympathy with each other.)

There were several reasons for this improvement. Eisenhower, having won the Presidential election, was more relaxed. I have already referred to his friendly reception of Caccia as our new Ambassador in Washington in November 1956, and to Sir William Elliot's account of his conversation with Eisenhower. Second, the realisation that the elimination of our colonial empire would simply add to American burdens was slowly penetrating their thinking. But the main reason, I believe, was Dulles's realisation of how badly the United States had handled the affair. It became a guilt complex. I have already referred to his conversation with me in the Walter Reed Hospital when he asked me why we had stopped (p. 219). It is known that he told Dean Rusk, American Secretary of State to Presidents Kennedy and Lyndon Johnson, how unhappy he was about Suez and excused himself on the ground that he was ill at the time. During the last few weeks of his life he spoke to the general commanding the Walter Reed Hospital, again expressing his regret at what had happened and saying that it was because he had been ill at the time. But I did not know

until I read Pineau's book *1956 Suez*, published in 1976, that
he had talked in the same sense to Pineau. Pineau describes how
some time after Suez he had a private talk with Dulles. They
talked about religion. Dulles was apparently surprised to find
that Pineau was not an atheist. In fact, their religious thinking
was very similar. Then Dulles said about Suez, after a long
silence: 'A Suez, nous nous sommes trompés. C'est vous qui
aviez raison.'*

Dulles certainly said much the same to me on several occasions,
and once or twice excused himself from blame on the ground
that he had been ill at the time.

There were tangible results from this attitude of Dulles. I
think that he became as intimate and friendly with me as with
anyone else with whom he had to deal. He was a strange man.
One had to be on the watch for the escape clause, the double
meaning, often inserted from habit rather than intention, but
we worked closely together. When our troops went into Jordan
in 1958 Dulles arranged for them to over-fly Israeli territory.
American troops had also gone into the Lebanon at President
Chamoun's request. I was in his room at the State Department
with the American military chiefs when the Turks said that they
proposed to invade Iraq through the passes, an operation which
was physically impossible without many months of preparation.
There was a completely open and frank discussion. We played
the hand together at the resulting special meeting of the
General Assembly. Our troops were withdrawn pursuant to a
resolution unanimously carried, which in the context of Middle
Eastern affairs almost amounted to a vote of thanks to us for our
intervention and preservation of peace. We laid the foundations
for the test-ban treaty. He took my constant discouragement of
the United States's involvement in the morass of Indo-China in
good part.

Over Quemoy and Matsui, although we started from a basic
difference in that Eden had said that these offshore islands

* 'We were wrong about Suez. You were the ones who were right.' (*1956
Suez*, p. 195.)

belonged to mainland China, we avoided open disagreement. I
said in the General Assembly that, whatever was the legal
position of the offshore islands, the dispute should not be
settled by force. He was tolerant though not enthusiastic about
our attempts to get some kind of personal relationship with the
Soviet leaders. In the last few months of his life he continued
to work and to travel to the limit of his endurance, although he
must have known the cost. He faced death bravely—truly a
remarkable man. In the four months from July to November
1956 he was at his worst but, as I have indicated, Eisenhower
bears a heavy responsibility for that. A week or two before he
died in May 1959, he sent me his photograph, with, written on
it: 'To Selwyn Lloyd. With affectionate regard and respect born
of four years of close association'.

Assessment of the debits and credits of the Suez operation is
limited, for one can only guess what would have happened if we
had tried to continue negotiations with Nasser. That would
have meant our conceding victory to him. If the Middle East
had seen him successfully defy the Western powers, his prestige
would have been enormous. I believe that within a matter of
months, not only would the regime of King Feisal, the Crown
Prince, and Nuri have been overthrown in Iraq, but King
Hussein, too, would have been eliminated in Jordan. The same
thing would have happened to King Idris in Libya and
President Chamoun would have been in grave danger in the
Lebanon. The oil shaikhdoms in the Gulf, incapable of defend-
ing themselves, would have been taken over by Nasser or his
nominees. The oil problems of 1974 might have arisen many
years earlier. The Sudan would also again have been in danger.
The royal house in Saudi Arabia would have been undermined.
    This chain of events would have been so alarming for the
Israelis that they would have intervened at some stage. I doubt
very much, however, whether the repercussions would have
been as limited as they were in 1967, when Israel brilliantly
defeated her three opponents—Egypt in Sinai, Jordan in
18

Jerusalem and the West Bank area, and Syria over the Golan Heights. I am also not sure whether Israel could have done it all in 1956 or 1957, successful though their Sinai campaign was. But this is conjecture. It remains my belief that the consequences of doing nothing would have been far worse than the results of what we did.

There is one criticism which must be faced. It has been said that the Suez operation was bedevilled by the lack of clear political aim. In fact, we had some very definite political aims. We wished to restore international control over the Canal. We wished to check Nasser and we wished to create the conditions for an Arab-Israeli settlement. Those aims, however, could only be mentioned incidentally. Our ostensible reason for intervening was to separate the combatants and to ensure the safety of the Canal and those using it.

The operation was not bedevilled by the lack of a clear political aim but by other quite different factors. Malta, our only deep-water harbour, was six days' sailing from Port Said. There was no military co-operation between us and Israel. If there had been, the capture of the Canal could have been effected much more speedily. The air drop could have taken place several days earlier. The United States's reaction was unexpected, to put it mildly. One had the feeling that Dulles had never shown Eisenhower his speeches about the use of force.

I accept no blame for Mediterranean geography. I believe that our misunderstanding of likely American reaction was more their fault than ours. I do, however, wonder whether I was wise to harbour doubt about co-operation between us and Israel for fear of Arab reaction. I was as much to blame for this as any other single person. I had in mind the mobs coming out in Cairo in 1952 and their mass-murders. I hated the efficacy of Radio Cairo—as powerful as Goebbels. My preoccupation was to safeguard Britons in Arab countries from massacre, and our strategic assets from destruction. I believed that an alliance between Israel and ourselves would produce exactly this feared result. I may well have been wrong; in the event there were no murders of Britons, and the only damage to our property, apart from the Canal itself, was the blowing up of the pumping stations on the pipeline from Iraq through Jordan — damage which was easy to repair.

As for the Russians, the friend whom they had armed had been defeated; but that was bound to happen in view of the strength of the opposing forces. The Russians had not come to his assistance. Their technicians had left Egypt hurriedly. Their initial assistance had consisted of speeches in the United Nations, including rather unctuous compliments to the United States for its leadership against Britain, France and Israel. Their threats to Britain and France only became really menacing when hostilities were almost over and it was clear that we were going to hand over to the UNEF. Nothing the Russians had said influenced the Cabinet in their decisions on 4th and 5th November.

Epilogue

There it is. Many of my friends have had doubts about my writing this book. I certainly have not wanted to ignite the dead embers of the controversies of yester-year. Although I said in the Preface that I wished I had written it much sooner, now that I have finished it perhaps it was right for me to hold back until Suez, 1956, could be looked at after twenty years and more.

One advantage of age is that one can see both sides of the argument, and can write more dispassionately. Some will disagree with me where I say we were right. Others will disagree where I say we were wrong. What I have tried to do is to set out as correctly as I can, after months and months of the reading of records and books, what I believe happened and why. I have written for the record, because my account has been missing from the record. Now, as Churchill wrote (inaccurately as it turned out) in the Visitors' Book at Chequers after his defeat in the 1945 General Election—

FINIS

That, alas, does not apply to disputes in the Middle East, but it does to my writing about them.

Appendix I

Dramatis Personae

(i) *Her Majesty's Government, 1956*

MEMBERS OF THE CABINET

PRIME MINISTER AND FIRST LORD OF THE TREASURY — Rt Hon. Sir Anthony Eden, K.G., M.C., M.P.

LORD PRESIDENT OF THE COUNCIL AND LEADER OF THE HOUSE OF LORDS — Most Hon. Marquess of Salisbury, K.G.

LORD PRIVY SEAL AND LEADER OF THE HOUSE OF COMMONS — Rt Hon. R. A. Butler, C.H., M.P.

CHANCELLOR OF THE EXCHEQUER — Rt Hon. Harold Macmillan, M.P.

LORD CHANCELLOR — Rt Hon. Viscount Kilmuir, G.C.V.O.

SECRETARY OF STATE FOR FOREIGN AFFAIRS — Rt Hon. Selwyn Lloyd, C.B.E., T.D., Q.C., M.P.

SECRETARY OF STATE FOR THE HOME DEPARTMENT AND MINISTER FOR WELSH AFFAIRS — Major Rt Hon. Gwilym Lloyd-George, M.P.

SECRETARY OF STATE FOR SCOTLAND — Rt Hon. James Stuart, M.V.O., M.C., M.P.

SECRETARY OF STATE FOR COMMONWEALTH RELATIONS — Rt Hon. Earl of Home.

SECRETARY OF STATE FOR THE COLONIES — Rt Hon. Alan Lennox-Boyd, M.P.

MINISTER OF DEFENCE — Rt Hon. Sir Walter Monckton, K.C.M.G., K.C.V.O., M.C., Q.C., M.P.*

MINISTER OF HOUSING AND LOCAL GOVERNMENT — Rt Hon. Duncan Sandys, M.P.

---

* From October, the Rt Hon. Antony Head, C.B.E., M.C., M.P. Sir Walter Monckton became Paymaster-General.

PRESIDENT OF THE BOARD OF TRADE — Rt Hon. Peter Thorneycroft, M.P.

MINISTER OF AGRICULTURE, FISHERIES AND FOOD — Rt Hon. Derick Heathcoat Amory, M.P.

MINISTER OF EDUCATION — Rt Hon. Sir David Eccles, K.C.V.O., M.P.

MINISTER OF LABOUR AND NATIONAL SERVICE — Rt Hon. Iain Macleod, M.P.

CHANCELLOR OF THE DUCHY OF LANCASTER — Rt Hon. Earl of Selkirk, O.B.E., A.F.C.

MINISTER OF WORKS — Rt Hon. Patrick Buchan-Hepburn, M.P.

MINISTERS NOT IN THE CABINET

FIRST LORD OF THE ADMIRALTY — Viscount Hailsham, Q.C.

SECRETARY OF STATE FOR WAR — Rt Hon. Antony Head, C.B.E., M.C., M.P.*

SECRETARY OF STATE FOR AIR — Rt Hon. Nigel Birch, O.B.E., M.P.

MINISTER OF PENSIONS AND NATIONAL INSURANCE — Rt Hon. John Boyd-Carpenter, M.P.

MINISTER OF SUPPLY — Rt. Hon. Reginald Maudling, M.P.

MINISTER OF HEALTH — Rt Hon. R. H. Turton, M.C., M.P.

MINISTER OF TRANSPORT AND CIVIL AVIATION — Rt Hon. Harold Watkinson, M.P.

MINISTER OF FUEL AND POWER — Rt Hon. Aubrey Jones, M.P.

POSTMASTER-GENERAL — Dr Rt Hon. Charles Hill, M.P.

MINISTER WITHOUT PORTFOLIO — Rt Hon. Earl of Munster.

MINISTER OF STATE FOR FOREIGN AFFAIRS — Most Hon. Marquess of Reading, C.B.E., M.C., T.D., Q.C.

MINISTER OF STATE, BOARD OF TRADE — Rt Hon. A. R. W. Low, C.B.E., D.S.O., T.D., M.P.

MINISTER OF STATE FOR FOREIGN AFFAIRS — Rt Hon. Anthony Nutting, M.P.†

* From October, the Rt Hon. John Hare.
† From October, the Rt Hon. Commander Sir Allan Noble.

MINISTER OF STATE, SCOTTISH OFFICE—Rt Hon. Lord Strathclyde.

MINISTER OF STATE FOR COLONIAL AFFAIRS—Rt Hon. John Hare, O.B.E., M.P.*

ATTORNEY-GENERAL—Rt Hon. Sir Reginald Manningham-Buller, Bt., Q.C., M.P.

LORD ADVOCATE—Rt Hon. W. R. Milligan, Q.C., M.P.

SOLICITOR-GENERAL—Sir Harry Hylton-Foster, Q.C., M.P.

SOLICITOR-GENERAL FOR SCOTLAND—William Grant, Esq., Q.C., M.P.

(ii) *Others frequently referred to in the book but whose function may not be clear from the text. The position held at the time appears first.*

ACHESON, DEAN: U.S. Secretary of State 1949–53, subsequently in private law practice.

CACCIA, SIR HAROLD (later LORD): Deputy Under-Secretary of State, Foreign Office. Later Ambassador in Washington 1956–61, and Permanent Under-Secretary of State, Foreign Office 1962–5.

DAYAN, MOSHE: Israeli Chief of Staff. Later Minister of Defence; now Minister of Foreign Affairs.

DIXON, SIR PIERSON ('BOB'): U.K. Permanent Representative at the United Nations, New York. Later Ambassador in Paris 1960–5.

DULLES, JOHN FOSTER: U.S. Secretary of State 1952–9.

EISENHOWER, DWIGHT D.: U.S. President 1953–61. Previously Supreme Commander Allied Powers in Europe.

FAWZI, MAHMUD: Egyptian Foreign Minister 1951–66. Later Prime Minister.

HAMMARSKJÖLD, DAG: Secretary-General of the United Nations 1953–61. Killed in aircraft crash, Ndole (Katangan–Northern Rhodesian—now Zambian—border) 1961.

* From October, the Rt Hon. John Mackay, C.M.G., J.P.

HEIKAL, MUHAMMAD HASSANIAN: Editor of *Al Ahram* 1957–74. Member of the Central Committee of the Arab Socialist Union (1968–74). Author of *Nasser: The Cairo Documents*, a study of Nasser, to whom he was close.

HENDERSON, LOY: U.S. Deputy Under-Secretary of State for Administration 1956.

HOOVER, HERBERT JNR: U.S. Under-Secretary of State 1956. Acting Secretary of State during Dulles's absence.

HOWE, SIR ROBERT: Governor-General of the Sudan 1947–55.

KEIGHTLEY, GENERAL SIR CHARLES: C.-in-C. Middle East Land Forces 1953–7, and Allied Commander-in-Chief of the Suez operation. Later Governor of Gibraltar.

KIRKPATRICK, SIR IVONE: Permanent Under-Secretary of State, Foreign Office.

LODGE, HENRY CABOT: U.S. Permanent Representative at the United Nations and member of the President's Cabinet. Later Ambassador to Vietnam 1963–4 and 1965–7, and to Federal Republic of Germany 1968–9.

LUCE, SIR WILLIAM: Adviser to the Governor-General of the Sudan (Sir Robert Howe) on Constitutional and External Affairs, 1953–6. Later Governor and C.-in-C. Aden.

MAKINS, SIR ROGER (later LORD SHERFIELD): Ambassador to the United States, 1953–6. Later Chairman of U.K. Atomic Energy Authority 1960–4.

MENZIES, SIR ROBERT: Prime Minister of Australia 1949–66.

MENON, V. K. KRISHNA: Indian Minister without Portfolio, 1956–7. Later Minister of Defence. Barrister, Middle Temple, and one-time Councillor, St Pancras. Close to Nehru.

MURPHY, ROBERT: Deputy Under-Secretary of State, U.S. State Department 1954–9.

MUSADDIQ, MUHAMMAD: Iranian Prime Minister 1951–3; nationalised the Anglo-Iranian Oil Company.

NASSER, GAMAL ABDUL: Ousted Neguib to become President of Egypt 1954 until his death in 1970.

NEHRU, JAWAHARLAL: Indian Prime Minister 1947–64. Father of Indira Ghandi (later Prime Minister) and brother of

Mrs Pandit, Indian High Commissioner to London 1954–1961.

NURI-ES-SAID: Prime Minister of Iraq 1954–7 and in 1958 until he and the King of Iraq were murdered 14 July 1958. He had been Prime Minister fourteen times since 1930.

PEARSON, LESTER ('MIKE'): Canadian Secretary of State for External Affairs 1948–57. Later Prime Minister.

PERES, SHIMON: Director-General Israeli Ministry of Defence 1952–9. Later Minister of Defence.

PINEAU, CHRISTIAN: French Minister of Foreign Affairs 1956–8.

STOCKWELL, GENERAL SIR HUGH: G.O.C. Commanding 1 Corps B.A.O.R. 1954–6, and Allied Commander, Ground Forces, Suez Operation. Later Deputy Supreme Allied Commander Europe 1960–4.

TEMPLER, GENERAL (later FIELD-MARSHAL) SIR GERALD: Chief of the Imperial General Staff 1955–8. Sent on mission to Jordan 1955.

WATERHOUSE, CAPTAIN RT HON. CHARLES: Conservative M.P. for S.E. Division of Leicester. Leader of the 'Suez Group' of M.P.s who supported military intervention to secure the Canal and criticised the withdrawal of the Anglo-French forces.

Appendix II

The Communiqué of 2nd August 1956: Three-power Invitation to the London Conference

Following a meeting of the Foreign Ministers of France, the United Kingdom and the United States, this communiqué was issued in London on 2nd August 1956, inviting twenty-one other nations to attend a conference in London to discuss the nationalisation of the Suez Canal:

The Governments of France, the United Kingdom and the United States join in the following statement:—

(i) They have taken note of the recent action of the Government of Egypt whereby it attempts to nationalize and take over the assets and the responsibilities of the Universal Suez Canal Company. This company was organized in Egypt in 1856 under a franchise to build the Suez Canal and operate it until 1968. The Universal Suez Canal Company has always had an international character in terms of its shareholders, directors and operating personnel, and in terms of its responsibility to assure the efficient functioning as an international waterway of the Suez Canal.

In 1888 all the great Powers then principally concerned with the international character of the canal and its free, open, and secure use without discrimination joined in the treaty and convention of Constantinople. This provided for the benefit of all the world that the international character of the canal would be perpetuated for all time, irrespective of the expiration of the concession of the Universal Suez Canal Company.

Egypt as recently as October 1954, recognized that the Suez Canal is 'a waterway economically, commercially, and strategically of international importance', and renewed its determination to uphold the convention of 1888.

(*ii*) They do not question the right of Egypt to enjoy and exercise all the powers of a fully sovereign and independent nation, including the generally recognized right, under appropriate conditions, to nationalize assets, not impressed with an international interest, which are subject to its political authority.

But the present action involves far more than a simple act of nationalization. It involves the arbitrary and unilateral seizure by one nation of an international agency which has the responsibility to maintain and to operate the Suez Canal so that all the signatories to, and beneficiaries of, the treaty of 1888 can effectively enjoy the use of an international waterway upon which the economy, commerce, and security of much of the world depends.

This situation is the more serious in its implications because it avowedly was made for the purpose of enabling the Government of Egypt to make the canal serve the purely national purposes of the Egyptian Government rather than the international purpose established by the convention of 1888.

Furthermore, they deplore the fact that, as an incident to its seizure, the Egyptian Government has had recourse to what amounts to a denial of fundamental human rights by compelling employees of the Suez Canal Company to continue to work under threat of imprisonment.

(*iii*) They consider that the action taken by the Government of Egypt, having regard to all the attendant circumstances, threatens the freedom and security of the canal as guaranteed by the convention of 1888. This makes it necessary that steps be taken to assure that the parties to that convention and all other nations entitled to enjoy its benefits shall in fact be assured of such benefits.

(*iv*) They consider that steps should be taken to establish operating arrangements under an international system designed to assure the continuity of operation of the canal as guaranteed by the convention of October 29, 1888, consistently with legitimate Egyptian interests.

(*v*) To this end they propose that a conference should promptly be held of parties to the convention and other nations largely concerned with the use of the canal. The invitations to such a conference, to be held in London on August 16, 1956, will be extended by the Government of the United Kingdom to the Governments named in the annex to this statement. The Governments of France and the United States are ready to take part in the conference.

ANNEX

Parties to the Convention of 1888. — Egypt, France, Italy, Netherlands, Spain, Turkey, United Kingdom, Union of Soviet Socialist Republics.

Other nations largely concerned in the use of the canal, either through ownership of tonnage or pattern of trade. — Australia, Ceylon, Denmark, Ethiopia, Federal Republic of Germany, Greece, India, Indonesia, Iran, Japan, New Zealand, Norway, Pakistan, Portugal, Sweden, United States.

Appendix III

Illegality of the Nationalisation of the Canal: Extract from the Speech by Selwyn Lloyd to the U.N. Security Council, 5th October 1956

But from the start the Suez Canal, although it runs through Egyptian territory, was not regarded as a purely Egyptian affair. On the contrary, its management and operation were largely, if not entirely, on an international basis.

Unless this is realised and seen in its historical setting, and unless it is realised that this was a fact to which the greatest importance was attached by all the interests making use of the Canal because it afforded to them a guarantee of the Canal's efficient and impartial operation, the real character and implications of the present Egyptian action and attitude cannot be seen in their proper perspective.

I now turn to the 1888 Convention. This contained a number of provisions, some of them providing for and guaranteeing rights of passage through the Canal on a basis of complete freedom and equality for the ships of all nations, without discrimination of flag; and others safeguarding the position of Egypt. I draw attention to the fact that the Convention constantly emphasises the notion of freedom of passage. Phrases that occur frequently are 'free use' (articles 1, 8, 11 and 12); 'free passage' (articles 4 and 8); 'free navigation' (article 4); 'liberty and ... entire security of ... navigation' (article 8); 'free and open' (article 1).

Such language indicates the existence of a system by which the enjoyment of these rights, and their effective application in practice, would be secured and guaranteed. In fact, this is exactly what we find, for the Convention was not an isolated instrument, nor was it, from a practical point of view, the sole guarantee of free and non-discriminatory passage through the Canal. It had been preceded, as we know, by the various concessions granted to and the agreements made with the Company by the Egyptian Government. Under these agreements the Company, subject to compliance by users with its regulations, was bound to grant passage without discrimination of any kind, and was obliged, for that purpose, to maintain the Canal in proper operating condition.

Nor was this all. Note must be taken of another international instrument which is relevant, and that is a declaration made by the Turkish Government as suzerain over Egypt—and therefore binding upon Egypt—attached to the report of the Commission on International Tonnage and Suez Canal Dues which met at Constantinople in 1873. By this declaration, the Turkish Government undertook that 'no modification of the conditions of passage through the Canal' in respect of the dues levied on navigation, pilotage, towage, anchorage etc., should be effected 'except with the consent of the Sublime Porte', which would not take any decision 'without previously coming to an understanding with the Powers interested therein'.

This was a clear recognition and confirmation, in an international instrument, of the interest of the user countries not merely in passage as such but in the conditions of operation of the Canal.

The Suez Canal Convention of 1888, therefore, constituted the completion rather than the initiation of a system which, taken as a whole, guaranteed passage rights through the Canal. It did not so much originate those rights as confirm them, and place them on a definite international treaty basis.

This position is clearly reflected in the Convention itself. I expect that members of the Security Council have already studied that Convention, but I may remind them of the words of the preamble, which states explicitly that the Powers desired to establish 'a definite system designed to guarantee at all times, and for all the Powers, the free use of the Suez Maritime Canal, and thus to complete the system under which the navigation of this Canal has been placed by the firman of His Imperial Majesty the Sultan, dated the 22nd February 1866 ... and sanctioning the concessions of His Highness the Khedive'. The firman referred to confirmed the important concessionary agreement entered into between the Company and Ismael Pasha, Viceroy of Egypt, dated the same day, 22 February 1866. That agreement in turn, by its article 17, confirmed the two previous principal concessions granted to the Company— covering also its statutes—respectively dated 30 November 1854 and 5 January 1856.

I do not think that anything could be clearer than the words of that preamble. And, as a matter of accepted legal principle, if one instrument is entered into expressly in order to 'complete the system' established by a previous instrument, it must be a necessary basis of the later instrument, and implicit in it, that the system in question will continue, at any rate for the period for which that system was originally established. This position is confirmed by article 14 of the Convention, which had the object of ensuring that the régime of the Convention would continue even after the termination of the Company's concession. By the very fact of so providing, this article recognised 'the duration of the acts of concession of the Universal Suez Canal Company', and assumed, as did the preamble, that operation by the Company would continue for the full period provided for by the Company's concessions.

I think it is also of interest to note in passing that these concessions, while providing that operation by the Company should come to an end after ninety-nine years if no contrary agreement was reached, nevertheless clearly contemplated the possibility that such an agreement might be reached—this is set out in article 16 of the 1856 firman and article 15 of the 1866 agreement—and provision was made for what would occur in that event. Indeed, one of these articles contemplated possible renewal for several successive periods of ninety-nine years.

So we find that, under the system of the Convention and the concessions, and the Turkish declaration of 1873 to which I have referred, the interests of the user countries were safeguarded not only in respect of passage but in respect of operation also, without which passage could not take place. For the right of passage would in practice have been a dead letter, and of no real value, unless the Canal itself was properly maintained, and unless its operation was of such a nature that passage could take place under secure and orderly conditions. This was the fundamental reason why the 1888 Convention assumed, and based itself upon the assumption of, operation by the Company for the period of its concession.

To put the matter in a different way, the Convention, together with the Company's concessions, constituted a balanced scheme. The position of Egypt was secured by various provisions of the Convention and by the fact that the Canal was within Egyptian territory and under Egyptian sovereignty. The position of the users, on the other hand, was safeguarded partly by the Convention and partly by the fact that the Canal was operated by a company so constituted as to be capable of providing for user interests. Operation by this Company for the period of its concession formed part of the basis of the Convention, as declared in its preamble. There was a balance in the scheme safeguarding the rights of Egypt and safeguarding the rights of users.

The Egyptian Government, by its action of 26 July 1956, has destroyed the balance of this scheme; it has taken out of the scheme the operation of the Canal by the Universal Suez Canal Company. It has thus removed one of the guarantees afforded under the régime of the Convention to user interests. This is contrary to the basis of the Convention. The Egyptian Government cannot require the user countries to recognise the consequences of its action or to accept a purely Egyptian authority for the operation of the Canal, or to pay the passage dues to that authority.

Our view of the legal position may therefore be summed up as follows. According to the scheme of the Convention, the Company was the proper entity to operate the Canal during the term of its concessions. The user countries are not obliged to accept an Egyptian public authority as the operating entity in lieu of the Company.

It therefore follows that the user countries are entitled, within the limits of the relevant international instruments, to set up their own association to safeguard their passage rights, and this is what they have done. It also follows that they are entitled to call upon Egypt to restore the guarantees it has impaired by nationalising the Company. If the Company itself cannot be restored, it should be replaced by an operating authority of an international character which will serve the same purpose. This is the legal foundation of the proposals which we now ask the Security Council to endorse and to recommend to the Egyptian Government as a just and equitable basis for negotiation.

That is the juridical aspect of the matter. Juridical aspects of matters are sometimes somewhat dull and dry to explain, but I have done my best to put as clearly as I could a situation which in law, I think, is clear beyond peradventure. But our apprehensions as to the future have been greatly increased by the way in which the Egyptian Government has behaved in practice.

Appendix IV

Six Principles for the Future of the Canal Proposed at the U.N. Security Council, 13th October 1956, by Britain and France

These principles, proposed by Britain and France on 13th October 1956, had their origin in the preparatory work of Britain, France and the United States for the London conference, and had appeared in very similar form in the Eighteen-Power Proposals put to Nasser by the Menzies mission.

Any settlement of the Suez question should meet the following requirements:

(1) there should be free and open transit through the Canal without discrimination, overt or covert—this covers both political and technical aspects;

(2) the sovereignty of Egypt should be respected;

(3) the operation of the Canal should be insulated from the politics of any country;

(4) the manner of fixing tolls and charges should be decided by agreement between Egypt and the users;

(5) a fair proportion of the dues should be allotted to development;

(6) in case of disputes, unresolved affairs between the Suez Canal Company and the Egyptian Government should be settled by arbitration with suitable terms of reference and suitable provisions for the payment of sums found to be due.

Index

Names borne at the time and used in this book comprise the main entries; a cross-reference is given when a significantly different name is in use. Principal events are usually to be found under the organisation, country or person mainly involved.